Mometrix
TEST PREPARATION

OSAT®

World History/ Geography (018) Secrets Study Guide

Dear Future Exam Success Story

First of all, **THANK YOU** for purchasing Mometrix study materials!

Second, congratulations! You are one of the few determined test-takers who are committed to doing whatever it takes to excel on your exam. **You have come to the right place.** We developed these study materials with one goal in mind: to deliver you the information you need in a format that's concise and easy to use.

In addition to optimizing your guide for the content of the test, we've outlined our recommended steps for breaking down the preparation process into small, attainable goals so you can make sure you stay on track.

We've also analyzed the entire test-taking process, identifying the most common pitfalls and showing how you can overcome them and be ready for any curveball the test throws you.

Standardized testing is one of the biggest obstacles on your road to success, which only increases the importance of doing well in the high-pressure, high-stakes environment of test day. Your results on this test could have a significant impact on your future, and this guide provides the information and practical advice to help you achieve your full potential on test day.

Your success is our success

We would love to hear from you! If you would like to share the story of your exam success or if you have any questions or comments in regard to our products, please contact us at **800-673-8175** or **support@mometrix.com**.

Thanks again for your business and we wish you continued success!

Sincerely,
The Mometrix Test Preparation Team

Need more help? Check out our flashcards at:
http://MometrixFlashcards.com/CEOE

TABLE OF CONTENTS

Introduction

Thank you for purchasing this resource! You have made the choice to prepare yourself for a test that could have a huge impact on your future, and this guide is designed to help you be fully ready for test day. Obviously, it's important to have a solid understanding of the test material, but you also need to be prepared for the unique environment and stressors of the test, so that you can perform to the best of your abilities.

For this purpose, the first section that appears in this guide is the **Secret Keys**. We've devoted countless hours to meticulously researching what works and what doesn't, and we've boiled down our findings to the five most impactful steps you can take to improve your performance on the test. We start at the beginning with study planning and move through the preparation process, all the way to the testing strategies that will help you get the most out of what you know when you're finally sitting in front of the test.

We recommend that you start preparing for your test as far in advance as possible. However, if you've bought this guide as a last-minute study resource and only have a few days before your test, we recommend that you skip over the first two Secret Keys since they address a long-term study plan.

If you struggle with **test anxiety**, we strongly encourage you to check out our recommendations for how you can overcome it. Test anxiety is a formidable foe, but it can be beaten, and we want to make sure you have the tools you need to defeat it.

Secret Key #1 – Plan Big, Study Small

There's a lot riding on your performance. If you want to ace this test, you're going to need to keep your skills sharp and the material fresh in your mind. You need a plan that lets you review everything you need to know while still fitting in your schedule. We'll break this strategy down into three categories.

Information Organization

Start with the information you already have: the official test outline. From this, you can make a complete list of all the concepts you need to cover before the test. Organize these concepts into groups that can be studied together, and create a list of any related vocabulary you need to learn so you can brush up on any difficult terms. You'll want to keep this vocabulary list handy once you actually start studying since you may need to add to it along the way.

Time Management

Once you have your set of study concepts, decide how to spread them out over the time you have left before the test. Break your study plan into small, clear goals so you have a manageable task for each day and know exactly what you're doing. Then just focus on one small step at a time. When you manage your time this way, you don't need to spend hours at a time studying. Studying a small block of content for a short period each day helps you retain information better and avoid stressing over how much you have left to do. You can relax knowing that you have a plan to cover everything in time. In order for this strategy to be effective though, you have to start studying early and stick to your schedule. Avoid the exhaustion and futility that comes from last-minute cramming!

Study Environment

The environment you study in has a big impact on your learning. Studying in a coffee shop, while probably more enjoyable, is not likely to be as fruitful as studying in a quiet room. It's important to keep distractions to a minimum. You're only planning to study for a short block of time, so make the most of it. Don't pause to check your phone or get up to find a snack. It's also important to **avoid multitasking**. Research has consistently shown that multitasking will make your studying dramatically less effective. Your study area should also be comfortable and well-lit so you don't have the distraction of straining your eyes or sitting on an uncomfortable chair.

The time of day you study is also important. You want to be rested and alert. Don't wait until just before bedtime. Study when you'll be most likely to comprehend and remember. Even better, if you know what time of day your test will be, set that time aside for study. That way your brain will be used to working on that subject at that specific time and you'll have a better chance of recalling information.

Finally, it can be helpful to team up with others who are studying for the same test. Your actual studying should be done in as isolated an environment as possible, but the work of organizing the information and setting up the study plan can be divided up. In between study sessions, you can discuss with your teammates the concepts that you're all studying and quiz each other on the details. Just be sure that your teammates are as serious about the test as you are. If you find that your study time is being replaced with social time, you might need to find a new team.

Secret Key #2 – Make Your Studying Count

You're devoting a lot of time and effort to preparing for this test, so you want to be absolutely certain it will pay off. This means doing more than just reading the content and hoping you can remember it on test day. It's important to make every minute of study count. There are two main areas you can focus on to make your studying count.

Retention

It doesn't matter how much time you study if you can't remember the material. You need to make sure you are retaining the concepts. To check your retention of the information you're learning, try recalling it at later times with minimal prompting. Try carrying around flashcards and glance at one or two from time to time or ask a friend who's also studying for the test to quiz you.

To enhance your retention, look for ways to put the information into practice so that you can apply it rather than simply recalling it. If you're using the information in practical ways, it will be much easier to remember. Similarly, it helps to solidify a concept in your mind if you're not only reading it to yourself but also explaining it to someone else. Ask a friend to let you teach them about a concept you're a little shaky on (or speak aloud to an imaginary audience if necessary). As you try to summarize, define, give examples, and answer your friend's questions, you'll understand the concepts better and they will stay with you longer. Finally, step back for a big picture view and ask yourself how each piece of information fits with the whole subject. When you link the different concepts together and see them working together as a whole, it's easier to remember the individual components.

Finally, practice showing your work on any multi-step problems, even if you're just studying. Writing out each step you take to solve a problem will help solidify the process in your mind, and you'll be more likely to remember it during the test.

Modality

Modality simply refers to the means or method by which you study. Choosing a study modality that fits your own individual learning style is crucial. No two people learn best in exactly the same way, so it's important to know your strengths and use them to your advantage.

For example, if you learn best by visualization, focus on visualizing a concept in your mind and draw an image or a diagram. Try color-coding your notes, illustrating them, or creating symbols that will trigger your mind to recall a learned concept. If you learn best by hearing or discussing information, find a study partner who learns the same way or read aloud to yourself. Think about how to put the information in your own words. Imagine that you are giving a lecture on the topic and record yourself so you can listen to it later.

For any learning style, flashcards can be helpful. Organize the information so you can take advantage of spare moments to review. Underline key words or phrases. Use different colors for different categories. Mnemonic devices (such as creating a short list in which every item starts with the same letter) can also help with retention. Find what works best for you and use it to store the information in your mind most effectively and easily.

Secret Key #3 – Practice the Right Way

Your success on test day depends not only on how many hours you put into preparing, but also on whether you prepared the right way. It's good to check along the way to see if your studying is paying off. One of the most effective ways to do this is by taking practice tests to evaluate your progress. Practice tests are useful because they show exactly where you need to improve. Every time you take a practice test, pay special attention to these three groups of questions:

- The questions you got wrong
- The questions you had to guess on, even if you guessed right
- The questions you found difficult or slow to work through

This will show you exactly what your weak areas are, and where you need to devote more study time. Ask yourself why each of these questions gave you trouble. Was it because you didn't understand the material? Was it because you didn't remember the vocabulary? Do you need more repetitions on this type of question to build speed and confidence? Dig into those questions and figure out how you can strengthen your weak areas as you go back to review the material.

Additionally, many practice tests have a section explaining the answer choices. It can be tempting to read the explanation and think that you now have a good understanding of the concept. However, an explanation likely only covers part of the question's broader context. Even if the explanation makes perfect sense, **go back and investigate** every concept related to the question until you're positive you have a thorough understanding.

As you go along, keep in mind that the practice test is just that: practice. Memorizing these questions and answers will not be very helpful on the actual test because it is unlikely to have any of the same exact questions. If you only know the right answers to the sample questions, you won't be prepared for the real thing. **Study the concepts** until you understand them fully, and then you'll be able to answer any question that shows up on the test.

It's important to wait on the practice tests until you're ready. If you take a test on your first day of study, you may be overwhelmed by the amount of material covered and how much you need to learn. Work up to it gradually.

On test day, you'll need to be prepared for answering questions, managing your time, and using the test-taking strategies you've learned. It's a lot to balance, like a mental marathon that will have a big impact on your future. Like training for a marathon, you'll need to start slowly and work your way up. When test day arrives, you'll be ready.

Start with the strategies you've read in the first two Secret Keys—plan your course and study in the way that works best for you. If you have time, consider using multiple study resources to get different approaches to the same concepts. It can be helpful to see difficult concepts from more than one angle. Then find a good source for practice tests. Many times, the test website will suggest potential study resources or provide sample tests.

Practice Test Strategy

If you're able to find at least three practice tests, we recommend this strategy:

UNTIMED AND OPEN-BOOK PRACTICE

Take the first test with no time constraints and with your notes and study guide handy. Take your time and focus on applying the strategies you've learned.

TIMED AND OPEN-BOOK PRACTICE

Take the second practice test open-book as well, but set a timer and practice pacing yourself to finish in time.

TIMED AND CLOSED-BOOK PRACTICE

Take any other practice tests as if it were test day. Set a timer and put away your study materials. Sit at a table or desk in a quiet room, imagine yourself at the testing center, and answer questions as quickly and accurately as possible.

Keep repeating timed and closed-book tests on a regular basis until you run out of practice tests or it's time for the actual test. Your mind will be ready for the schedule and stress of test day, and you'll be able to focus on recalling the material you've learned.

Secret Key #4 – Pace Yourself

Once you're fully prepared for the material on the test, your biggest challenge on test day will be managing your time. Just knowing that the clock is ticking can make you panic even if you have plenty of time left. Work on pacing yourself so you can build confidence against the time constraints of the exam. Pacing is a difficult skill to master, especially in a high-pressure environment, so **practice is vital**.

Set time expectations for your pace based on how much time is available. For example, if a section has 60 questions and the time limit is 30 minutes, you know you have to average 30 seconds or less per question in order to answer them all. Although 30 seconds is the hard limit, set 25 seconds per question as your goal, so you reserve extra time to spend on harder questions. When you budget extra time for the harder questions, you no longer have any reason to stress when those questions take longer to answer.

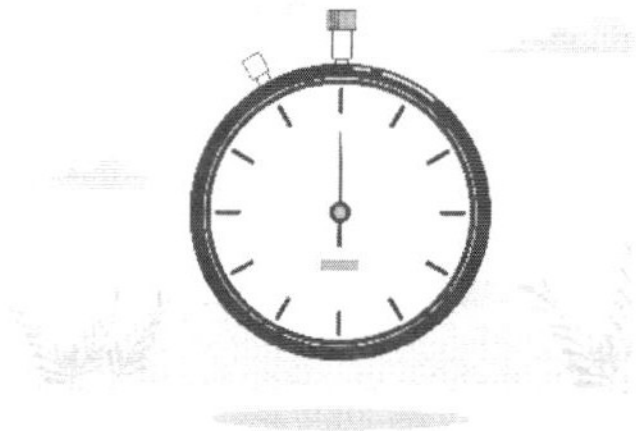

Don't let this time expectation distract you from working through the test at a calm, steady pace, but keep it in mind so you don't spend too much time on any one question. Recognize that taking extra time on one question you don't understand may keep you from answering two that you do understand later in the test. If your time limit for a question is up and you're still not sure of the answer, mark it and move on, and come back to it later if the time and the test format allow. If the testing format doesn't allow you to return to earlier questions, just make an educated guess; then put it out of your mind and move on.

On the easier questions, be careful not to rush. It may seem wise to hurry through them so you have more time for the challenging ones, but it's not worth missing one if you know the concept and just didn't take the time to read the question fully. Work efficiently but make sure you understand the question and have looked at all of the answer choices, since more than one may seem right at first.

Even if you're paying attention to the time, you may find yourself a little behind at some point. You should speed up to get back on track, but do so wisely. Don't panic; just take a few seconds less on each question until you're caught up. Don't guess without thinking, but do look through the answer choices and eliminate any you know are wrong. If you can get down to two choices, it is often worthwhile to guess from those. Once you've chosen an answer, move on and don't dwell on any that you skipped or had to hurry through. If a question was taking too long, chances are it was one of the harder ones, so you weren't as likely to get it right anyway.

On the other hand, if you find yourself getting ahead of schedule, it may be beneficial to slow down a little. The more quickly you work, the more likely you are to make a careless mistake that will affect your score. You've budgeted time for each question, so don't be afraid to spend that time. Practice an efficient but careful pace to get the most out of the time you have.

Secret Key #5 – Have a Plan for Guessing

When you're taking the test, you may find yourself stuck on a question. Some of the answer choices seem better than others, but you don't see the one answer choice that is obviously correct. What do you do?

The scenario described above is very common, yet most test takers have not effectively prepared for it. Developing and practicing a plan for guessing may be one of the single most effective uses of your time as you get ready for the exam.

In developing your plan for guessing, there are three questions to address:

- When should you start the guessing process?
- How should you narrow down the choices?
- Which answer should you choose?

When to Start the Guessing Process

Unless your plan for guessing is to select C every time (which, despite its merits, is not what we recommend), you need to leave yourself enough time to apply your answer elimination strategies. Since you have a limited amount of time for each question, that means that if you're going to give yourself the best shot at guessing correctly, you have to decide quickly whether or not you will guess.

Of course, the best-case scenario is that you don't have to guess at all, so first, see if you can answer the question based on your knowledge of the subject and basic reasoning skills. Focus on the key words in the question and try to jog your memory of related topics. Give yourself a chance to bring the knowledge to mind, but once you realize that you don't have (or you can't access) the knowledge you need to answer the question, it's time to start the guessing process.

It's almost always better to start the guessing process too early than too late. It only takes a few seconds to remember something and answer the question from knowledge. Carefully eliminating wrong answer choices takes longer. Plus, going through the process of eliminating answer choices can actually help jog your memory.

Summary: Start the guessing process as soon as you decide that you can't answer the question based on your knowledge.

How to Narrow Down the Choices

The next chapter in this book (**Test-Taking Strategies**) includes a wide range of strategies for how to approach questions and how to look for answer choices to eliminate. You will definitely want to read those carefully, practice them, and figure out which ones work best for you. Here though, we're going to address a mindset rather than a particular strategy.

Your odds of guessing an answer correctly depend on how many options you are choosing from.

Number of options left	5	4	3	2	1
Odds of guessing correctly	20%	25%	33%	50%	100%

You can see from this chart just how valuable it is to be able to eliminate incorrect answers and make an educated guess, but there are two things that many test takers do that cause them to miss out on the benefits of guessing:

- Accidentally eliminating the correct answer
- Selecting an answer based on an impression

We'll look at the first one here, and the second one in the next section.

To avoid accidentally eliminating the correct answer, we recommend a thought exercise called **the $5 challenge**. In this challenge, you only eliminate an answer choice from contention if you are willing to bet $5 on it being wrong. Why $5? Five dollars is a small but not insignificant amount of money. It's an amount you could afford to lose but wouldn't want to throw away. And while losing $5 once might not hurt too much, doing it twenty times will set you back $100. In the same way, each small decision you make—eliminating a choice here, guessing on a question there—won't by itself impact your score very much, but when you put them all together, they can make a big difference. By holding each answer choice elimination decision to a higher standard, you can reduce the risk of accidentally eliminating the correct answer.

The $5 challenge can also be applied in a positive sense: If you are willing to bet $5 that an answer choice *is* correct, go ahead and mark it as correct.

Summary: Only eliminate an answer choice if you are willing to bet $5 that it is wrong.

Which Answer to Choose

You're taking the test. You've run into a hard question and decided you'll have to guess. You've eliminated all the answer choices you're willing to bet $5 on. Now you have to pick an answer. Why do we even need to talk about this? Why can't you just pick whichever one you feel like when the time comes?

The answer to these questions is that if you don't come into the test with a plan, you'll rely on your impression to select an answer choice, and if you do that, you risk falling into a trap. The test writers know that everyone who takes their test will be guessing on some of the questions, so they intentionally write wrong answer choices to seem plausible. You still have to pick an answer though, and if the wrong answer choices are designed to look right, how can you ever be sure that you're not falling for their trap? The best solution we've found to this dilemma is to take the decision out of your hands entirely. Here is the process we recommend:

Once you've eliminated any choices that you are confident (willing to bet $5) are wrong, select the first remaining choice as your answer.

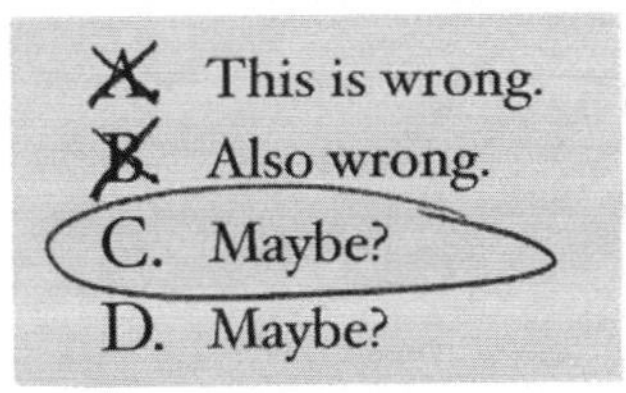

Whether you choose to select the first remaining choice, the second, or the last, the important thing is that you use some preselected standard. Using this approach guarantees that you will not be enticed into selecting an answer choice that looks right, because you are not basing your decision on how the answer choices look.

This is not meant to make you question your knowledge. Instead, it is to help you recognize the difference between your knowledge and your impressions. There's a huge difference between thinking an answer is right because of what you know, and thinking an answer is right because it looks or sounds like it should be right.

Summary: To ensure that your selection is appropriately random, make a predetermined selection from among all answer choices you have not eliminated.

Test-Taking Strategies

This section contains a list of test-taking strategies that you may find helpful as you work through the test. By taking what you know and applying logical thought, you can maximize your chances of answering any question correctly!

It is very important to realize that every question is different and every person is different: no single strategy will work on every question, and no single strategy will work for every person. That's why we've included all of them here, so you can try them out and determine which ones work best for different types of questions and which ones work best for you.

Question Strategies

Read Carefully

Read the question and the answer choices carefully. Don't miss the question because you misread the terms. You have plenty of time to read each question thoroughly and make sure you understand what is being asked. Yet a happy medium must be attained, so don't waste too much time. You must read carefully and efficiently.

Contextual Clues

Look for contextual clues. If the question includes a word you are not familiar with, look at the immediate context for some indication of what the word might mean. Contextual clues can often give you all the information you need to decipher the meaning of an unfamiliar word. Even if you can't determine the meaning, you may be able to narrow down the possibilities enough to make a solid guess at the answer to the question.

Prefixes

If you're having trouble with a word in the question or answer choices, try dissecting it. Take advantage of every clue that the word might include. Prefixes can be a huge help. Usually, they allow you to determine a basic meaning. *Pre-* means before, *post-* means after, *pro-* is positive, *de-* is negative. From prefixes, you can get an idea of the general meaning of the word and try to put it into context.

Hedge Words

Watch out for critical hedge words, such as *likely, may, can, often, almost, mostly, usually, generally, rarely*, and *sometimes*. Question writers insert these hedge phrases to cover every possibility. Often an answer choice will be wrong simply because it leaves no room for exception. Be on guard for answer choices that have definitive words such as *exactly* and *always*.

Switchback Words

Stay alert for *switchbacks*. These are the words and phrases frequently used to alert you to shifts in thought. The most common switchback words are *but, although*, and *however*. Others include *nevertheless, on the other hand, even though, while, in spite of, despite*, and *regardless of*. Switchback words are important to catch because they can change the direction of the question or an answer choice.

✓ FACE VALUE

When in doubt, use common sense. Accept the situation in the problem at face value. Don't read too much into it. These problems will not require you to make wild assumptions. If you have to go beyond creativity and warp time or space in order to have an answer choice fit the question, then you should move on and consider the other answer choices. These are normal problems rooted in reality. The applicable relationship or explanation may not be readily apparent, but it is there for you to figure out. Use your common sense to interpret anything that isn't clear.

Answer Choice Strategies

✓ ANSWER SELECTION

The most thorough way to pick an answer choice is to identify and eliminate wrong answers until only one is left, then confirm it is the correct answer. Sometimes an answer choice may immediately seem right, but be careful. The test writers will usually put more than one reasonable answer choice on each question, so take a second to read all of them and make sure that the other choices are not equally obvious. As long as you have time left, it is better to read every answer choice than to pick the first one that looks right without checking the others.

✓ ANSWER CHOICE FAMILIES

An answer choice family consists of two (in rare cases, three) answer choices that are very similar in construction and cannot all be true at the same time. If you see two answer choices that are direct opposites or parallels, one of them is usually the correct answer. For instance, if one answer choice says that quantity *x* increases and another either says that quantity *x* decreases (opposite) or says that quantity *y* increases (parallel), then those answer choices would fall into the same family. An answer choice that doesn't match the construction of the answer choice family is more likely to be incorrect. Most questions will not have answer choice families, but when they do appear, you should be prepared to recognize them.

✓ ELIMINATE ANSWERS

Eliminate answer choices as soon as you realize they are wrong, but make sure you consider all possibilities. If you are eliminating answer choices and realize that the last one you are left with is also wrong, don't panic. Start over and consider each choice again. There may be something you missed the first time that you will realize on the second pass.

✓ AVOID FACT TRAPS

Don't be distracted by an answer choice that is factually true but doesn't answer the question. You are looking for the choice that answers the question. Stay focused on what the question is asking for so you don't accidentally pick an answer that is true but incorrect. Always go back to the question and make sure the answer choice you've selected actually answers the question and is not merely a true statement.

✓ EXTREME STATEMENTS

In general, you should avoid answers that put forth extreme actions as standard practice or proclaim controversial ideas as established fact. An answer choice that states the "process should be used in certain situations, if..." is much more likely to be correct than one that states the "process should be discontinued completely." The first is a calm rational statement and doesn't even make a definitive, uncompromising stance, using a hedge word *if* to provide wiggle room, whereas the second choice is far more extreme.

⊘ Benchmark

As you read through the answer choices and you come across one that seems to answer the question well, mentally select that answer choice. This is not your final answer, but it's the one that will help you evaluate the other answer choices. The one that you selected is your benchmark or standard for judging each of the other answer choices. Every other answer choice must be compared to your benchmark. That choice is correct until proven otherwise by another answer choice beating it. If you find a better answer, then that one becomes your new benchmark. Once you've decided that no other choice answers the question as well as your benchmark, you have your final answer.

⊘ Predict the Answer

Before you even start looking at the answer choices, it is often best to try to predict the answer. When you come up with the answer on your own, it is easier to avoid distractions and traps because you will know exactly what to look for. The right answer choice is unlikely to be word-for-word what you came up with, but it should be a close match. Even if you are confident that you have the right answer, you should still take the time to read each option before moving on.

General Strategies

⊘ Tough Questions

If you are stumped on a problem or it appears too hard or too difficult, don't waste time. Move on! Remember though, if you can quickly check for obviously incorrect answer choices, your chances of guessing correctly are greatly improved. Before you completely give up, at least try to knock out a couple of possible answers. Eliminate what you can and then guess at the remaining answer choices before moving on.

⊘ Check Your Work

Since you will probably not know every term listed and the answer to every question, it is important that you get credit for the ones that you do know. Don't miss any questions through careless mistakes. If at all possible, try to take a second to look back over your answer selection and make sure you've selected the correct answer choice and haven't made a costly careless mistake (such as marking an answer choice that you didn't mean to mark). This quick double check should more than pay for itself in caught mistakes for the time it costs.

⊘ Pace Yourself

It's easy to be overwhelmed when you're looking at a page full of questions; your mind is confused and full of random thoughts, and the clock is ticking down faster than you would like. Calm down and maintain the pace that you have set for yourself. Especially as you get down to the last few minutes of the test, don't let the small numbers on the clock make you panic. As long as you are on track by monitoring your pace, you are guaranteed to have time for each question.

⊘ Don't Rush

It is very easy to make errors when you are in a hurry. Maintaining a fast pace in answering questions is pointless if it makes you miss questions that you would have gotten right otherwise. Test writers like to include distracting information and wrong answers that seem right. Taking a little extra time to avoid careless mistakes can make all the difference in your test score. Find a pace that allows you to be confident in the answers that you select.

✓ KEEP MOVING

Panicking will not help you pass the test, so do your best to stay calm and keep moving. Taking deep breaths and going through the answer elimination steps you practiced can help to break through a stress barrier and keep your pace.

Final Notes

The combination of a solid foundation of content knowledge and the confidence that comes from practicing your plan for applying that knowledge is the key to maximizing your performance on test day. As your foundation of content knowledge is built up and strengthened, you'll find that the strategies included in this chapter become more and more effective in helping you quickly sift through the distractions and traps of the test to isolate the correct answer.

Now that you're preparing to move forward into the test content chapters of this book, be sure to keep your goal in mind. As you read, think about how you will be able to apply this information on the test. If you've already seen sample questions for the test and you have an idea of the question format and style, try to come up with questions of your own that you can answer based on what you're reading. This will give you valuable practice applying your knowledge in the same ways you can expect to on test day.

Good luck and good studying!

World History

World History Pre-1400

Lower Paleolithic Period

The **Paleolithic period** is the earliest period of human development, as well as the longest. It is also commonly referred to as the **Old Stone Age**. It lasted from about 2.5 million years ago until about 300,000 years ago. Development during this period was excruciatingly slow. The Paleolithic period is usually divided into three sections: the Lower, Middle, and Upper. The **Lower Paleolithic period** is characterized by the appearance of stone tools; the chopping tools found at the Olduvai Gorge in Tanzania are from this period and date back over a million years. They were probably made by **Australopithecus**, an ancestor of modern humans. Anthropologists have also found stone tools believed to have been made by Homo erectus between 100,000 and 500,000 years ago.

Middle and Upper Paleolithic Periods

The Middle Paleolithic period occurred about 300,000 years ago until about 40,000 years ago. During this time, the Mousterian culture of Neanderthal men was active in Europe, North Africa, Palestine, and Siberia. These ancestors of modern man lived in caves and had the use of fire. They hunted prehistoric mammals and had slightly more sophisticated tools than their forebears, including crude needles for sewing furs together. These people may have practiced some sort of religion. In the **Upper Paleolithic** period, about 40,000 years ago until about 10,000 years ago, Neanderthals were replaced by varieties of Homo sapiens, including Cro-Magnon man and Grimaldi man. A number of diverse cultures flourished during this period, and the first manmade shelters arose. This was also the period in which people first crafted jewelry and illustrated drawings on the walls of caves.

Solutrean and Magdalenian Phase of the Paleolithic Period

During the **Upper Paleolithic period**, hunters entered Europe from the east and conquered the more primitive cultures living there. These victorious hunters were known as the **Solutreans**. These people are noted for their fine spearheads, which they used to hunt wild horses. The Solutreans were, in turn, replaced by the **Magdalenians**, the most advanced phase of the Paleolithic period. The Magdalenians subsisted mainly through fishing and reindeer hunting. They developed extremely precise tools and sophisticated weapons, such as the atlatl, a device that made it possible to throw a spear over a great distance. Most of all, though, the Magdalenians are known for their cave paintings in modern-day France.

Mesolithic Period

The Mesolithic period, otherwise known as the **Middle Stone Age**, began roughly 10,000 years ago and ended with the introduction of farming (dates vary by culture). In some areas, the use of farming was already beginning at the end of the Paleolithic era, and therefore there may not be a true **Mesolithic period**. The most extensive examples of this kind of culture are found in Northern Europe, where the end of the **Ice Age** created much greater changes in the ability to live off of the land. The remains of the Mesolithic period are mainly just middens (rubbish heaps), as well as some deforestation. The people of the Mesolithic period made small tools out of flint; fishing tackle, canoes, and bows have been found at some sites.

Neolithic Period

The Neolithic period, also known as the **New Stone Age**, refers to that stage of human cultural evolution in which man developed stone tools, settled in villages, and began making crafts. In order to begin living in towns, man had to learn how to domesticate animals and sustain agriculture; formerly, in the Paleolithic and Mesolithic periods, man had subsisted through hunting, fishing, and gathering. The **Neolithic period** is said to have ended when urban civilizations began, or when metal tools or writing began. Because the designation of Neolithic depends on these factors, anthropologists date its occurrence differently for different regions and populations. At present, anthropologists believe that the earliest Neolithic culture was in southwest Asia between 8000 and 6000 BC.

Spread of Neolithic Culture

Most anthropologists date the beginning of **Neolithic culture** at somewhere between 8000 and 6000 BC. It began with the domestication of plants (wheat, barley, and millet) and animals (cattle, sheep, and goats). The Neolithic culture in the valley between the Tigris and Euphrates Rivers gradually evolved into a more urban civilization by 3500 BC. Meanwhile, Neolithic cultural advances spread through Europe, the Nile Valley, the Indus Valley, and the Huang He Valley. In these regions, the innovations of the Neolithic period were intermixed with the particulars of the region; in the Huang He region, for instance, rice cultivation was a product of advances in agriculture. By 1500 BC, Neolithic culture had spread to Mexico and South America. In these areas, corn, beans, and squash were the major crops.

Sumerians of Mesopotamia

Mesopotamia, the region between the Tigris and Euphrates Rivers in what is now considered the Middle East, contained several different early civilizations of which the **Sumerians** were one of the more prominent. They developed the system of writing known as **cuneiform**, by which they elaborated their theories on mathematics and astronomy. The Sumerians also had a detailed system of **laws** and traded widely with other groups throughout the region. They even traded with civilizations as far away as Egypt and India. There was no coin or currency system at this time, thus trade was conducted on the barter system, in which goods are exchanged for one another, directly.

Babylonian Civilization of Mesopotamia

After the Sumerian civilization declined, the next dominant civilization was **Babylon**. The Babylonians conquered the Sumerians and established a city on the Euphrates River in approximately 1,750 B.C. One of the most famous Babylonian rulers was **Hammurabi**, who established the famous **Code of Hammurabi**, an extremely detailed set of laws. This marked the first time that a set of rules governing every aspect of social life was applied to an entire people. The Babylonians are also known for their construction of **ziggurats**, long pyramid-like structures that were used as religious temples. Over time, the Babylonians acquired a reputation as a sensuous and hedonistic people, and the name Babylon has come to stand for any debauched civilization.

> **Review Video:** Early Mesopotamia: The Babylonians
> Visit mometrix.com/academy and enter code: 340325
>
> **Review Video:** Early Mesopotamia: The Sumerians
> Visit mometrix.com/academy and enter code: 939880

Pyramids of Egypt

The incredible engineering skills of the Egyptians are most famously displayed in the **pyramids** clustered along the Nile River. These were built roughly between 2700 and 2500 BC. The largest of the structures, the **Khufu pyramid** at Giza, is estimated to have taken 20 years and 100,000 laborers to construct. Today, it stands at 450 feet; some of its height has been lost to erosion. These pyramids were built as burial sites for the pharaohs, who were believed to continue their rule in the afterlife. Peasants worked on the pyramids in exchange for food and shelter. The shape of the pyramids was meant to symbolize the slanting rays of the sun, with sloping sides meant to help the ka (soul) of the pharaoh climb to the sky and join the gods.

Review Video: Ancient Egypt
Visit mometrix.com/academy and enter code: 398041

Religion in Africa

Sub-Saharan Africa was composed of disparate tribes. Most of Africa practiced **animistic religion**, in which it is believed that deities are embodied in the animals that people depend upon for food and service. Ritual and participatory worship were important; common activities included drumming, dancing, divination, and sacrifices. These religions typically had well-developed concepts of good and evil; they believed that some evil, disasters, and illnesses were produced by witchcraft, and that specialists (known as diviners) were required to combat the power of these malevolent beings. Many African peoples shared an underlying belief in a **creator deity**, whose power was expressed through the **ancestors** who founded the tribe. These deceased ancestors were a link between the living and the deities. African tribal religions showed a remarkable resilience when they began to come into contact with monotheistic religions.

Indus Valley Civilizations

The **Indus River Valley** is an area bordered by the Himalayan Mountains in what is now Pakistan. The people of this region developed a system of writing, as well as systems of weight and measurement which were useful in trade. They exchanged goods with the people of Mesopotamia in the west, as well as with the people of Tibet in the east. The Aryans invaded this region and brought with them iron technology and the Sanskrit language. The introduction of iron tools made it possible to cultivate the forests of the **Ganges River Valley** in what is now India.

Early Cities of Mohenjo-Daro and Harappa in the Indus Valley

Both the Indus Valley and Egyptian civilizations featured extremely well-planned **cities**. In the Indus Valley, the cities of **Mohenjo-Daro** and **Harappa** were located along the Indus River, in what is now Pakistan. Each of these cities was built around 2500 BC and housed approximately 30,000 citizens. They were each designed in a grid-like pattern, with streets running east-west and north-south. Both Mohenjo-Daro and Harrapa had bathhouses, sewer systems, and organized garbage collection. The structures in these cities were built with oven-fired bricks, which made them durable. Unlike in Egypt, where technological advances were used to enhance religious practice, the people of the Indus Valley used their technology to improve sanitation.

Earliest Civilization in What Would Become China

The earliest civilizations in what would become China flourished along the banks of the **Huang He (Yellow) River** before the year 2000 BC. The first Chinese dynasty was the **Xia** (Hsia), succeeded by the **Shang** dynasty. In this period, the rulers established an intricate system of government and a comprehensive judiciary. The basic components of this system would be preserved in Chinese civilization for centuries. The distinctive Chinese style of writing also developed during this period. Like Egyptian hieroglyphs, the Chinese pictographs were meant to resemble their definition. Over time, though, the Chinese characters have come to resemble their definitions less and less.

Zhou Dynasty

The Zhou dynasty, which ran from roughly 1030 to 221 BC, is generally considered to be the third Chinese dynasty, after the Shang. The **Zhou** were brought into power by the commander **Wu**, who declared that the decadent Shang monarchs had forfeited the mandate of heaven (in other words, God's approval of their reign). The Zhou dynasty is generally divided into two parts: The **Western Zhou** ran a feudal-type state in the central plain and the area around the Yellow River. The later **Eastern Zhou** had a more difficult time maintaining control of rival states within its control. The Zhou dynasty was the period in which Chinese civilization spread to most parts of Asia. Both **Confucius** and **Lao Tzu** were active during this period. China became the preeminent state during this period.

Han Dynasty

The Han dynasty ran from approximately 206 BC to AD 220. It began when a peasant, **Liu Pang**, led a successful insurrection against the Qin dynasty leaders. The **Han** shifted the capital of China to Changan (Xian). This was the period in which **Confucianism** became the dominant political and social ideology in China. The Han developed a code of laws and a form of government based upon the proper Confucian relations between king and subject, husband and wife, and father and son. The Han dynasty saw China accrue fantastic wealth and become one of the most sophisticated and resplendent countries the world has seen. Eventually, though, peasant revolts weakened the Han and made them susceptible to overthrow.

Daoism

Next to Confucianism, **Daoism** (also Taoism) is the most important philosophy to have emerged out of China. **Taoist thought** is based on the 6th century-BC writings of **Lao Tzu**, specifically on the Tao Te Ching. Lao Tzu was a student of Confucius and taught that individuals should discover the essential nature of things and of themselves and should not seek to challenge the natural harmony of life. A proper Taoist should be patient and austere. Unlike Confucianism, Daoism contains an element of mysticism and so may be called a religion. Taoism introduced the concept of the **yin and yang**, the contrasting male and female elements that make up everything in existence and which must be harmonized in order to achieve self-realization.

Early Civilizations of Mesoamerica and South America

Mesoamerica, which is now known as Central and South America, were both host to developed civilizations 3,000 years before the arrival of Columbus. These civilizations were largely dependent upon water-supported agriculture. The most important crop in the region was **maize**. The first dominant group in this region, the **Olmecs**, was based in what is now the gulf coast of eastern Mexico. The Olmecs were known for making large and elaborate stone carvings. There were also major civilizations at this time in what is now Peru. In the Andes Mountains of that region, the **Chavin** culture developed intricate stone temples and pyramids. These sites have been explored carefully by archaeologists.

Hinduism

Hinduism is the traditional religion of India. It is expressed in an individual's philosophy and behavior, rather than in the performance of any specific rituals. **Hinduism** does not claim a founder but has evolved slowly over thousands of years; the first Hindu writings date back to the third millennium BC. There are a few concepts that are common to all permutations of Hinduism, such as the **Vedas**, which are considered to be the sacred texts of the religion. The chief aim in life for a Hindu is to be liberated from the cycle of suffering and rebirth. Hindus believe in **reincarnation** and that a person's conduct in this life will affect his or her position in the next (**karma**). Although Hinduism is frequently associated with the caste system, the two are actually unrelated.

Hindu Caste System

The Hindu caste system is a means of organizing society. It divides the populace into four groups, each associated with a part of the body of the Hindu god Purusha. The highest class is the **Brahmins**, associated with the mouth of the god. In the original system, the brahmin class was made up of priests. The second caste is the **Kshatriyas**, made up of rulers and soldiers; this caste is associated with the arms of Purusha. Next are the **Vaishyas**, associated with the legs of the god. This caste was composed of landowners, merchants, and artisans. The last group is the **Shudras**, associated with the feet of the god. This caste was composed of servants and slaves. Women do not have a place in the traditional Hindu caste system.

Judaism

Judaism was founded by **Abraham** in the 20th century BC. Abraham was called out from among the Chaldeans to enter into a covenant with God, whereby he and his descendants would receive special treatment and an inheritance of land. Abraham then moved to Canaan (near present-day Israel). Later, his descendants would move to Egypt and be enslaved. They were eventually liberated from slavery in Egypt by God through Moses, and they conquered the land of Canaan under the leadership of Joshua. Moses received from God a set of strict laws, the **Ten Commandments**; all of this is described in the **Torah**, the essential Jewish Scripture. There are also several other important books, including the Talmud, and many important commentaries by learned Jewish theologians.

Creation of Ancient Israel

Around the year 1020 BC, **Saul** became the first king of the Jewish nation, known as **Israel**. Saul's successor **David** conquered the city of Jerusalem and united all of the tribes of Israel, making Jerusalem their capital. In the 10th century BC, David's son **Solomon** built the first Jewish Temple in Jerusalem; this building was used to house the **Ark of the Covenant**, which housed the original Torah. Israel would be taken over by the **Assyrians** in the 8th century BC, and later by the **Babylonians**. Finally, in 538 BC, the Persian King Cyrus allowed the Jews to return to Jerusalem and rebuild the Temple. Israel would subsequently be taken over by the **Greeks** under Alexander, and later by the **Romans** under Pompey.

Vedic Age

The Vedic Age is the period recounted in the Indian Vedas, the earliest known records of Indian history. The dates of the **Vedic age** are considered by most to be between 2000 and 1000 BC. The oldest Vedic text is the **Rig-Veda**, which bears many Indo-Iranian elements. It is a collection of religious hymns and stories and describes a nomadic people who were ruled by a king who depended on their consent. His main duty was to protect the people. Religion in this period primarily consisted of chanting and the performing of sacrifices. During this period, elaborate rules concerning marriage were created, and the rigid social stratification that would become known as the **caste system** evolved.

Buddhism

Buddhism was created by **Gautama Siddhartha** (otherwise known as Buddha) in about 528 B.C. It was in part a response to Hinduism, which Buddha felt had become bloated with worldliness and politics. Traditional Buddhism is based upon the **Four Noble Truths**: existence is suffering, suffering is caused by desire, an end of suffering will come with Nirvana, and Nirvana will come with the practice of the **Eightfold Path**. The steps of the Eightfold Path are as follows: right views, right resolve, right speech, right action, right livelihood, right effort, right mindfulness, and right concentration. Buddhism has no deities. Buddhism did not receive any official sanction for a long time but did eventually spread and take hold in India, China, Japan, and elsewhere.

PERSIA

Persia is the European name for the region that is now Iran. This area has been the site of a number of vibrant cultures. The **Medes** were the first to develop there, lasting from approximately 700 to 549 BC, when they were expelled by the army of Cyrus. This great king then established the **Achaemenid dynasty**, which itself was destroyed by Alexander the Great in 330 BC. After this, a succession of peoples including the **Parthians**—rivals to Rome—inhabited the region, until a durable **Sasanian dynasty** was established in AD 224. Persia was in constant conflict with the **Byzantine Empire**, and would eventually be overtaken by the **Arabs** in the 7th century AD.

ZOROASTRIANISM

Zoroastrianism was the state religion of Persia during the **Sasanian dynasty** between the years AD 224 and 651. It is based upon the prophecies of **Zoroaster** (also known as Zarathustra, c. 628-551 BC), a Persian who claimed to have encountered the divine being Ahura Mazda. Zoroastrians believed that the world was composed of good and evil spirits, who are in constant conflict. Fire was sacred to the Zoroastrians. Many of the concepts of Zoroastrianism would be included in Christianity, especially by the Manichean sect, who also saw the world as a struggle between absolute good and absolute evil. Zoroastrianism receded in popularity with the rise of Islam.

CITY-STATE OF ATHENS IN ANCIENT GREECE

Ancient Greece was dominated by two city-states, **Athens** and **Sparta**. These two had very distinct cultures. Athens was a coastal city with a democratic form of government which amassed wealth by trading overseas. Athens is also known as the city that gave life to philosophy and the arts. **Socrates** engaged in his famous dialogues in the streets of Athens, and though he was eventually executed by the Athenian government for supposedly corrupting the youth, his thoughts achieved immortality in the writings of his student **Plato**. In turn, Plato's student **Aristotle** developed a strict form of reasoning that has formed the basis of much subsequent Western thought. Athens is also renowned for the architectural marvel that is the **Parthenon**.

SPARTA IN ANCIENT GREECE

While Athens was known for its devotion to the arts and its democratic form of government, its rival city-state **Sparta** was devoted to agriculture and the military. Sparta was not located on the coast, and therefore the Spartans had little contact with distant peoples. Spartan society was governed by a strict class system. Most people (**helots**) worked the land of other people as virtual serfs. In the upper classes, participation in **military training** was compulsory. Indeed, Spartan youths left their families to begin military training at a young age. The Spartans did not produce any noteworthy philosophers, but as a culture, they stressed the good of the group over that of the individual. This is in stark contrast to most Athenian thought, which celebrates the achievements of the individual.

Review Video: Ancient Greece
Visit mometrix.com/academy and enter code: 800829

GREECE IN THE PERICLEAN AND HELLENISTIC AGES

The **Periclean Age** in Greece, so named because Pericles was the leader of Athens during the period, took place in the 5th century BC. It was during this period that most of the great contributions to Western culture were made, including the philosophy of Socrates, the medical work of Hippocrates, and the great dramatic works of Aeschylus, Sophocles, and Euripides. The **Hellenistic Age** (4th century BC), on the other hand, is more commonly known for the military conquests made by **Alexander the Great**. If it were not for the conquests of Alexander during the Hellenistic Age, many of the innovations and achievements of the Periclean Age may not have had such a great influence on the West. It should be noted that the Hellenistic Age was not without its own great thinkers; in fact, Alexander studied as a boy under Aristotle.

Major Wars of Greece in the Periclean and Hellenistic Ages

During the **Age of Pericles**, an alliance of Greek city-states was challenged by the mighty Persians. Miraculously, the outnumbered Greeks were able to defeat the Persians at Thermopylae and Marathon, and staved off conquest. The war with the Persians impoverished the Greeks, however, and increased rivalries among the city-states. In Athens, the requirements for citizenship were loosened, though slavery remained. Conflict between Sparta and Athens culminated in the **Peloponnesian War**, won by Sparta. Eventually, the whole of Greece would be conquered by **Philip of Macedon**, who allowed the Greeks to maintain their culture and traditions. **Alexander the Great** was the son of Philip and became the master of an empire larger than any the world had ever seen. During his reign, he united many disparate peoples through a common law and exchange policy. He died at the age of 33, and his empire was divided into three parts amongst his generals.

Roman Republic

Roman civilization dates from the founding of the city in 753 BC until the defeat of the last Emperor, **Romulus Augustus**, in AD 476. The republic itself lasted from the overthrow of the monarchy in 509 BC until the empowering of the first Emperor, **Octavian Augustus**, in 27 BC. The area along the Tiber River where Rome would be built was previously inhabited by a group known as the **Etruscans**. Rome took its name from the legendary **Romulus**, who is said to have founded it after triumphing over his brother Remus. The basic structure of Roman society consisted of **patricians** at the top of the social hierarchy, who were descendants of the founders of the republic and often wealthy. Beneath the patricians were the **plebeians**, which consisted of all other freemen. Finally, at the bottom of the social hierarchy were **slaves**. Women were not included in most social or economic business, although a Roman woman's rights were often significantly preferable to her contemporaries in other civilizations. The **Roman Republic**, which was the first political arrangement of Rome, was led by two consuls who were chosen annually. The **consuls** presided over the **Senate**, made up of a permanent group of those who had been previously elected to a high-ranking magistracy (originally primarily patrician in composition), and the **Assembly**, which was solely for the plebeians. Rome had extensive laws covering individual and property rights.

Review Video: Roman Republic Part One
Visit mometrix.com/academy and enter code: 360192

Review Video: Roman Republic Part Two
Visit mometrix.com/academy and enter code: 881514

Expansion of Rome

Punic Wars

The first real challenge to the territorial expansion of Rome was the city of **Carthage**, located across the Mediterranean in North Africa. Carthage was founded by the Phoenicians. There were three major conflicts, known as the **Punic Wars**, fought between Rome and Carthage. Rome won the **First Punic War** and acquired Sicily in the process. The Carthaginian effort in the **Second Punic War** was led by Hannibal and included his famous crossing of the Alps. Hannibal was quite successful in Italy, but a combination of a war of attrition throughout Italy and the counterattacks on

Carthaginian holdings in Spain and the city of Carthage itself by the Romans forced Hannibal to retreat to North Africa to defend Carthage. In the **Third Punic War**, Rome finally destroyed Carthage; in fact, it is often rumored that the victorious Romans burned Carthage to the ground and then salted the fields of their vanquished foe, a tribute to the Senator Cato the Elder's repeated cry at the end of various speeches of "*Ceterum censeo Carthaginem esse delendam*" ("Moreover, I have determined that Carthage must be destroyed").

Review Video: The Punic Wars
Visit mometrix.com/academy and enter code: 879745

Greece, Gaul, and Spain

After defeating Carthage once and for all, Rome met little resistance as it continued to acquire more territory. This was partly due to the superiority of Roman weaponry, and in part because the Romans were good at bringing conquered peoples into the fold. Rome typically allowed conquered people to maintain their native cultures, so long as they paid tribute to Rome. Rome defeated the Macedonians and took **Greece**, then conquered large portions of **Gaul** (France) and **Spain**. The vastness of the Roman Empire necessitated some advances in infrastructure technology. Romans are justly famous for their solid and durable **roads** and **aqueducts** (systems for delivering water), many of which survive today.

Grand Alliance of Julius Caesar in Rome

As Rome continued to expand, class conflicts developed between the nobility and the poor. In this era of unrest, it became possible for individual leaders to claim more power than the law had allowed previously. In 60 B.C., the famous general Julius Caesar formed the three-person alliance known as the First Triumvirate to govern Rome. The other two members were **Gnaeus Pompey Magnus** and **Marcus Licinius Crassus**. During this period, Caesar led a successful campaign against the Gauls (a people in modern-day France) and made himself richer than the entire Roman State on the proceeds from his conquest. After Crassus was killed in battle, Caesar pushed Pompey out and assumed total control of Rome, crowning himself dictator-for-life. Though Caesar was very popular with the mob, his decision to claim lifelong power alienated him from the nobility in the Senate. He was assassinated by a group of senators, led by **Marcus Iunius Brutus**, in 44 B.C.

Second Roman Triumvirate

After the assassination of Caesar in 44 B.C., Rome was mired in chaos. Those who had conspired to kill Caesar had hoped to return to the republican form of government, but instead another trio of leaders came to the fore, this time as a governmental commission of "three men for reconstituting the Republic," known as the **Triumvirate**. The Triumvirate was composed of **Marc Antony**, one of Caesar's greatest generals and a Consul at the time; **Octavius**, the nephew and testamentary heir of Caesar; and **Marcus Aemilius Lepidus**, a third wheel who was quickly made a non-entity. While Octavius stayed in Rome, Antony left for Egypt, where he stayed for a time as the guest and lover of **Cleopatra**. Eventually, infighting between Octavius and Antony led the former to mount a campaign against Egypt. When they realized that they were defeated, Antony and Cleopatra committed suicide to avoid the shame of being paraded in Octavian's triumph. Lepidus having been marginalized, Octavius (now known as Augustus) became the first **Emperor**.

Pax Romana

After the ascension of Augustus, Rome entered a period of relative tranquility. Augustus dubbed this era, which lasted about forty years, the **Pax Romana**. Rome remained an empire, although the conquered peoples were able to obtain Roman citizenship without having to forfeit their native customs. It was at this period that Rome reached its greatest geographic proportions, stretching all the way up to present-day Scotland. This was also the greatest period for **Roman artistic achievement**; both Virgil and Ovid were active during the Pax Romana, and, indeed, the Aeneid of Virgil was written in part to glorify Augustus. It was at this time that the polytheist religion of Rome was challenged first by the **Judaism** of the conquered Hebrews, and later by the early **Christians**.

Constantine and the Christians

The Roman Emperor **Constantine**, in response to the inconvenient vastness of his dominion, established an eastern capital: **Constantinople**, in AD 330. Having received a sign in the heavens which promised him victory over his rivals for the office of Emperor should he convert to Christianity, Constantine famously issued the **Edict of Milan**, in which he called for the end of the persecution of Christians, after a sound victory as promised. After this act, Christianity flourished in the Roman Empire and became the official religion of the state. A movement called **monasticism** developed within the religion, advocating the renunciation of worldly goods in favor of contemplation and prayer. After the death of Constantine, the empire once again proved unwieldy for one man, and therefore it split as it had previously, with the western half being governed from Rome and the eastern half from Constantinople. This arrangement would prove untenable, however; a Germanic tribe of **barbarians** eventually sacked Rome, and the western Roman capital fell in AD 476.

Byzantine Empire

The eastern half of the Roman Empire became known as the **Byzantine Empire**. After the fall of Rome, **Emperor Justinian** led successfully from Constantinople for a number of years. The Justinian era is especially remembered for the contributions to law and religious artwork, in particular the development of mosaics. In the years after the fall of Rome, the **Catholic Christian Church** gradually rose to fill the power vacuum. In what had been the Western Roman Empire, the Church acted completely independent of any political body, while even in the Byzantine Empire the Church was increasing in power. Only the influence of the Byzantine Emperor kept the Church from being the most powerful group in all of Europe.

Rise of Christianity

Early Christianity was a mass of competing doctrines, including various groups such as the Gnostics and Arians who all sought to have their view legitimized as the truth. Eventually, the **orthodox church**, through an ecumenical council of bishops, created in the 4th century AD the canon of New Testament texts which exists today. The apostles had created a hierarchy of bishops, priests, and deacons who stressed obedience to duly constituted church authority. By the middle of the 2nd century, Christianity began to attract intellectuals in the **Roman Empire**. Although Christians were still liable to be persecuted in the farther reaches of the empire, many turned to the Church as the empire crumbled, as the Church was all that was left of civilization, and would rebuild Europe over the next millennium.

Kingdom of Kush

Kush was a powerful African kingdom that lasted in some form from 2000 BC until AD 350. For a long time, **Kush** was based around the city of **Kerma**, in what is now Sudan. Kushites became wealthy because of their mineral resources and because of their advantageous location in the northwest corner of Africa, where they were at the crossroads of several intercontinental trade routes. There was a great deal of contact between Kush and **Egypt** in this period. In 767 BC, King Kashta of Kush defeated the Egyptians, and the Kushites had control of the entire Nile Valley. Kush would soon be weakened by the Assyrians, however, and would eventually fall prey to the **Romans**; in AD 350, the new capital of Kush, Meroe, was sacked.

AKSUM (AXUM)

Aksum, a town in what is now northern Ethiopia, was the capital city of one of Africa's most powerful kingdoms between the 1st and 6th centuries AD. The kings of **Aksum** were said to have descended from **Menelik**, one of the sons of the famous King Solomon. These people controlled almost all of the trade on the **Red Sea** and made a tremendous profit on the exchange of ivory. In the 4th century AD, Aksum eliminated the kingdom of **Kush** and became the predominant power in Africa. It was also during this century that Aksum was **Christianized**; it remains a hub of Ethiopian Christianity to this day. In its later stages, Aksum's control extended into southern Arabia and would eventually give way to the Persians and the Arabs.

NOK CULTURE

One of the most successful cultures of the African Iron Age was the **Nok culture**. The Nok developed **ironworking** technology before anyone else, and also created a rich artistic culture that spread throughout the West African forest region. The Nok were mainly active between the 5th and the 1st centuries BC. Their creation of iron farm implements made it possible for farmers to develop surplus crops, and thus urban centers could develop. This increase in agricultural productivity also made it possible for there to be more specialization of labor. Therefore, not only were civilizations more stable, but they were also better able to protect themselves, as they now had both better weapons made of iron and more time to train warriors.

ANCIENT GHANA

Beginning in the 7th century AD, **Ghana** was a major trading power in west Africa. It was mainly located in the areas that are now known as Mali and Mauritania. The people of Ghana grew rich by exchanging ivory and gold from the south and salt from the north. Eventually, Ghana would become an empire and would collect lavish tributes from all of the lands within its control. In the 11th century, the capital of Ghana was **Kumbi**. In 1076, however, Kumbi fell to the Almoravids, a Muslim tribe. The whole of Ghana would eventually be subsumed into the burgeoning empire of **Mali**.

ANCIENT MALI

Today, Mali is the largest nation in West Africa. Indeed, throughout African history, **Mali** has been a major power. Until the 11th century, it was a part of the empire of Ghana, a wealthy trading nation. Mali would eventually rise to prominence in its own right. The economy of Mali was based upon the rich mineral resources (especially gold) of the region. Mali reached its highest prominence during the reign of **Mansa Musa** (AD 1312-7). This ruler introduced Islam to his people, which at this time lived as far north as Morocco. The city of **Timbuktu** became a cultural center for the region, as well as a crossroads for trade routes that stretched across the Sahara. Over time, internal disputes would divide Mali into several smaller kingdoms.

SONGHAI EMPIRE

The Songhai empire flourished in West Africa between the 14th and 16th centuries. Centered in the valley of the Niger River, the **Songhai** were first organized by Christian **Berbers** in the 7th century. Four hundred years later, they established their capital at **Gao** and became an Islamic nation. Except for a brief period in which they were ruled by the empire of Mali, the Songhai controlled over a thousand miles along the Niger. Like most of the African powers, the Songhai made their money through trade. **Muhammad I**, who ruled from 1493 to 1528, expanded the empire to its greatest area. One of the weaknesses of the Songhai, however, was that they did not have a traditional means of succession, and thus frequent infighting among the powerful eventually led to the empire's demise.

The Huns

The Huns were a nomadic people who moved east across central Asia during the 4th century AD. The **Huns** were divided into several branches. The **White Huns** overran the Sasanian Empire and conquered many cities in the northern part of the Indian subcontinent. Another group roamed eastern Europe and established a strong empire on the Hungarian Plain around AD 400. The Huns were known for their amazing horsemanship and for being aggressive on the battlefield. It was under the guidance of **Attila** (440s) that the Huns reached their highest level of prominence. During this period, they collected tribute from many of the areas within the Roman Empire. Soon after the death of Attila, however, the Huns became complacent and lost most of their territory.

The Mongols

The Mongols, who descended from the Huns, were a nomadic group that roamed east-central Asia. Around the year AD 1206, the various **Mongol** tribes were united under **Genghis Khan**, whose empire then stretched from the Black Sea to the Pacific Ocean, and from Tibet to Siberia. After the death of Genghis, the Mongol lands were divided up. This did not, however, slow expansion; Mongols eventually controlled parts of Iran as well. **Kublai Khan** was another prominent Mongol leader; he destroyed the Song dynasty in China and replaced it with the Yuan. By the 14th century, the Mongol Empire was beginning to disintegrate. Like many of its kind, it proved too large to govern. The Ming and subsequently the Qing dynasties put the remaining Mongols under Chinese control.

Emergence of Russia

In the Middle Ages, Russia had a complicated and inefficient system of succession, which meant that the various lands were constantly being fought over, and authority was often dubious. For a long time, **Russia** was dominated by the **Mongols** (Tatars), who kept the local governments weak in order to continue receiving tributes. Moscow was able to parlay loyalty to the Tatars and colonization of other feudal estates into a great deal of power during this period. Supported by their Tatar overlords, the **Muscovite princes** were able to partition off their new lands in such a way that it became very difficult for nobles to consolidate their landholdings, which prevented any wealthy lords from ever challenging the princes of Moscow.

Steppe Peoples and Seljuk Turks

Between the years AD 1000 and 1450, invaders from the **steppes** conquered parts of Asia, the Middle East, and Europe. These people had originally been nomads, but in this period, they began to settle and become tradesmen. The clans that made up this group were loosely based on family ties; once they became stationary, they began to appoint powerful chiefs for leadership support. Near AD 1000, the **Seljuk Turks** moved from Central Asia into the Middle East. This group then controlled the trade routes between Asia, Africa, and Europe, and charged tolls on these routes, building an empire with their wealth. In 1071, the Seljuk Turks defeated the Byzantines at the **Battle of Manzikert**; a Christian defeat which would be part of the motivation for the **First Crusade.** The Seljuk Turks were known as excellent fighters and mediocre rulers; local leaders frequently ignored the central government and fought one another for control of land. This infighting weakened the group until they became prey to new nomadic invaders from Central Asia.

Poland and Hungary in Eastern Europe During the Middle Ages

During the Middle Ages, a number of different leaders tried to unite the various lands of **Poland.** These attempts were always defeated by the nobility, who preferred the country to be an oligarchy rather than a monarchy. Poland was also much involved during this period in a battle with the **Teutonic knights** over the Baltic coastline. **Hungary** was a feudal state by the beginning of the

14th century, and the various patches of land which constituted the country were ruled as if they were independent. Bishops in the **Eastern Orthodox Church** were among the largest landholders. Ostensibly, the nobility was in charge of the defense of the Hungarian people, though they rarely supplied the money and material for war.

ORIGINS AND EXPANSION OF ISLAM

The religion of Islam was founded by the prophet **Muhammad** in AD 610. **Islam** is a monotheistic religion based on the **Koran**, a book of scripture according to the Muslim god, **Allah**. The practice of Islam is based on "**Five Pillars**": faith in Allah, a pilgrimage to the city of Mecca, a yearly fast during the month of Ramadan, the giving of alms, and prayer five times a day. Muhammad also asserted that Islam should be spread throughout the world. Indeed, as the Christian Church was becoming the dominant factor in Europe, Islam was spreading throughout North Africa, the Middle East, parts of Asia, and even Spain. The simultaneous ascensions of Christianity and Islam inevitably led to conflict, most notably in the **Crusades**.

Review Video: Islam
Visit mometrix.com/academy and enter code: 359164

ISLAMIC CIVILIZATION

After the formation of Islam in the 7th century AD, it took 3 or 4 centuries to develop the institutional structures of the religion. **Islamic law** was created, and a new class of Muslim religious leaders and scholars emerged who took a prominent place in society. The Islamic civilization drew elements from its surroundings, namely the culture of the Greeks, Iranians, Christians, Jews, and Zoroastrians. At first, the Islamic Empire was ruled by a single **caliph** and a small Arab elite. As the empire expanded, however, this became untenable, and the lands were divided into a number of independent political entities. Also, factions began to emerge among Muslims, most notably between the **Sunnis** and **Shiites**, who rivaled over the true successor to Muhammad, among other issues. Because the entire Islamic world operated with a common system of trade, it quickly became very wealthy.

Review Video: The Islamic Empire
Visit mometrix.com/academy and enter code: 511181

FEUDALISM IN WESTERN EUROPE

Feudalism was the system of social and economic organization that developed in Europe in the Middle Ages (roughly AD 750 to 1300). **Feudalism** is characterized by rigid hierarchies among the various classes. At the top of the hierarchy was the **king**, and below him **lords**, who oversaw a smaller area of land. Below the lords were **noblemen** who had been granted control over farmland in exchange for their pledge of allegiance to the king. These noblemen were known as **vassals** and **subvassals**. The land managed by each vassal was known as a **fief**, and the home of the vassal was known as the **manor**. Each manor and the community surrounding it comprised a self-sufficient unit. The laws of **primogeniture** were enforced at this time, meaning that the ownership of the fief would descend to the firstborn son of the lord. Finally, the land was cultivated either by **peasants** or **serfs**; peasants were free farmers, while serfs were basically slaves who were forced to work for the lord and were bound to their lands.

CHARLEMAGNE

The emergence of the feudal system in Western Europe meant that instead of a centralized power, there were many local authorities. **Charlemagne** (AD 742-814) was a Germanic leader who tried to unify the former Western Roman Empire. In AD 800, **Pope St. Leo III** crowned Charlemagne

Emperor of Rome during Christmas Mass at St. Peter's Basilica in Rome, establishing a political relationship with the **Church** that would last throughout the Middle Ages. Charlemagne allocated a great deal of power to regional leaders and did not tax his subjects. For this reason, he was unable to make many internal improvements during his reign. Nevertheless, Charlemagne is credited with promoting the arts, especially within the thriving monasteries, without which much of antiquity would not have been transcribed and thus preserved. After the death of Charlemagne, his lands were divided up among his three grandsons according to the **Treaty of Verdun**.

Holy Roman Empire

The Holy Roman Empire was the name given to the holdings of **Otto the Great** in 962, who had unified the central area of Charlemagne's empire. As in Charlemagne's day, this was a disparate group of territories, and proved difficult to govern. Otto incorporated the **Church** into his government, though he continually sought to minimize its power. One of the legacies of Otto's reign would be the rivalry between the Church and state. Gradually, the Church leaders acquired power, until they were exercising great control over the day-to-day activities of most citizens. Perhaps inevitably, this great power began to corrupt many of the Church's leaders. Indicative of the state of the Church was the often unpunished offense of **simony**, in which prestigious and important offices were bought and sold.

Review Video: The Middle Ages: The Holy Roman Empire
Visit mometrix.com/academy and enter code: 137655

Western Europe in the 12th and 13th Centuries

In the 12th century AD, the various **fiefs** in Western Europe increasingly came into contact with one another. As advances in transportation technology made trade with distant neighbors possible, there developed more necessity for specialization. Rather than be entirely self-sufficient, lords found it was more economically advantageous to perfect the cultivation of one crop and exchange that for everything else. As **trade** became more important, so did the merchants in towns, known as burghers, who wielded considerable political power. Trade arrangements led to alliances between various towns, and the whole of Western Europe became more homogenous. The distinction between **classes** also became much less pronounced during this period. There were drawbacks, however: the increasing number of people in towns, as well as the more frequent travel between towns, contributed, no doubt, to the **bubonic plague epidemic** of the mid-14th century.

Faith and Learning in Western Europe During the Late Middle Ages

Surprising though it may seem, one of the best things that happened to Christian thought during the Middle Ages was its contact with **Islam**. The complex philosophies of Muslim scholars helped spur the evolution of **Christian theology**. These, in addition to the rediscovery of ancient philosophers such as Aristotle, led Christians to begin to glorify **reason** as the God-given tool for investigating religious faith. Many assertions made by the new rational theologians, however, were dubbed **heresy** by many Church leaders, as more and more Christian thinkers were bemoaning the materialistic ways of the Church leaders. One of the leading Christian thinkers of the Middle Ages was **St. Thomas Aquinas**, whose *Summa Theologica* outlined rational explanations for the belief in God and in the miracles of Christianity.

Formation of Universities in the Middle Ages

The rapid evolution in Christian thought that took place during the Middle Ages gave rise to the formation of the first **universities**. For the first time in Western Europe, young men would move to large cities to study theology, law, and medicine at formal institutions. In addition to this trend, the academic method known as **scholasticism** was developed, in which scholars would use logic and deductive reasoning in order to analyze a work or determine something of an abstract nature. Among the so-called scholastics, two schools of thought developed: those scholars who adhered to the ideas of Plato were known as **realists**, and those who followed Aristotle were known as **nominalists**. The word *realist* is somewhat confusing when used to refer to the work of Plato, who believed that our perceptions of objects were merely perceptions of the barest shadows of their reality. Another development of Christianity in this period was **mysticism**; Christian mystics believed that they could achieve union with God through self-denial, contemplative prayer, and alms-giving.

Germany, Italy, and France in the 13th Century

During the 13th century, France was transformed from a group of disparate fiefs into a centralized monarchy by **Philip Augustus** (Philip II). His heir, Philip IV, would establish the **Estates General**, a governing body composed of representatives from each province. The Estates General contained noblemen as well as wealthy commoners. Meanwhile, Germany endured an **interregnum**, or period between kings, after the ruler died without a clear successor. Italy, as well, spent this period as a collection of strong and independent townships. In a decentralized state, it became easier for wealthy merchants to wield power. In Germany, the **Hanseatic League**, an association of merchants, set regional trade policy.

Magna Carta

England, unlike many of the other regions of Western Europe, had been accustomed to a strong monarchy. This tradition was challenged in AD 1215, when noblemen forced King John to sign the **Magna Carta**, a document which gave feudal rights back to the nobles and extended the rule of law to the middle-class burghers. The Magna Carta made the formation of the **Houses of Parliament** possible. Over time, Parliament would evolve into a two-house structure: the **House of Lords**, which contained nobles and clergy, and the **House of Commons,** which contained knights and burghers. The House of Lords was mainly occupied with legal questions, while the House of Commons dealt mainly in economic issues.

Feudalism End in Western Europe

In the late 13th century, increased contact between regions and greater representation in government culminated in a number of **peasant revolts** and **serf uprisings**. During this period, members of the clergy became even more secular and open in their greed for fame and power. This alienated many common citizens from the Church. The invention of **gunpowder** also changed the social arrangements in Western Europe; fewer noblemen were willing to participate in combat, and so the code of chivalry gave way to **mercenary soldiers**. Noblemen largely turned their attention to acquiring some of the fantastic wealth available in trade. The quality that men strived for in these days was called **virtue**, meaning a solemn dedication to the arts and sciences.

Papal Bull "Unam Sanctam" and the Crisis in the Western Church

Around the year 1300, the power of the Pope in political affairs was weakening because of the rise of strong monarchs and a spirit of nationalism. **Pope Boniface VIII** attempted to force kings to obey him but was unsuccessful. In response, Boniface issued a papal bull in 1296 that instructed **King Philip IV** of France to not tax the church; Philip ignored this command. Boniface would not relent, and issued the bull "**Unam Sanctam**," in which he declared that there are two powers on the earth, the temporal and the spiritual, with the latter always superior, and that there is no salvation outside of loyalty to the Roman Pontiff. Once again, Philip refused the claims of the Pope and decided to silence him by having him kidnapped and brought to France. Boniface was able to escape captivity but died soon afterward. This significantly weakened the political authority of the papacy.

Babylon Captivity and Schism and the Crisis in the Western Church

After the death of Pope Boniface VIII, King Philip IV of France persuaded the College of Cardinals to select a French archbishop as the next pope. This pope, **Clement V**, moved the papacy to Avignon, France, where it would remain for 67 years. Debate raged during this period as to whether a pope could be legitimate in any city other than Rome. Also, Clement's court became notorious for its extravagance. In 1378, a new pope was chosen; an Italian, who chose the name **Urban VI** to indicate that he planned on keeping the papacy in Rome. Upset with Urban's policy, 13 French cardinals selected a new pope, the French-speaking **Clement VII**. Now, there were two popes, and each one declared the other illegitimate. This confusion lasted from 1378 until 1417, with the Pope in Rome and an antipope in Avignon.

Hundred Years' War

England made a claim on the French throne in 1337, and the result was a **war** (or series of wars) that lasted for 116 years. France was angry, in return, that England had not upheld its feudal obligations to the French throne, to whom the English king was technically a distant vassal. France had the support of the Pope, but England used the innovation of the longbow to score some significant victories. It was during this war that the charismatic figure **Joan of Arc** emerged. Joan was a French peasant who led troops to several unlikely victories after being visited by God. Her deeds rallied the spirits of the French, and France eventually won. The catastrophic losses suffered by both sides had major consequences: England withdrew from contention as a land power, electing instead to develop a **navy**; in France, **Louis IX**—St. Louis—took advantage of the chaos to consolidate power in the monarchy.

Effects of the Black Death and Johannes Gutenberg

Toward the end of the Middle Ages, two events greatly shaped future events. The **bubonic plague**, also known as the Black Death, killed between 30% and 60% of the European population. The influx of people to squalid cities made the rapid spread of this disease possible. The seemingly random devastation caused by the disease caused many people to question their faith, and the power of the Church suffered as a result. The other monumental event was the invention of the **printing press** by Johannes Gutenberg in about 1436. This invention was used first to produce a cheap copy of the Bible. Soon, though, printing presses with movable type were being used to print all sorts of things, and the literacy rate in Europe rose dramatically. It immediately became possible to disseminate ideas quickly.

Review Video: An Overview of the Black Death
Visit mometrix.com/academy and enter code: 431857

Feudalism in Japan

Feudalism developed in Japan after wars in the 11th century left much of the land in the control of military leaders. These men did not actually own the land, but a complex set of rights were given to them, whereby they had the exclusive right to cultivate and profit from the land. Many Japanese were disenchanted with the central government at this time, so the idea of powerful regional leaders appealed to them. A code of ethics specific to feudalism emerged, and Japanese peasants were required to pledge loyalty to a particular lord rather than to a political ideal. One particular feudal administration, the **Minamoto**, acquired almost the entirety of Japan and replaced the central government for most people.

MAYAS

The Mayas were based in Mexico's Yucatan Peninsula, Tabasco, and Chiapas, as well as in what is now Guatemala and Honduras. Between the years AD 200 and 950, they developed a sophisticated civilization, with complex religions, architecture, arts, engineering, and astronomy. The **Mayas** did have a form of hieroglyphic writing, but most of their history and folklore was preserved orally. The Mayas are responsible for creating an extremely accurate **calendar** and for first conceiving the number **zero**. The Maya civilization was supported by agriculture, but it was run by a class of priests and warriors. In the 9th century, the Mayas were overrun by Toltecs from the north, who created the legend of the feathered serpent **Quetzalcoatl**.

MAYA RELIGION

The Mayas conceived of the universe as a flat, square earth, whose four corners and center were dominated by a god. Above the sky, there were 13 levels, and below were 9 underworlds, each dominated by a god. The sun and moon, deities in their own right, passed through all of these levels every day. Each male god had a female goddess counterpart. The Mayas also had patron gods and goddesses for various occupations and classes. Maya rulers had religious powers. Religious rituals often entailed human sacrifice and self-mutilation. The Mayas also played a ritual ball game that had religious importance; the losers of this game stood to lose their lives. Mayas developed their cities as tributes to the gods.

AZTECS

When the **Toltec empire** had been eradicated around the year 1150, the power in Mesoamerica shifted to the valley of Mexico, around three lakes. By about 1325, the **Aztecs** had seized control of this area. The Aztec civilization was organized into **city-states**, much like early medieval Europe; political intrigue and state marriages were as common among the Aztecs as among the French. The Aztecs were known as fierce warriors and were hated by their neighbors because of their brutality. According to legend, the Aztecs settled in **Tenochtitlan** after a scout saw an eagle with a serpent in its beak perched on a cactus there. The Aztecs formed alliances based on threats and forced tributes.

INCAS

The Incas inhabited a huge area, from present-day Ecuador to central Chile to the eastern side of the Andes Mountains. The **Incas'** territory expanded especially after the 14th century AD. The Incas were engaged in frequent conflicts with rival groups, and they frequently enslaved the groups that they defeated. They eventually formed a permanent underclass of **serfs** in order to ensure that the lands of the military leaders would be cultivated. Incas typically dispersed rival groups in order to prevent being attacked. The Incan religion contained a god in heaven, a cult of ancestors, and a number of sacred objects and places. The Incas called themselves the **children of the Sun**.

TANG DYNASTY

The Tang dynasty was in control of China from AD 618 to 907. One of the main projects pursued by the **Tang** rulers was the **unification** of the far-flung and diverse Chinese states. The early portion of the Tang dynasty is considered one of the high points in Chinese history; the economy and the arts both flourished. Under the leadership of Tang generals, Chinese soldiers would claim parts of Afghanistan, Tibet, and Korea. The Tang were also somewhat unique as Chinese leaders in that they encouraged the introduction of foreign ideas into Chinese culture. **Printing** was invented in China during this period, and thus ideas could be disseminated much more easily. The end of the Tang dynasty came after a period of internal governmental conflict.

Song Dynasty

The Song dynasty of China lasted between the years AD 960 and 1279. The **Song** rulers are credited with reuniting many portions of China that had become disjointed. Historians usually distinguish between the Northern and the Southern Song. The leaders of the Song dynasty made a deliberate effort to reduce the emphasis on military conquest; instead, they focused on developing China's **civil service**. The Song dynasty saw a rejuvenation of **Confucian philosophy** in China, as well as a renewed interest in the **arts**. Some people compare the Song dynasty with the European Renaissance. The Song was the only dynasty in China not to be ended by internal conflict; the Song were ousted by a rebel leader instead.

Mauryan Empire

The Mauryan Empire lasted approximately between the years 321 and 185 BC. in India. It was established by the powerful leader **Chandragupta Maurya** and featured a strong military and an efficient bureaucracy. The **Mauryan empire** eventually spread as far west of the Indus River as present-day Afghanistan. At its greatest expansion, the Mauryan empire comprised almost the entirety of what is now India. The leader **Ashoka** (c. 272-232 BC) converted to Buddhism, and his rule was prosperous for rich and poor alike. After the death of Ashoka, however, the Mauryan Empire splintered, as the southern lands sought autonomy and the northern lands were subject to constant foreign invasions.

World History 1400 to 1914

Beginning of the Renaissance

In the 14th century, the turmoil caused by war and plague weakened the power of Christian theology. In its place came the philosophy of **humanism**, in which the emphasis is placed on individual potential and determination while detracting from one's attention to the realm of the divine. Humanist thought contributed to a resurgence in the arts and sciences, which eventually came to be known as the **Renaissance**. In the 14th and 15th centuries, the center of this resurgence was in **Northern Italy**, in large part because this was the crossroads of several important trade routes. Specifically, the city-states of Milan, Florence, and Venice cultivated excellent artists. Talented youths typically studied in these cities with their expenses paid by a wealthy patron; the most famous patrons were the **Medici** family in Florence.

Review Video: The Renaissance
Visit mometrix.com/academy and enter code: 123100

Italian Artists of the Renaissance

The early part of the Renaissance was dominated by the artists congregated in Northern Italy. Among them were several immortal talents. **Donatello** (1386-1466) sculpted a marvelous statue of David and was the first artist in this period to depict the naked human body (religious concerns had kept recent artists from doing so). **Botticelli** (1444-1510) is the painter of the famous Birth of Venus. **Leonardo da Vinci** (1452-1519) excelled in a number of different fields, but he is perhaps best known for painting the Mona Lisa and the Last Supper. **Michelangelo** (1475-1563), though, was probably the most famous painter and sculptor of the time; he painted the ceiling in the Sistine Chapel and sculpted the most famous statue of David.

Literature and Science in the Renaissance

Although the Renaissance is typically associated with achievements in visual art, the period also saw a magnificent outpouring of literary and scientific talent. One of the most significant works to emerge from this period was *The Prince*, by the Florentine **Niccolo Macchiavelli**. This book outlined a practical plan for political management, one that would be emulated by ruthless leaders in the future. Some of the other noteworthy authors were **Erasmus** (*In Praise of Folly*), **Sir Thomas More** (*Utopia*), **Montaigne**, **Cervantes** (*Don Quixote*), **Ben Johnson**, **Christopher Marlowe**, and, of course, **William Shakespeare**. At the same time, remarkable advances were being made in the sciences. **Copernicus** incited controversy by suggesting that the Earth revolved around the Sun; **Kepler** and **Galileo** would acquire hard data to support this claim.

Age of Exploration

The Age of Exploration is also called the **Age of Discovery**. It is generally considered to have begun in the early 15th century and continued into the 17th century. Major developments of the Age of Exploration included **technological advances** in navigation, mapmaking, and shipbuilding. These advances led to expanded European exploration of the rest of the world. **Explorers** set out from several European countries, including Portugal, Spain, France, and England, seeking new routes to Asia. These efforts led to the discovery of new lands, as well as **colonization** in India, Asia, Africa, and North America.

Review Video: Age of Exploration
Visit mometrix.com/academy and enter code: 612972

Role of Economics in the Age of Exploration

At the same time that the Renaissance was reinvigorating European cultural life, a desire to explore the world abroad was growing. Indeed, the ability to make long voyages was facilitated by the advances in **navigational technology** made around this time. The main reason for exploration, though, was **economic**. Europeans had first been introduced to eastern goods during the Crusades, and the exploits of Marco Polo in the 13th century had further whetted the western appetite for contact with distant lands. This increasing focus on exploration and trade caused a general shift in the balance of power in Europe. Landlocked countries, like Germany, found that they were excluded from participating in the lucrative new economy. On the other hand, those countries which bordered the **Atlantic** (England, France, Spain, and Portugal) were the most powerful players.

Obstacles to Exploration by Europe Before 1400

Before 1400, few Europeans knew anything about the world. When **Christopher Columbus** read of the exploits of the Italian Marco Polo, however, he was inspired to seek out new trade routes. Also, **Prince Henry** of Portugal established a navigation institute that encouraged sailors to explore. For a long time, extended sea voyages were restricted by a lack of navigational and seafaring technology; the inventions of the compass, astrolabe, and caravel remedied this situation. There was also a high cost associated with long travels (around 1400); however, new monarchs in France, England, Spain, and Portugal decided that they were willing to pay a high price to get a piece of the spice trade. Finally, the question of a motive for exploration was answered by the increasing fervor for missionary work, as well as the economic necessity of developing new trade routes.

Major European Explorers

Vasco da Gama was the first European to sail around the Cape of Good Hope, on the southern tip of what is now South Africa. This made it possible to reach Asia by boat. **Balboa** explored Central America and was the first European to view the Pacific Ocean. **Magellan** is remembered as the first to circumnavigate the globe. **Cortes** was a powerful commander who subjugated the Aztecs in what is now Mexico; he used great brutality to achieve his ends. **Pizarro**, like Cortes, was a conquistador; he conquered the Incas in what is now Peru. **Amerigo Vespucci**, from whose name the word

America was derived, mapped the Atlantic coast of South America and was able to convince stubborn Europeans that these lands were not a part of India.

Joint-Stock Companies at the Time of the Age of Exploration

As exploration created new opportunities for amassing wealth, **Portugal** enjoyed special favor because of its excellent location and cordial relations with many of the Muslim nations of North Africa. The ruler of Portugal at this time was even known as Prince Henry "the Navigator" (1394-1460). In order to solidify trade arrangements, European rulers began to think about colonizing foreign lands. In order to fund these expensive trips, a new kind of business known as the **joint-stock company** was developed. In a joint-stock company, a group of merchants would combine their resources to pay for the passage of a vessel. These groups would later be influential in securing colonial charters for many of their agents. One of the most powerful examples was the **Muscovy Company of England**, which controlled almost all trade with Russia.

Mercantilism at the Time of the Age of Exploration

As foreign trade became the most important part of every nation's economy, the economic theory of **mercantilism** became popular. According to mercantilism, a nation should never import more than it exports. Of course, it is impossible for every country to achieve this goal at the same time, so European countries were in fierce competition at all times. The solution that most nations pursued was to establish **colonies**, because these could supply resources for export by the mother country without really being considered imports. This rush to colonize had disastrous consequences for the indigenous peoples of the Americas and Africa. Europeans often looted the Native Americans for anything of value, and their need for cheap labor to cultivate the land there spawned the **African slave trade**.

Reformation

A response to corruption in the Catholic Church and lapses in enforcement of the basic tenets of the faith, such as those against simony, the **Reformation** was a movement that called for a return to what many believed to be a simpler message of salvation that they felt to be more scripturally accurate. Many people in this time were outraged by the vast landholdings and stuffed coffers of the Church, which they felt should be concerned with tending to the spiritual health of its members. In 1440, the invention of the **printing press** had made it possible for ideas to be disseminated more widely, and authors of the Renaissance had sharply criticized the greed of the clergy. People were also angered by the selling of **ecclesial offices** and especially the selling of **indulgences**, in which a person would pay money to have one's time in purgatory shortened. Selling salvation was indeed against the tenets of the Church, but was often largely unenforced. The general distrust of the Church in this period is known as **anticlericalism**.

Martin Luther

Martin Luther was a German friar who first became famous for criticizing the Catholic Church's sale of indulgences. In **1517**, in accordance with the tradition of theological debate, **Luther** posted his critique of this practice on the door of his local church; the document known as the "**Ninety-five Theses**" won him immediate fame. Luther then set about undermining the institution of the Church, arguing that individuals did not need the help of clergy to establish a strong relationship with God. Luther went even further, stating that faith, rather than obedience to arbitrary Church rules, would be what got individuals into heaven. The final straw for the Church came when Luther directly challenged the Pope, declaring that no one man could be the perfect interpreter of Scripture. Luther was excommunicated but continued to spread his message. Germany was then wracked by a war between the Lutherans of the north and the Catholics of the south. The **Peace of Augsburg** in 1555 was the resolution to this conflict, in which the subjects of a prince would follow that prince's faith, a practice referred to as *cuius regio, cuius religio*—literally, "whose jurisdiction, whose religion."

Review Video: Martin Luther and the Reformation
Visit mometrix.com/academy and enter code: 691828

PROTESTANTS

Inspired by Luther, many other critics of Catholic excess joined together throughout Europe. These groups were known collectively as **Protestants**. One of the largest sects of Protestants was the **Calvinists**, named after founder John Calvin. This group believed in the idea of predestination, or that God had already fixed each person's eternal destiny, and that only the Elect would join Him in heaven. Naturally, most people believed themselves to be among the Elect. In England, **King Henry VIII** split from the Catholic Church after his request for an annulment from Catherine of Aragon was denied by the Pope. Henry established the **Church of England** with himself as leader, and had five more wives before his death.

Review Video: The Protestants
Visit mometrix.com/academy and enter code: 583582

COUNTER-REFORMATION

After being bombarded by Protestant attacks for years, the **Catholic Church** finally began to make some positive changes. This program was known as the **Counter-Reformation**, and it was aimed at stopping the spread of Protestantism. For instance, the sale of indulgences was halted, and more authority was given to local bishops. The Church reaffirmed many of its core teachings (such as the earning of indulgences, transubstantiation, veneration of the Virgin Mary, the necessity of works, etc.) yet admitted its errors with regard to simony and abuses of clerical power, which were quickly remedied. One of the most influential men of this movement was **Sir Ignatius Loyola**, a Spaniard who founded the **Society of Jesus (the Jesuits)** to promote the Catholic interpretation of Scripture. The **Council of Trent** was a 20-year meeting that determined the official Catholic interpretation on all matters of theology. The Counter-Reformation also saw the re-emergence of the **Inquisition**, in which heretics were sought out and punished.

Review Video: The Counter-Reformation
Visit mometrix.com/academy and enter code: 950498

INTRODUCTION OF THE ERA OF EUROPEAN MONARCHIES (1500-1650)

Between the years 1500 and 1650, most of the major European powers were led by **absolute monarchs**, who claimed a divine right to rule. These European monarchies often consolidated their power by marrying into one another. The strength of the monarchies fostered a resurgent spirit of **nationalism** and consequently led to more frequent conflicts between nations. In 1500, **Spain** was probably the most powerful nation in Europe, because of her lucrative colonies and impressive Armada. Over the next century and a half, however, **France** and **England** would emerge as the dominant powers in the region. **Germany** and **Russia**, though largely excluded from shipping, were still powerful during this period.

Review Video: Absolute Monarchs: An Overview
Visit mometrix.com/academy and enter code: 678546

Review Video: Absolute Monarchs: France
Visit mometrix.com/academy and enter code: 953883

Review Video: Absolute Monarchs: Germany
Visit mometrix.com/academy and enter code: 562601

Review Video: Absolute Monarchs: Russia
Visit mometrix.com/academy and enter code: 974242

Review Video: Spanish Government in the 1500s
Visit mometrix.com/academy and enter code: 735727

Powers of Spain Between 1500 and 1650

The height of Spanish power began with the reign of **King Ferdinand** and **Queen Isabella**; these monarchs promoted exploration and became fantastically rich as a result. The Hapsburg **King Charles V** would increase Spain's prominence and territory, because he had acquired lands in France, Austria, and Germany through inheritance. Spain was drawn into a number of conflicts over these new possessions, however: France disputed his claim to parts of Italy, and the Ottoman Turks challenged his Armada in the Mediterranean. Charles V would finally be forced to abdicate the throne, leaving his brother **Ferdinand I** in control of Austria and Germany, and his son **Philip II** in control of Spain and some western lands. During Philip's reign, most of these possessions would be lost; particularly bitter was the loss of the Netherlands, which quickly became a trading power in their own right.

Pizarro and the Incas

Francisco Pizarro (c. 1478-1541) was a Spanish explorer. He lived for a time in what is now Panama, where he heard tales of the fabulous wealth enjoyed by the **Incas** in the Andes Mountains. **Pizarro** was determined to conquer this empire, and with 168 men he reached the Incan city of Tumbes in 1532. At this time, the Incas were in the middle of a civil war. Pizarro used this to his advantage; he massacred one side and took their leader prisoner. In order to free himself, the leader arranged a huge ransom, which Pizarro collected and then ignored, killing the leader anyway. Soon, Spaniards conquered the Incan city of **Cuzco** and installed a puppet regime. After some turmoil, Pizarro took over the leadership of **Peru** until his assassination in 1541.

Cortez and His Relationship with the Aztecs

Hernán Cortez (1485-1547) was a Spanish conquistador. He assisted in the conquest of **Cuba** and lived there until 1518, when he was assigned to lead an expedition into **Mexico**. He and 700 men landed on the Mexican shore, and he promptly had his ships burnt in order to indicate his sincerity about establishing a foothold in the country. **Cortez** then led his troops into **Tenochtitlan**, the capital of the **Aztec Empire**. They were received graciously by the Aztec ruler, **Montezuma**, whom they immediately enslaved. The Aztecs tried to revolt against the Spanish influence, but Cortez formed a coalition with other anti-Aztec groups and brutally eliminated the Aztec uprising. Cortez went on to rule "New Spain" for a number of years.

Government of France Between 1500 and 1650

While England was undergoing a turbulent transition from an absolute to a limited monarchy, **France** was governed by a succession of powerful and talented Bourbon monarchs. The **Estates General**, the French counterpart to the British Parliament, was not especially powerful. During a period in which the Bourbon heir was too young to govern himself, the charismatic **Cardinal Richelieu** governed France. Cardinal Richelieu was a Catholic, of course, but he did not persecute the French protestant Huguenot sect. Rather, he compromised with his enemies in an attempt to consolidate the power of the French crown. Cardinal Richelieu also established a strong bureaucracy, known as the ***noblesse de la robe***.

Government of Germany Between 1500 and 1650

Unlike many of the other Western European powers in 1500, **Germany** was still essentially just a collection of disjointed city-states. The **Hapsburg** family was powerful there, but the lands they called their **Holy Roman Empire** were not well organized, and the Hapsburgs were weak compared to other European leaders. The **Peace of Augsburg**, which had quelled disputes between Lutherans and Catholics, was destroyed by the **Thirty Years' War** (1618-48), which began when Protestants challenged the authority of the Hapsburg emperor. Germany would become so chaotic and disjointed during this period that other nations would step in, whether to seize some land or to help out one side or the other. The brutality of this war left Germany in a state of turmoil.

Russian Rule Between 1500 and 1650

As the nations of Western Europe were beginning to rely on foreign trade almost exclusively to support themselves, **Russia** remained a feudal nation. After the Mongols were overthrown, Russia was ruled by a succession of **Czars**, and Russia was largely excluded from the cultural rejuvenation of the Renaissance period. Instead, Russians suffered through the reign of **Ivan the Terrible** (1530-84), a fierce ruler who pushed the borders out in the east with horrible brutality and suffocated any rivals or critics. Ivan's reign was so oppressive that Russia could not develop a merchant class to rival those of the Western European powers, despite having some impressive natural resources.

Scientific Revolution

The rapid advance in learning known as the **Scientific Revolution** was a product of the systematic form of inquiry known as the **scientific method**. With the scientific method, learning is incremental: a question is posed, a hypothetical solution is offered, observations are made, and the hypothesis is either supported or refuted. The consistency of the method made it easy for scientific discoveries to be transferred from one country to another. Along with a standardized form of **measurement**, the development of the scientific method gave scientists a common language. Scientists also benefited from the development of powerful **telescopes** and **microscopes**.

Major Figures

After **Copernicus** startled the world by challenging the geocentric (that is, earth-centered) model for the universe, Italian **Galileo Galilei** supplied scientific experiments that proved the accuracy of Copernicus' theory. One of the philosophical heroes of the Scientific Revolution was Frenchman **Rene Descartes**, who attempted to base his beliefs about the world upon empirical and provable facts: most famously, "I think, therefore I am." **Francis Bacon** was an English intellectual who wrote copiously on the possibilities for science to improve the human condition. **Sir Isaac Newton** excelled in many fields but is best known for his theories of motion and gravitation. Newton helped create the general idea that objects in the world behave in regular and predictable ways.

Review Video: The Scientific Revolution
Visit mometrix.com/academy and enter code: 974600

England During the Tudor and Stuart Rulings

For many years, England was ruled by the **Tudor** family. **Henry VIII**, the founder of the Anglican Church, had been a Tudor, and his daughter **Elizabeth** continued his policies. During the Elizabethan age in England, trading and exploration increased, and the Spanish Armada, sent to overthrow Elizabeth as a protestant heretic, was defeated. After Elizabeth died in 1603, the **Stuart** family ascended to the throne. The Stuart period would be marked by conflict. Both **James I** and **Charles I** butted heads with Parliament over the issue of taxation, and there were also continual conflicts between **Puritans** (followers of John Calvin) and **Anglicans** (adherents of the Church of England). The Puritans joined with Parliament in opposition to the monarchy.

Cromwell and William and Mary

The alliance of Parliament and the Puritans was led by **Oliver Cromwell**. His army was successful in deposing and executing **King Charles I**, and Cromwell was subsequently installed as **Protector of England**. Cromwell's rule was undermined by Anglican nobles and clergy who disliked his Puritanism. After the death of Cromwell, England was ruled by the two sons of Charles I, **Charles II** and **James II**, the latter of which was forced to abdicate by Parliament. After this period of relative chaos, **William and Mary** of the Netherlands were asked to rule England in a limited monarchy. This shift in power was known as the **Glorious Revolution**. The **Declaration of Rights** that limited the power of the monarchy gave Parliament more power and made possible a long period of tranquility.

The Enlightenment

Between the years 1600 and 1770, political and social philosophy in Europe underwent a tremendous change, known collectively as the **Enlightenment**. Just as Northern Italy had been the center of the Renaissance, so now **Paris** was the hub of progressive thought. The collection of philosophers, who sought to bring every subject under the authority of reason, included both **deists** (those who believed in God) and **atheists** (those who did not). The study known as **political science** first emerged during this period. Intellectuals began to question the divine right that had been claimed by absolute monarchs in the past; they sought to determine which was the best form of government for all the citizens of the country.

Review Video: Age of Enlightenment
Visit mometrix.com/academy and enter code: 143022

Major Figures

One of the most sparkling wits of the Enlightenment period belonged to the Frenchman **Voltaire** (1694-1778). He challenged the authority of the Church, declaring that people should tolerate the views of others and that no one man or group had a monopoly on absolute truth. **Thomas Hobbes** (1598-1679) was one of the most influential political theorists of the period. In his masterpiece "Leviathan," he declared that the base impulses of the people had to be restrained by a powerful and just monarch. **John Locke** (1632-1704), on the other hand, declared that men were born with natural rights which could not be justly denied them. **Rousseau** (1712-78), a Swiss philosopher, asserted that the government only ruled so long as it did so to the satisfaction of the general will of the people.

Peace of Westphalia and Louis XIV

The monarchs of the Enlightenment period found themselves under increasing pressure to be tolerant and benevolent. In Western Europe, so-called "enlightened despots" governed in order to promote the best interests of their subjects; this was probably done more to retain power than to express any profound solidarity with the commoners. France had become the central power on the European continent after the **Peace of Westphalia** (1648), which ended the **Thirty Years' War** and weakened Germany. The long reign of **Louis XIV** of France was characterized by grandiosity and the cultivation of the arts. Louis spent considerable effort trying to acquire new territories for France and glory for himself, and so alarmed the other European powers with his swiftness from victory to victory that many former enemies allied against France.

Creation of Prussia and Contributions of Frederick the Great

The **Peace of Westphalia** (1648) established the independence of several small sections of Germany; chief among these new states was Prussia. **Frederick the Great** (1712-86) became the ruler of **Prussia** in 1740 and displayed marvelous efficiency and benevolence. He made a genuine effort to allow for the coexistence of all the religious groups in Prussia, and also worked to improve the lives of the serfs. Frederick also encouraged immigration to Prussia, which brought in new ideas and technological advances. Prussia, which had long suffered economically because of its lack of a coastline, now became a producer of luxury goods like porcelain and silk.

Russia During the Rule of Peter the Great and Catherine the Great

Peter the Great (1672-1725) was responsible for the transformation of Russia from an impoverished agricultural nation to a strong commercial nation. Peter was enamored of the ways of the western European nations and made several trips to other capitals to learn the intricacies of Enlightenment politics and trade. **St. Petersburg** was intended to be a Russian city in the style of Paris or Berlin. Peter's innovations revitalized the economy, but they also set a standard for decadence that would be carried on by future czars. **Catherine II**, otherwise known as Catherine the Great, ruled from 1762 to 1796 and implemented many Enlightenment policies in education and the arts. Nevertheless, in the remote provinces of Russia, the **feudal system** endured, and the economy remained stunted.

French Revolution

Causes

Before the revolution, France was governed by an absolute monarch and, with regard to matters of taxation, the **Estates General**, which had been formed in order to represent the common people. The Estates General was composed of three estates: the clergy (**First Estate**), nobility (**Second Estate**), and everyone else (**Third Estate**). Unfortunately, this body had been marginalized by a series of powerful monarchs, and it was arranged such that the largest group by far, the Third Estate, only had one-third of the vote. In any case, the Third Estate usually found its desires opposed by the other estates. Another source of anger for the middle class and peasants was the **tax structure**; the nobles and clergy were not forced to pay taxes, and thus the burden of France's depressed economy fell upon the Third Estate.

King Louis XVI and National Assembly

Aware of the injustice of the French tax policy, **King Louis XVI** tried to pass some reforms but was repeatedly thwarted by the greedy nobles and clergy. The **Third Estate** was infuriated and refused to vote in the Estates General anymore. Instead, prominent members of the middle class banded together to form the **National Assembly**, which purported to represent the interests of common Frenchmen. At the same time, the peasants were in full revolt. On July 14, 1789, they stormed the

Parisian prison known as the **Bastille**. The success of this riot inspired more peasants to clamor for representation, and the diversion it caused kept the government from dealing with the National Assembly.

Declaration of the Rights of Man

After the storming of the Bastille and the formation of the National Assembly in 1789, the French middle and lower classes joined together and established a new government with the slogan "**Liberty, Equality, Fraternity**." This government quickly reformed the tax code and declared that government offices would henceforth be filled on the basis of merit. The National Assembly also eliminated serfdom and drafted a **Declaration of the Rights of Man**, which was similar to the American Bill of Rights. The National Assembly then seized the lands that belonged to the Church and eliminated the feudal rights of the aristocracy. Soon, there was dissension within the Third Estate, and the revolution became more radical and violent.

French Revolution and the Reign of Terror

As the government established by the Third Estate descended into chaos, the radical Jacobin leader **Robespierre** took charge. He had an idealistic vision of what France could become, and he was willing to kill thousands in order to see it realized. The **guillotine** provided a swift way to execute scores of opponents, a group that included anyone who dared challenge the Jacobin party line or was suspected of retaining their Catholic faith in the new culture of state-mandated atheism. Among those executed were **King Louis XVI** and his wife, **Marie Antoinette**. After a while, the French tired of the violence and turmoil of the **Reign of Terror**, and Robespierre himself fell victim to the guillotine. A group of five prominent men, known as the **Directory**, was established to restore calm. This group would last until 1799, when it was overthrown in a coup that would eventually bring **Napoleon Bonaparte** to power.

Rise of Napoleon Bonaparte

Napoleon Bonaparte (1769-1821) began his career as a French military commander, scoring major victories in Austria and England. Upon his return to the chaos of France, he led a coup and was installed as the leader of France. He was subsequently elected by a popular vote. Almost immediately, **Napoleon** reformed French education, agriculture, and infrastructure. The main object of Napoleon's rule, however, was the acquisition of territory both in Europe and in the New World. Napoleon's troops quickly conquered Austria, Portugal, Spain, and Prussia. Napoleon, who modeled himself after Charlemagne in many ways, then crowned himself **emperor**. The French empire proved too large to manage, however, and Napoleon further weakened himself with a disastrous campaign against Russia.

> **Review Video: The French Revolution: Napoleon Bonaparte**
> Visit mometrix.com/academy and enter code: 876330

Independence Struggle in Latin America

When Spain fell to Napoleon's forces in 1809, the provinces of **Chile** and **Buenos Aires** both declared themselves independent. At this time, **Peru** was the stronghold of Spanish power in the New World, and therefore the rebels attacked the government there. Led by the Argentinean **Jose San Martin**, rebels entered Lima and declared Peru an independent state in 1821. The greatest military leader of the independence movement, however, was **Simon Bolivar**. He had traveled extensively in Europe and used his knowledge of the enemy to run the Spaniards out of Colombia, Venezuela, and Central America. Bolivar eventually seized control of Peru and hoped to form a great union of South American nations, but this alliance was eventually torn asunder by internal feuds.

FALL OF NAPOLEON

After Napoleon's debacle in Russia debilitated his military, revolts sprung up in many of the nations that he had conquered, and Napoleon was overthrown. The leaders of the countries that had overthrown Napoleon met in Vienna to decide how to respond to him. These three men, **Prince von Metternich** of Austria, the English **Duke of Wellington**, and **Alexander I** of Russia, were constantly in disagreement, however, and Napoleon used this opportunity to return from his exile on the Isle of Elba in the Mediterranean and reclaim power. Finally, Napoleon was defeated at **Waterloo** and sent into permanent exile. The allies met again at the **Congress of Vienna** in 1815 where France was not treated too harshly, and it was determined that a balance of power should be maintained in Europe to ensure that no one in the future tried to dominate the continent.

OPIUM WAR

The Opium War lasted between the years 1839 and 1842. It began because the British kept trafficking **opium** from India into China because they wanted to trade with the Chinese, and opium was the only product that China could not produce for itself. The Chinese government, however, was appalled by the effect that the drug had on its citizens and mounted a serious anti-opium campaign. When British merchants appealed to their leaders, the British navy was sent in order to force the Chinese to accept the opium. The British ended up seizing several Chinese cities, including Shanghai and Nanking. The war ended with the **Treaty of Nanking** in 1842; China was forced to cede Hong Kong to the British, and several Chinese ports had to be left open for trade.

Review Video: Anti-Colonial Struggles: The Opium War
Visit mometrix.com/academy and enter code: 111806

TAIPING REBELLION

The Taiping Rebellion lasted in China between the years 1850 and 1864. It was a religious and political rebellion against the government of the **Manchus**, led by the Christian **Hung Hsiu-ch'uan**. The rebels advocated the public ownership of land and a self-sufficient economy. They wanted to rid China of the encroaching influences of foreign merchants. Hung's troops were able to conquer Nanking and make it the capital of their "Great Peaceful Heavenly Dynasty." Internal feuds weakened the Taiping, however, and the western powers (concerned that they would lose the Chinese market) helped to oust them in 1864. The **Taiping Rebellion** was by far the bloodiest war of the 19th century.

MEIJI REFORM

In 1854, an American group led by **Commodore Matthew Perry** forced Japan to open its ports to foreign merchants. Japan had been closed to the West for 200 years. The Japanese people were not pleased with this development, and they blamed the **Tokugawa shogun** (the military leader of the period). In 1867, the shogun resigned and **Emperor Matsuhito** declared that he was now in charge. The Japanese capital was moved from Kyoto to Edo (which was renamed Tokyo). The ensuing period in Japanese history is known as the **Meiji Period**. During it, the feudal system was abolished, and Western ideas became popular. The samurai had their land right revoked and were eventually eliminated altogether. In the late 19th century, Japanese leaders began to turn their attentions to expansion onto the Asian continent; in the Sino-Japanese war, they conquered parts of China and Korea.

BOXER REBELLION

The Boxer Rebellion was a peasant uprising in China around the turn of the 20th century. The rebels aimed to overthrow the **Manchu government** and to cast all foreigners out of China. The rebels were known as the **Boxers** because they practiced certain mystical boxing rituals. After Japan had defeated China in 1895, the Japanese had exercised a great deal of influence on the Chinese economy. Around 1900, Boxers began to kill foreign merchants and diplomats. An international force was assembled to defeat the Boxers. During the ensuing fight, the city of **Peking** was almost entirely destroyed. Eventually, the western powers prevailed and forced the Boxer leaders to sign an incredibly unfavorable treaty.

Review Video: Anti-Colonial Struggles: The Boxer Rebellion
Visit mometrix.com/academy and enter code: 352161

Industrial Revolution

English Textile Industry

The **Industrial Revolution** in Europe in the 19th century produced immediate and far-reaching changes in the social structure. **England** was perhaps the first to feel the effects of rapid industrialization; the factory system for manufacturing textiles was implemented, meaning that individuals were only required to do one in the series of tasks required to prepare a piece of cloth. This division of labor increased productivity. New energy sources, such as the steam engine, also made fabulous increases in productivity possible. Coal was introduced as an aid to the iron-smelting process, and the mass production of cotton textiles was soon propelling the English economy.

Social Changes

With the success of the textile industry, more and more workers were needed in the European cities, and therefore people began to abandon their country lives and take factory jobs in town. This rapid **urbanization** created a new **middle class** in Europe, and it also created a number of problems. Most cities did not have the infrastructure to support such an explosion in population, and as such, disease, crime, and poverty were common. The booming success of industry made many people rich as investors and merchants, and therefore the middle class assumed even more political power in Europe. **Social mobility** was infinitely more possible in this economic environment, encouraging many people to stick with jobs that were demeaning and not especially lucrative.

Working Class and Luddites

As people flooded the cities to work in the booming factories, large landowners consolidated the farmlands they left behind. **Working-class** individuals were probably not pleased with their new lives; 18-hour days, low wages, and dangerous machinery were among the problems faced by this new underclass. Oftentimes, women and children were employed for the most menial jobs, and they were paid less than men. A small rebellion, led by a group called the **Luddites**, tried to resist the tide of industrialization and were known for vandalizing factory equipment. Still, most individuals were enticed by the prospect of upward mobility that the new, fluid class system offered, and were willing to endure hardship in exchange for hope.

Review Video: The Industrial Revolution
Visit mometrix.com/academy and enter code: 372796

Review Video: Industrialization
Visit mometrix.com/academy and enter code: 893924

NATIONALISM IN 19TH-CENTURY EUROPE

In the 19th century, the spirit of nationalism that had been building in Europe since the Middle Ages reached a critical mass. **Nationalism** refers to pride in the traditions, culture, language, and past of a certain nation of people, and not necessarily to pride in one's country. This is important to note, because in the 19th century, there were many nations of people thrown together as parts of a larger kingdom. The rising tide of nationalism, then, was a concern to the ruling **monarchs**, who hoped to hold together disparate nations under their control. Russia, for instance, contained a wide variety of cultures and languages under one leadership.

Review Video: Historical Nationalism
Visit mometrix.com/academy and enter code: 510185

CLASSICAL LIBERALISM IN 19TH-CENTURY EUROPE

The political and economic philosophies of the Enlightenment laid the foundation for 19th-century **classical liberalism**. **Adam Smith's** "The Wealth of Nations," written in 1776, introduced the concept of the "invisible hand," suggesting that market forces, if left largely to operate freely, could lead to economic prosperity. Although Smith's work preceded the Industrial Revolution, his ideas influenced later classical liberals who championed free-market policies. Another influential thinker, **Thomas Malthus**, in "An Essay on the Principle of Population" (1798), wrote that unchecked population growth would outstrip food supply, leading to famine and disease. While his work was later used to justify laissez-faire economic policies, Malthus himself advocated for population control measures rather than the outright suffering of the poor.

SOCIAL LIBERALISM IN 19TH-CENTURY EUROPE

Social liberalism developed in the late 19th century as an alternative to classical liberalism. **Social liberalism** declares that political problems can be solved by the work of liberal institutions in the government. Unlike the classical liberals, social liberals believe that the government should exercise some influence on the **economy** and should extend some basic **welfare services** to the people. Social liberalism aimed to improve life for the poor and disadvantaged. Social liberals were also very outspoken on issues of civil rights and individual liberties. Some of the most famous social liberals are **Jeremy Bentham**, **John Stuart Mill**, and **John Dewey**.

EMERGENCE OF SOCIALISM IN 19TH-CENTURY EUROPE

Socialism is a political philosophy which declares that the economic means of production should be owned by the workers. This control may either be exercised directly by the workers through local councils or by the state with the consent of the workers. Socialists hope thereby to create a state of **social equality** and an even **distribution of wealth**. Not surprisingly, this movement was most popular among the working classes in 19th-century Europe. Socialists at this time declared that capitalism served only the interests of the very wealthy and exploited everyone else. In their view, a socialist society would provide a greater reward for hard work and would create harmonious societies. Socialism and communism come from the same ideological lineage, but they differ in some ways. Generally speaking, socialism and communism both hope to have the means of production controlled by a collective or governing organization and not owned privately. **Socialism** would allow for individuals to continue to have private property, whereas **communism** would eliminate private property and have the collective or state regulate the distribution of wealth.

Review Video: Communism vs. Socialism
Visit mometrix.com/academy and enter code: 917677

Emergence of Marxism in 19th-Century Europe

The political theories of socialism and communism both take their inspiration from the works of **Karl Marx** (1818-83). Marx declared that economics has been the primary determinant in history and that the history of society is nothing more than a "history of class struggle." Marx asserted that problems have been created in situations where the material that a worker produces is worth more than the compensation he receives for his work. The surplus goes to the capitalist owner, and the worker is caught in a situation where he can never get ahead. The inevitable result, according to Marx, is a revolution of the working class (which he called the **proletariat**) and the installation of an economic system similar to socialism or communism.

Review Video: Karl Marx
Visit mometrix.com/academy and enter code: 362061

19th-Century British Politics

During the 19th century, the memory of Napoleon and the balance of power established by the **Congress of Vienna** prevented any large conflicts. The **Industrial Revolution** had made Britain the wealthiest and most powerful nation in Europe. The rise of a rich middle class caused the British Parliament to alter voting laws so that more of the wealthy would have influence. This was done with the **Reform Act of 1832**; in 1833, Britain abolished slavery in its colonies. This was not enough for the many working-class Britons, however, and they lobbied long and hard for universal suffrage until it was finally granted in the 1880s. The British movement for universal suffrage was known as **Chartism**.

Review Video: 19th Century Politics: Britain
Visit mometrix.com/academy and enter code: 266214

19th-Century French Politics

Internal turmoil caused France to miss out on much of the wealth of the Industrial Revolution. After the demise of Napoleon, **Louis XVII** had been restored to the throne by the **Congress of Vienna**. He was succeeded by the archconservative **Charles X**, who was quite unpopular and was chased off the throne in the **July Revolution of 1830**. In his place came **Louis Philippe**, who administered over a fairly stable country for eighteen years until he was deposed in the revolution of 1848. Next came **Napoleon III**. Elected the emperor of France in 1851, he remained in power until the French defeat in the **Franco-Prussian War of 1870**. From 1870 until 1940, France would be governed by a constitutional and democratic government that was, for the most part, conservative.

19th-Century German Political System

Ever since the end of Charlemagne's empire, Austria and Germany had not been unified as a single nation. This was finally achieved by the Prussian **Otto von Bismarck** after a long period of suppression of German nationalists. Bismarck's unification of **Prussia** was mainly aimed at defeating the rival Hapsburgs, who controlled Austria. When Prussia won the **Austro-Prussian** and **Franco-Prussian wars** in quick succession, Bismarck declared that he had achieved his ends and unified the German empire. He oversaw the creation of the **Reichstag**, a legislative body that would provide representation to the middle and lower classes. Germany threw itself into the project of industrialization.

19th-Century Italian Political System

Italy, like Germany, had really been more of a disjointed collection of independent city-states than a nation in its own right. In the 19th century, however, there was a drive to unify the region. A leader from the Piedmont region, **Camillo Cavour**, tried to bring the various city-states together through diplomacy rather than combat. This process took a very long time but was eventually completed in the 1870s. **Northern Italy**, which had intimate contact with Germany, became industrialized during this period, and the city of Milan enjoyed immense growth. **Southern Italy**, on the other hand, remained largely rural. This distinction between the two halves of Italy would be a source of conflict in the future.

19th-Century Russian Political System

At the beginning of the 19th century, much of Russia was still mired in an impoverished, quasi-feudal state. After the death of **Alexander** in 1825, the **Decembrists** tried to force the incoming Czar to adopt a constitution allocating some power to the people. The next czar was **Nicholas I**, who used secret police to try to eliminate the roots of the popular insurrection. This policy of suppression only further isolated Russia from the rest of Europe, which was at that time reducing the power of the monarch. Russia later lost the **Crimean War** to Britain, France, and the Ottoman Empire, and many Russians bemoaned the backward state of their country. Finally, a new czar, **Alexander II**, freed the serfs and tried to industrialize. This happened slowly.

Russian Revolution of 1905

At the turn of the 20th century, **Russia** was torn by the trends of industrialism and imperialism. The country was still being operated as an absolute monarchy, and was behind on social reforms common to the rest of Europe. Russia was trying to undergo rapid industrial expansion in the cities. Russia experienced a humiliating defeat of their navy in the **Russo-Japanese War,** causing increased labor unrest and dissatisfaction with the strong monarchy. The socialist party in Russia split into the **Bolsheviks,**who favored immediate socialist reform, and the **Mensheviks,** who favored gradual reforms and cooperation. When a peaceful demonstration against the czar was brutally suppressed, rebel forces made up of political activists, peasants, and workers became energized, leading to the **Russian Revolution of 1905.** This revolution continued with revolts by peasants and soldiers, until the czar promised to create a constitutional monarchy with a powerful legislative body, known as the **Duma**. These changes promised civil liberties and a parliamentary process, but the Tsar soon after went back on his word and limited the power of the Duma, leading to increased civil unreast.

World History 1914 to Present

Entangling Alliances Prior to WWI

In the early years of the 20th century, relations among the various European powers were complex. Ever since the **Franco-Prussian War**, won by Prussia, the two sides had been enemies. At the center of their conflict was the territory of **Alsace-Lorraine**, which each side claimed as its own. In order to bolster their position in the region, each side entered into networks of alliances. After years of negotiations, two main alliances contained the major European powers: the **Triple Alliance** (Germany, Austria, Italy) and the **Triple Entente** (France, Britain, Russia). These two alliances would end up being the opposing sides in the great war of the ensuing years.

The Balkans and Beginning of WWI

In the years before the First World War, the **Balkans** were attempting to gain independence from the Hapsburg empire of Austria. This insurrection culminated in the assassination of Austrian **Archduke Franz Ferdinand** in 1914 by **Gavrilo Princip**, a member of a Serbian nationalist group. At this point, a chain reaction of war declarations (spurred by the comprehensive alliances of the time) ensued. Austria declared war against Serbia, Germany and Turkey joined with the Austrians,

Russia declared war on these countries in support of Serbia, France joined with Russia, and Britain and Italy joined forces with France, even though Italy had been a member of the Triple Alliance.

Combat and Exit of Russia During WWI

Despite the fact that almost every nation in Europe had entered into World War I, most Europeans thought the conflict would be brief. Instead, advances in **weapons technology** made the war bloody and excruciatingly slow. Much of the fighting was done from **trenches**, and some battles would see the deaths of thousands of soldiers at a time. The war was also slow because the sides were very evenly matched; that is, until 1917, when the United States entered on the side of Britain. Also, in 1917, the Russians exited the war via the **Brest-Litovsk Treaty**. Russia was basically exhausted after suffering through a Revolution in 1917 in which the **Bolsheviks** came to power. The entry of the US provided the British and French with supplies and troops, and Germany was soon forced to call for a truce.

Treaty of Versailles

As the First World War wound down, a disgruntled German populace ousted the emperor and installed a moderate socialist government. This government, known as the **Weimar Republic**, would last until 1933. At the **Paris Peace Conference**, the victors of the war (the US, Britain, France, and Italy) exacted some revenge on Germany. The **Treaty of Versailles** penalized Germany economically and territorially; Alsace-Lorraine became independent, and the German military was dismantled. The Treaty of Versailles would need to be modified by two subsequent agreements: the **Treaty of Locarno,** which outlined a more reasonable reparations plan for Germany, and the **Kellogg-Briand Pact,** which asserted that diplomacy rather than force would be used to resolve conflicts.

Western Europe and Italy After the First World War

In the years after the First World War, the general mood in Europe was one of wariness. Most nations were exhausted by the conflict, and few felt that the signing of the **Treaty of Versailles** and the formation of the **League of Nations** had created a permanent peace. In the 1920s, Britain, Germany, France, and the United States were all liberal democracies without a strong executive. Unlike the United States, however, the European nations suffered a profound economic depression. One nation that saw no diminution in nationalism was **Italy**. In part out of a fear of communism, Italians supported the rise of the fascist dictator **Benito Mussolini**. **Fascism** is defined as an extreme-right movement characterized by totalitarian rule with an emphasis on national unity and identity. Fascism generally manifests in dictatorial rule and suppression of the free speech and rights of dissenters. It originated in Italy and promised to the Italians a return to the glory days of Rome, when they were a mighty power ruled by a dominating executive. Of course, in order to maintain his authority, Mussolini had to brutally suppress any opposition.

Russian Revolution of 1917

After the **Revolution of 1905**, Russia had enjoyed a few years of relative peace. After a while, however, the peasants became dissatisfied with the weakness of the Duma, and after strikes and protests, **Czar Nicholas II** was forced to abdicate the throne. In place of the monarchy, a **provisional government** was set up to work alongside more progressive local councils, known as **Soviets**. These two groups were constantly at odds, however, especially during Russia's participation in the **First World War** (the Soviets wanted to withdraw and focus on national issues, while the Provisional Government felt obliged to fight). During this period, **Vladimir Lenin** rose to prominence as the Marxist leader of the **Bolshevik Party**. In the **Russian Revolution of 1917**, Lenin and his supporters ousted the provisional government and exited the war. Lenin then began the immense project of nationalizing the Soviet economy.

Lenin and Stalin

After his success in the Revolution of 1917, **Lenin** began to advocate the revolt of the working class in other nations. Naturally, this did not endear the new Russian government to the leaders of other nations. Russia became increasingly isolated both economically and politically from the rest of the world. Domestically, Lenin established the **New Economic Policy**, which blended capitalism and communism. This plan worked well enough in agriculture, but it never achieved much success in industry. After Lenin's death, **Joseph Stalin** came to power and began an ambitious plan of collectivizing farms and nationalizing factories (known as the **Five Year Plans**). Stalin was ruthless in the pursuit of his goals; he established labor camps to house his opponents. It is estimated that 20 million people were killed by Stalin's regime during the period now known as the **Great Terror**.

China in the Early 20h Century

In 1911, the **Manchu dynasty**, which had been significantly weakened by the **Boxer Rebellion**, was finally overthrown. A period of instability followed, in which **Sun Yat-sen** declared the creation of a republic with its headquarters in Nanking. Sun Yat-sen began a political party aimed at improving life for the common people; it was known as the **Kuomintang**. During this period, both Mongolia and Tibet declared their independence from China. The Chinese people became disenchanted with the Kuomintang government after what they saw as unfavorable agreements following World War I. After the death of Sun Yat-sen in 1925, a national government was established at Canton; the **communist party** was a major participant in this government.

Rule of the Kuomintang and the Sino-Japanese War in 20th-Century China

In 1926, the military leader **Chiang Kai-shek** led campaigns in central and northern China, in the hopes of unifying the country. During this period, Chiang broke with the **communist party**, and Communists were persecuted in Shanghai. In 1927, a national government led by the **Kuomintang**, who had previously fallen out of favor, was established in Nanking. The peasants were not pleased with this leadership, and they were organized as the **Red Army** under **Mao Tse-tung** in the south. In what is known as the **Long March**, Mao led his army north to Yenan, where they would gather strength. The situation in China was made even more volatile by the Japanese invasion in 1937. In what is known as the "**Rape of Nanking**," Japanese troops killed over 200,000 Chinese. The people were outraged, and the partisan splits between Mao's communists and Chiang's government only widened.

Japan in the Years Before WWII

In 1926, amid growing nationalism, **Hirohito** became the Emperor of Japan. The next year, the Japanese prime minister declared that Japan should dominate Asia, and four years later, Japanese forces invaded **Manchuria**. Some historians consider this to be the beginning of the Second World War. After establishing a puppet regime in Manchuria, the Japanese withdrew from the League of Nations and attacked China. The **Sino-Japanese War** ensued. In 1938, Japan outlined its new vision of **Co-Prosperity Spheres**; Japan would be the industrial center of Asia and would acquire its raw materials from its colonies in the rest of Asia. Japan promoted this idea as an opportunity to break from European imperialism, but it was really just the substitution of one master for another. In 1940, Japan would complete its transformation into a **fascist state** by dissolving all political parties.

Events Leading to World War II in Europe

Still shell-shocked from the First World War, the nations of western Europe were slow to respond to the growing menace of **Nazi Germany**. In general, they pursued a policy of appeasement and isolation. The British prime minister **Neville Chamberlain** was especially committed to using diplomacy over war. Then, in 1936, Hitler sent troops to occupy the **Rhineland**, a strip of territory on the German border. At around the same time, **Mussolini** invaded Ethiopia; the two aggressors, Germany and Italy, entered into an agreement making them the **Axis Powers**. In 1938, Germany annexed Austria and indicated that it was about to attack Czechoslovakia. In response to these actions, Chamberlain brought together Mussolini and Hitler for the **Munich Conference of 1938**. These talks would only briefly suspend German aggression.

WEIMAR REPUBLIC AND THE RISE OF HITLER

After the abdication of the emperor, Germany was ruled by a legislative body known as the **Weimar Republic**. Most Germans felt that this group had been too willing to accept punishment in the treaties that followed the war. Germans also thought that this government was responsible for the **inflation** which crippled the German economy in the post-war period. Germany, then, was vulnerable to the charms of a leader who told them they had nothing about which to be ashamed. This leader was **Adolf Hitler** (1889-1945). A failed artist, Hitler became the head of the **National Socialist**, or **Nazi**, party. His speeches were expressions of ardent nationalism, although often Hitler seemed to be calling for a return to an ideal German state that had never actually existed.

BELIEF SYSTEM OF THE NAZI PARTY

Led by **Adolf Hitler**, the Nazi party championed the **Aryan race** as superior to all others, especially the "insidious" Jews. Hitler suggested that the noble ambitions of the true German people required ***lebensraum***, or living space. In other words, Germany needed more territory. In its early days, the Nazi party was part of the German republican system; Nazi candidates ran for office and served in the **Reichstag** (German parliament). As Germany suffered through a terrible economic depression in the early 1930s, however, the people became impatient. In 1933, the Reichstag was set on fire, and the Nazis used the opportunity to claim total control of the government. Hitler had already been appointed Chancellor in January 1933. He was able to quickly improve the German economy, mostly through the expansion of the weapon-building industry. At the same time, the new government began to quietly round up Jews, Gypsies, and homosexuals.

HOLOCAUST

As **Germany** sank deeper and deeper into dire economic straits, the tendency was to look for a person or group of people to blame for the problems of the country. With distrust of the **Jewish people** already ingrained, it was easy for German authorities to set up the Jews as scapegoats for Germany's problems.

The Holocaust is the name given to the systematic killing of Jews, Gypsies, homosexuals, and others by the Nazis. **Anti-Semitism** had existed in Europe for millennia, but the Nazis gave it renewed emphasis and, after making numerous false claims about Jews, began persecuting them upon Hitler's rise to power in 1933. Jews were disenfranchised, forced into ghettos, had their property taken, and were finally sent to work and be killed in **concentration camps**. Approximately 6 million Jews were killed during the **Holocaust**. As the situation for the Germans became more dire in the Second World War, Hitler sought to implement what he called the "final solution," in which hundreds of thousands were killed just before the fall of Nazi Germany.

The Allies were aware of rumors of mass slaughter throughout the war, but many discounted the reports. Only when troops went in to liberate the prisoners was the true horror of the concentration camps brought to light.

Review Video: The Holocaust
Visit mometrix.com/academy and enter code: 350695

Consequences of the Holocaust

Many of the Nazi leaders were tried and convicted at the **Nuremberg trials** for their roles in the Holocaust. West Germany would later issue a **Federal Compensation Law**, through which billions of dollars were paid to survivors. During and after the Holocaust, Zionist Jews fled to **Palestine**. Public sympathy with their plight would be one of the main reasons for the creation of **Israel** in 1948. The total destruction of the Jewish community in Europe caused many Jews to question their faith, and those that remained in Europe are markedly more secular than their ancestors. The shock of the Holocaust has also caused many institutions, including the Roman Catholic Church, to consider their own latent anti-Semitism. Unfortunately, the anti-genocide legislation created in response to the Holocaust was not strict enough to rally international support against the **Rwandans** (who slaughtered hundreds of thousands of Tutsis in 1994) or the **Bosnian Serbs and Croats** (who killed thousands of Muslims in the early 1990s).

Pacific Arena in WWII

The **Japanese**, like the Germans, became seduced by the notion of their own racial superiority during the 1930s. As in Germany, this inevitably led to a lust for territorial expansion. By 1941, Japan had conquered Korea, Manchuria, and parts of China. Japan was also threatening to invade American interests in the Philippines. The United States imposed **economic sanctions** on Japan, making it difficult for the Japanese war industry to function. In response, the Japanese launched a surprise attack on the United States by bombing the US naval base of **Pearl Harbor**. After the attack on Pearl Harbor, the United States declared war upon Japan (and Germany, in turn, declared war on the United States). The Japanese made huge territorial gains before the US turned the tide at the **Battles of Midway and Guadalcanal**. The war in the Pacific would take much longer than the war in Europe due to the island-hopping nature of the fight. The unwillingness of the Japanese to surrender made it almost impossible for America to entirely vanquish them without enormous loss of life. So, the United States decided to drop atomic bombs on **Hiroshima** and **Nagasaki** to force Japan to surrender and finally end the war in the Pacific in August 1945.

Beginning and Initial Years of World War II in Europe

After **Chamberlain** had tried to forestall German aggression at the **Munich Conference of 1938**, Germany nevertheless invaded Czechoslovakia in 1939. It was also during this year that Hitler signed a secret agreement with **Stalin** pledging not to attack Russia so long as Russia stayed out of German affairs. Hitler then declared war on and conquered Poland. At this step, Great Britain and France were finally forced to declare war upon Germany. Germany at this point was a dominating military adversary. New advances in motorized military vehicles made it possible for Germany to conquer large areas of land quickly in a new form of warfare called **Blitzkrieg** (lightning war). The **Axis powers** conquered almost the entire European continent, including France, over the course of 1940. Only Great Britain remained in opposition, and the Nazis undertook a ferocious aerial assault on the British, who were by then led by **Winston Churchill**, but failed to do enough damage to make an invasion of the island country practical. Instead, Hitler turned east and decided to violate his truce with Stalin, invading **Russia** in 1941. The Germans overwhelmed much of the Soviet military and advanced deep into Russian territory in a huge surprise offensive.

Middle Years and Conclusion of World War II in Europe

The tide turned against Hitler once the United States entered the war. The harsh Russian winter halted the German advance into Russia short of Moscow in 1941. The Germans made further gains in the summer of 1942 but were decisively beaten at the **Battle of Stalingrad** and were slowly pushed back out of Russia from then on. American and British troops landed in North Africa in 1942 and used that as a springboard to invade Italy in 1943. In 1944, the Americans and British opened yet another front with a massive invasion of northern France in the **D-Day landings**. Fighting numerically superior forces on multiple fronts, the Germans steadily lost ground and the Allies pushed into Germany from both East and West in 1945. Surrounded and with the war lost, Hitler committed **suicide** in his bunker in Berlin in April 1945, and the remaining German forces **surrendered** shortly afterward.

India and Pakistan After WWII

In 1947, after years of peaceful protests led by **Mahatma Gandhi**, India was given its independence and partitioned into two states, **India** and **Pakistan**. The following year, Gandhi would be assassinated in India. In 1965, border disputes would flare into the **Indo-Pakistani War**. In 1971, Pakistan would fend off attacks from Bengali rebels, who sought to achieve independence. The next year, however, **Bangladesh** would be established as an independent state. In 1984, India had its own internal problems; after the Indian army occupied the **Golden Temple** sacred to the Sikhs, the Indian leader **Indira Gandhi** was assassinated by her Sikh bodyguards. **Anti-Sikh riots** resulted, and much blood was shed.

Beginnings of The Cold War

After the defeat of the Axis powers in WWII, the United States and Russia entered into a long and often secret conflict, in which each side used diplomatic, economic, and occasionally military forces to try to assert itself as the dominant world power. The first issue on which these nations butted heads was the **rebuilding of Europe**. Germany was divided into an eastern and western section; the western half was democratic and looked to the US for guidance, while Eastern Germany became a communist nation in the USSR's sphere of influence. Russia worked to bring all of its neighbors (including Poland, Czechoslovakia, Hungary, Romania, and Bulgaria) under its control. The western borders of these nations formed what Churchill referred to as the **iron curtain**, dividing communist Eastern Europe from democratic Western Europe.

Truman Doctrine, Marshall Plan, NATO, and Warsaw Pact

In order to stop the spread of communism in Europe and elsewhere, President Truman asserted his policy of "containment" in the so-called **Truman Doctrine**. This meant that the US would support the anticommunist governments throughout the world. The **Marshall Plan** advanced this policy by supplying aid to war-ravaged countries in Western Europe. When the **Eastern Bloc countries** prevented aid from reaching West Berlin, the US, England, and France organized the **Berlin Airlift** to overcome this obstacle. In 1949, the Western European and North American nations entered into a mutual defense treaty, NATO (North Atlantic Treaty Organization). As a response, the Eastern Bloc nations joined with the Soviet Union in the **Warsaw Pact**.

Communist Revolution in China

China was torn by civil strife all throughout the Second World War. At one point, the American government had to renounce its trade rights in **China** in order to persuade China not to sign a peace treaty with Japan while the US still needed Chinese support. Once Japan had been defeated, the **Red Army** under Mao moved into **Manchuria** (which had recently been vacated by the Soviets). The major cities were still occupied by Nationalist forces, supported by the Americans. In 1946, fighting resumed between the opposing factions, and the **Nationalists** under Chiang were eventually forced to abandon central China. In 1949, the Red Army forced Chiang Kai-shek to leave the mainland and find refuge in Taiwan. On October 1, 1949, the communists declared the official creation of the **People's Republic of China**.

ARMS RACE, CUBAN MISSILE CRISIS, AND BAY OF PIGS IN THE COLD WAR

During the **Cold War**, the United States and the Soviet Union each tried to deter an attack by the other by building up fantastic arsenals of **nuclear missiles**. The two nations would also expend considerable effort trying to be the first in space. Finally, in the late 60s and early 70s, the two nations would begin talks aimed at mutual disarmament. This occurred in part because relations between China and the USSR had cooled. Before this period of détente, however, there had been a couple of serious threats to global peace. In 1961, the US had financed an unsuccessful invasion of Cuba at the **Bay of Pigs**. This led the Soviet Union to establish missile bases on communist Cuba; the US and USSR almost declared war on one another during the **Cuban Missile Crisis of 1962**.

END OF THE COLD WAR

Over time, the leaders of the Soviet Union and United States began to realize the total annihilation that would ensue if nuclear war was declared, and it was agreed that both sides would **disarm**. The two treaties that were signed during the 1970s are known as the **Strategic Arms Limitation Talks (SALT) I and II**. When **Mikhail Gorbachev** came into power in the USSR in 1985, he established a policy of **glasnost**, or "openness." In response to US President Ronald Reagan's military build-up using the might of the US economy, Gorbachev understood that the Soviet Union could not economically compete militarily under a communist system and overcome the military might of the United States. He thus advocated **perestroika**, a gradual metamorphosis of the Soviet economy. In 1991, these reforms culminated in the disintegration of the ruling Communist party, and the **disbanding of the Soviet Union**. This occurred two years after the **Berlin Wall**, which for more than forty years had separated communist and anticommunist Germany, was finally torn down.

Review Video: The End of the Cold War
Visit mometrix.com/academy and enter code: 278032

MIDDLE EAST FROM 1947 TO 1977

After WWII, the United Nations announced that **Palestine** would be partitioned in order to make room for a new Jewish state. **Israel** was created in 1948. In 1951, the Iranian leader **Mossadegh** nationalized the oil interests, making his government extremely wealthy and powerful. This move would be emulated by future leaders. In 1967, in the **Six-Day War**, Israel routed a coalition of Arab nations, seizing the West Bank, Sinai, and Jerusalem. In 1972, Palestinian terrorists murdered 12 Israeli athletes at the Olympics in Munich. In 1973, the oil-producing Arab nations placed an embargo on shipments to the West, causing major energy crises in the US and Europe. Also, in 1973, Israelis and Arabs battled again in the **Yom Kippur War**. In 1977, Egyptian leader **Anwar Sadat** became the first Arab leader to visit Israel.

MIDDLE EAST FROM 1978 TO 1985

In 1978, American President **Jimmy Carter** hosted successful peace talks between Egypt and Israel at **Camp David**. The next year, however, a fundamentalist Islamist regime would take power in Iran, and many Americans would be taken hostage, only released upon the election of **Ronald Reagan**. Between 1980 and 1988, Iran and Iraq engaged in a bloody and brutal war, begun when the Iraqi leader **Saddam Hussein** seized territory in eastern Iran. Also, during this period, Afghan rebels were engaged in a prolonged, ultimately successful fight for independence from the Soviets. In 1982, Israel attacked Lebanon, which was harboring the Palestinian leader **Yasser Arafat**. Lebanon would be forced to oust Arafat the next year. Israel would continue attacking Arafat and the **Palestinian Liberation Organization**, and the PLO would continue to sponsor terrorist activities against Israel.

Middle East from 1987 to 2003

In 1987, Syrian troops entered Lebanon and stopped the civil war. Also, during this year, 402 pilgrims died during riots in the Saudi Arabian sacred city of Mecca. In 1988, the Palestinian resistance (known as the Intifada) began in earnest against Israel. Iraq invaded Kuwait in 1990, and after UN sanctions were levied, the US invaded in 1991. The Iraqi soldiers set fire to thousands of Kuwaiti oil wells while retreating. In 1992, Arafat and Israeli PM Yitzhak Rabin shook hands in Washington, and Arafat would soon return to Gaza after years of exile. In 1995, the Israelis and Palestinians signed an agreement giving the Palestinians autonomy in the West Bank and Gaza areas. Despite continuing violence, another agreement was reached in 1998, this one stating that the Palestinians would be granted land in exchange for keeping the peace. Violence continued, however, and in 2003, Israel began construction of a barrier between itself and the Palestinian territories.

New Europe after 1991 through 1998

In 1991, **Gorbachev** resigned as the last president of the USSR, and a number of the Soviet provinces, including Lithuania and Latvia, declared independence. The **Maastricht Treaty**, formally announcing the creation of the European Union, was signed in 1992, and the next year a unified European stock market opened. In the **"Velvet" Revolution of 1993**, Slovakia separated from Czechoslovakia, which became the Czech Republic. Meanwhile, the former USSR was enduring civil strife until **Boris Yeltsin** seized power in 1993. In 1994, Russian troops attacked **Chechnya**, which was trying to achieve independence. In 1998, President Clinton helped broker a peace agreement between the **British** and **North Irish rebels**.

New Europe After 1999

In 1999, the Czech Republic, Poland, and Hungary all joined **NATO**, further eliminating the old divides between western and eastern Europe. The conflict in Chechnya increased during this year, and Yeltsin was succeeded as Russian leader by the former KGB agent Vladimir Putin. An **International Criminal Court** was created in the Hague (Netherlands) in 2002, despite the vehement opposition of the United States. In the late '90s, many of the western European governments had become quasi-socialist, and they spent much of their time debating the immense increase in **immigration**. Meanwhile, the former Soviet states have had a rough transition from command to market economies, and are still somewhat economically depressed.

Emergence of the Pacific Rim After 1991

In the 1990s and early years of the 21st century, Japan and China emerged as two major economic powers. Despite suffering a prolonged recession, **Japan** continued to be one of the world's manufacturing leaders. However, several internal scandals have shaken Japanese confidence and have caused many to question the close relations between corporations and government. In **China**, the suffocating communist regime has relaxed its economic strictures somewhat, and the result has been an economic boom. China created several **special economic zones** along its eastern coast to lure foreign business. Now however, Chinese firms are control a sizable portion of the market in their own right.

First World, Second World, and Third World

First-world nations are those that have advanced capitalist economies and are fully industrialized. The former Soviet states, which are slowly developing capitalist economies after having inefficient socialist economies for so long, are classified as **second-world nations**. This term has fallen out of general use, as these nations have slowly become more similar to first-world nations. The relatively poor and non-industrialized nations of Latin America, Africa, and Asia, most of which were colonized or involved in other exploitative trade arrangements with the Western empires at one time, are known as the **third-world nations**. Although these nations are far more numerous than those of the first or second world, they wield much less political power.Underdevelopment

Third-world countries that do not have the modern economic conditions possessed by the wealthier nations are said to suffer from **underdevelopment**. That is, they do not have the industrial, social, or political strength that is required to be a self-sustaining party in the global economy. In some countries, underdevelopment is clearly the result of **dysfunctional politics**; third-world nations are more likely to be ruled by a small group or by a dictator. Underdeveloped nations are typically those that were colonized at one time. Because their economy during the colonial period was so heavily based upon exporting raw materials, they never created a manufacturing base and found themselves unequipped for independence. Experts are at odds as to whether first-world nations should aid underdeveloped countries by funneling money to them or by helping them to develop modern economies.

Specific Technological Advances Since 1991

In 1993, the first **web browser** was developed, beginning the era of internet communications that has revolutionized every area of human life. The internet did not become widely used, however, until 1997 and 1998. In 1997, a Scottish lab successfully **cloned** a lamb from adult sheep DNA, opening the door to the cloning of other animals, or human organs for medical purposes, and even for the cloning of entire human beings. This last possibility was strengthened in 2001, when the work of **sequencing the DNA** of the human genome was finally finished. Although **embryonic stem-cell research** has been limited in the US (other sources than embryos remain legal), other countries are using cells from human embryos to search for cures for disease. Another leap in genetic technology came in 2012 with the advent of CRISPR, a tool for directly editing the genes of any organism. In 2008, a new technology was used to implement Bitcoin called blockchain. This is a powerful method for sharing and storing information in an incredibly secure way, among many other uses. One of the most astonishing acheivements in science in recent history was in 2016 when the LIGO observatory used incredibly sensitive detectors to sense gravitational waves from distant colliding black holes.

Modernization

Modernization is the process by which societies develop sophisticated industrial technology, as well as the political, cultural, and social systems that are most effective in sustaining and advancing that technology. For a long time, sociologists noted that the most modernized countries, namely the Western empires, were the most successful, and that other societies should strive to emulate them. In recent decades, however, more sensitive sociologists have declared that **modernization** need not be equated with Westernization, and that the indigenous cultures of South America and Africa, for example, need not be cast off for these places to enjoy prosperity. One way sociologists can assess the relative modernization of a society is by comparing the **gross national product** (GNP), which is the total value of all economic activity within a society. Often, GNP is divided by total population to determine a society's **per capita gross national product**.

State Theory of Modernization and World System Theory of Modernization

The state theory of modernization supports the ideals of **capitalism** by maintaining that whenever the government is restricted from seizing private property, capitalism will develop and free markets will arise as people modernize and strive to become more productive. The **world system theory of modernization**, also known as the **dependency theory**, states that some nations modernize at the expense of less-developed nations, and that so long as this exploitation continues, the less-developed nations will be unable to improve their lot. This theory essentially takes the

Marxist view of the capitalist society, in which those who own the means of production are able to maintain dominance over the workers, and applies it to the interactions of nations.

Globalization

Globalization is the process whereby all the social groups in the world are being brought into closer connection with one another. This has occurred mainly through the advances in transportation and communication technology, although the era of colonialism also had the effect of shrinking the world. This phenomenon has, in some cases, made it more difficult for repressive regimes to isolate themselves; during the Tiananmen Square uprising in China, for instance, Western media was able to communicate with the student rebels and present their story to the rest of the world. Many observers lament **globalization**, however, because they feel it will homogenize culture and crowd out fascinating, but not economically successful, societies.

Review Video: Globalization
Visit mometrix.com/academy and enter code: 551962

Automation

Automation is when machines are employed to do work formerly done by humans. This is typically done when an industry seeks to have greater worker productivity, but it may have some costly side effects. The work that remains for people after automation is frequently repetitive and mindless. Sociologists studying the phenomenon have observed increased alienation and lowered self-esteem among workers whose jobs have been automated. Also, automation reduces the need for specialization by driving employees out of their previously unique fields; this creates both unhealthy competition for menial jobs and confusion over social roles among the workers. Unfortunately, the pressures of the **capitalist market** make it impossible for most businesses to avoid automation.

Hyperurbanization

Hyperurbanization has occurred when the development of population growth in urban areas has moved too quickly and has outpaced the necessary accompanying growths in industry and business. The inevitable result of **hyperurbanization** is unemployment and inadequate public services. This has been a particular problem in **third-world countries**, which are experiencing mass internal migration from the countryside to the cities. In fact, the urbanization currently taking place in China may be the largest movement of people in the history of the world. It is impossible for any society, no matter how wealthy, to keep up with such a migration and provide adequate roads, health care, education, water, food, and electricity.

Historiography

Introduction to Historiography

Historiography is the study of the methods and approaches that historians use to create histories. It involves examining how historical evidence is chosen, interpreted, evaluated, analyzed, and used in the writing of history. Historiography is not concerned with the events that make up history but rather the manner in which that history was recorded. The sources, techniques, and theoretical frameworks used to record the history of a certain subject constitute that subject's historiography.

Common Terminology Used When Studying History

When studying history, it is important to have a clear understanding of various terms that can be used interchangeably. The term **time** refers to the continuous passing of events in the past, present, and future. Time is a scientific measure that conventionally uses minutes, hours, days, and years as its **standard measures**. Time passes with or without significant events taking place. **History** is distinct from time as it is the record of **significant events** throughout the past. The term **chronology** refers to the arrangement of events in their correct order. As history contains uncertainty, the chronology of particular events is up for debate. Terms used to describe the ebb and flow of history are change and continuity. **Continuity** refers to periods of time that are relatively stable in history with no major changes, whereas times of **change** refer to rich periods in history with significant events that alter the common practices of that time, often leading into a new era. When describing what has changed for a civilization over time, it is common to focus on political, economic, social, and technological aspects. For instance, the United States government was established in 1776 and continues today. This demonstrates a change at the beginning of the timeline related the United States, but since then, there has been political continuity as it has existed for roughly 250 years. Other aspects of life in this period may have experienced other changes, such as the innovation of electricity, steam engines, and automobiles. When a portion of time has relatively stable conditions such that it can be summed up by a common characterization, it is called a **period of time**; this process of summing up time into periods is called **periodization**.

Civilization, City-States, and Empires

Since history is the study of recorded events throughout time, it is naturally tied to organized society with a developed language to record the events. The development necessary to record history generally coincides with early civilization. A **civilization** is a human society that has established complex means of surviving as a group. These **functions** are developing a food supply, a social structure, a shared language, a culture, and technology. The first known complex civilization is Mesopotamia, which was more easily developed due to its fertile farmlands, access to water through an available river. Mesopotamia is a good example of a **city-state**, which is essentially an independently sovereign city that does not depend on another government. Mesopotamia, as an early civilization, was the central hub and government in its region. The model of city-states still exists today, though they are often comparatively less significant in size and economy compared to other nation-states. Examples of modern city-states include Monaco, Vatican City, and Singapore. As the early civilizations continued to develop, they would eventually grow into **empires**, which are larger sovereign states with multiple territories, though they are usually governed centrally by a monarch or emperor.

Interpreting Timelines

Timelines are a useful tool for visualizing the chronology of events as well as a great method to map out periods and view changes or continuity throughout history. Timelines can focus on either small or large ranges and can be multifaceted so that one period or type of event can be compared with another. A key element of a timeline is having a consistent interval mapped out. For instance, if we wanted to construct a timeline to map the events that happened for a single day, we would likely use hours to plot out the continuum. One might start the timeline at 12am and end the timeline at 12am the next night to show the picture of the entire day. Each event or period, such as sleeping, waking up, eating, going to work, and special occurrences can be marked on the timeline to plot out the day. If someone wanted to compare multiple days, these timelines could be lined up and compared and contrasted to find what is common to all days and what is unique. These same concepts can be applied to historical timelines as well. Instead of mapping just one day, one might consider mapping the events leading up to and throughout a particular war. The significance of events should change with the focus of the timeline. Seeing events plotted on a steady continuum of time can be very helpful in understanding the pacing of events throughout history.

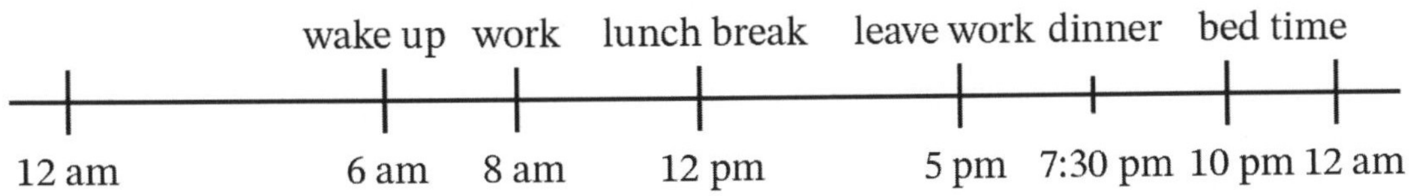

Relationships Between Historical Events and Their Implications

As one aspect of society changes, it frequently proves to have significant effects on other parts of society. One of the easiest ways to see this effect is the innovation of new technologies. An example of a highly impactful technology is the printing press. Prior to this invention, all written documents had to be written by hand, which was time-consuming and costly. Books were very expensive and rare, which put the burden of education on mainly religious authorities and very wealthy classes of people. This new innovation allowed for more written works to be spread, which caused a need for literacy and education, ultimately evoking huge cultural and political changes. Technology tends to be a much quicker influencer of change in civilization, as it is sudden and can have dramatic impacts on how things are done. Cultural, political, and economic effects tend to move more gradually but likewise have strong effects that can change civilization forever.

Primary and Secondary Sources of Historical Information

When studying history, it is important to consider the reliability, validity, and availability of sources of information. **Primary sources** are first-hand accounts of an event, such as a transcript of a speech, a recording, statistics, or a work of art. **Secondary sources** are indirect records, such as text books, newspapers, and other forms of reviews of the primary sources. Secondary sources of information can still be valid and useful, but are more open to **interpretation** and **bias**. Information from recent history, such as the election of a president in the 2010s is very reliable, as there are many sources of information that are in consensus about the objective event. Furthermore, many people still alive are primary sources since they were alive and witnessed the election. This is not true of less modern history, such as the election of Abraham Lincoln in 1860. There are still plentiful records of the information, but all witnesses to the election have passed away at this point. This event took place in an era where newspapers and legitimate documentation was widespread and available. The clarity and objectivity of sources are indisputable because they are so abundant. If, however, we only had political cartoons and election campaign brochures to go by, the reliability and accuracy of the information may be up for debate because the source materials are only secondary sources of information and are likely to contain biases. Generally, the further back in history one researches, the fewer sources are available due to lack of documentation, technological limitations, and language barriers. With fewer sources, and possibly conflicting information, historians must put together the most reasonable explanation of what took place during the period in question, given the amount of information available to them.

Types of Sources of Information Used in Historical Research

- **Almanacs**—books that are published each year to express current information for consideration in the coming year. These often act as time capsules for that particular year and can give historians insight into economic and technological details of the time.
- **Encyclopedias**—resources that cover a variety of topics broadly for the purpose of giving the reader an overview. Wikipedia is an internet-based version of an encyclopedia that is useful for finding leads or obtaining general information about a topic.

- **Bibliographies**—a list of resources used in composing a scholarly work. These are usually primary and secondary sources that can be used to check an author's sources or to give leads on similar research. Similar concepts include works-cited pages and literature reviews.
- **Periodical Guides**—a series of publications over time, usually in the form of magazines or journals. These usually broach a more specific category of information, such as on research methods, psychology, or medical procedures, and are intended to help members of a particular field stay up-to-date with current research in their field.
- **Biographical Dictionaries**—a resource that contains a list of important names to know about the given subject and a description of how they contributed to the field. For instance, if one were interested in the Revolutionary War, a biographical dictionary would include information on each of the founding fathers and other significant individuals of the time.
- **Maps**—representations of land and territories that can display a variety of factors, including geographical features, political features, economics, demographics, and many more aspects. Digital maps can generally be manipulated to show multiple features at once.

Uses and Limitations of Various Historical Source Materials

Historical source materials are a type of primary source material that offer historians the opportunity to study people, places, and events that occurred in the past. Unfortunately, there are limitations to what these materials can tell us. A limitation of **historical source materials** is that they may be biased by those who created them. For example, those who create historical documents such as letters may leave out details or exaggerate parts in order to make their points more convincing. Another limitation might be that some historical sources only provide evidence for certain points of view, as they were recorded by those with specific interests and perspectives.

- An **oral history** provides an account of an event that happened in the past, which is told by the person who was there when it happened. Oral histories are important because they allow us to learn about things that may not be written in books or recorded in documents.
- **Newspapers** are important source materials for scholars because they provide a detailed account of the past, which cannot be found in books or other sources. Newspapers are not always reliable as they may not be based on fact, while others might omit certain information or give undue weight towards one side of an issue at the expense of another.
- **Diaries** and personal **journals** can provide valuable information for historians because they are detailed histories of people's lives. However, the reliability of these accounts is always in question because they were created by just one person and aren't always written with the intention of sharing.
- **Artifacts** can be defined as objects created by humans, which can give hints at the peoples' material culture and intangible culture. Material culture includes things like buildings or furniture while intangible culture includes things like music or dance. The benefits of artifacts are that they can offer insights into how people lived in the past. They can also be used to shed light on the thoughts, feelings, fears, tensions, customs, rituals, and other social practices at that time.
- **Tax lists** and **census data** are useful sources of insight into how people lived during a certain time. They provide us with reliable information about the income, demographics, and beliefs of the people living in a particular time.

- **Personal correspondence** has been an important form of historical information for historians. It gives an insight into the lives and interactions of ordinary people. The main benefits of using personal correspondence as a source for history is that it provides an authentic portrayal of the author's thoughts and feelings during a time period or in response to significant events.

Historical Interpretation and Biases

History is a discipline that relies on the interpretation of **facts** to create **narratives**. Due to the types and availability of sources, history tends to leave itself open to **subjectivity**. Often, this means that **biases** are introduced at either the source of information, the interpretation of the information, or at the explanation of the information. For instance, if the only **sources of information** about an event are newspapers, the author of these historical sources may have been biased, causing the **interpretation** of the actual events to be skewed from the start. Similarly, the person interpreting the source may have their own biases that they introduce or even **teach** to others in the process of communicating the historical narrative. Commonly described biases in modern interpretation of history generally revolve around sociopolitical issues such as Eurocentrism, popular political parties, economic biases, and cultural favoritism.

Historical Revisionism

Historical revisionism is the act of reinterpreting a historical account through established historical methodologies. This is often done when new information is discovered or old information is reinterpreted in such a way that it warrants reconsidering the previously accepted history of an event or period. Historical revisionism is an essential and necessary process in creating accurate histories. Revisionism can, sometimes, be used incorrectly and in a way that leads to a less accurate interpretation of historical events. An example of this would be when the historical record is denied or deliberately distorted. This can involve using falsified records, purposefully misrepresenting the meaning of a piece of historical evidence, manipulating statistics, or unjustly denying the validity of historical evidence. A common example of this is Holocaust denial, which is an antisemitic theory that the Holocaust was either fabricated or greatly exaggerated.

Chapter Quiz

Ready to see how well you retained what you just read? Scan the QR code to go directly to the chapter quiz interface for this study guide. If you're using a computer, simply visit the online resources page at **mometrix.com/resources719/osatwhistgeog** and click the Chapter Quizzes link.

Geography

Cartography and Map Skills

MAPS AND GLOBES

A **map** is a diagrammatic representation of all or part of the three-dimensional world on a two-dimensional (flat) surface. A given map conveys data about certain characteristics of a region, such as human settlement patterns, climate variations, or geologic quality, which is difficult to observe otherwise. Maps can also display spatial relationships between locations and natural or human-made formations. The science of mapmaking is called cartography. General cartography entails the creation of maps for a general audience; thematic cartography involves the creation of maps with specific geographic themes. Because Earth is a spherical object, flat maps cannot accurately convey all shapes, distances, and directions. A **globe** is a representation of Earth drawn to scale, which means that shapes, distances, and directions are accurately denoted. Globes are round objects mounted upon rotational axes. They are most often used to display topographical (surface) features of the planet; however, they have also been employed as representations of the ocean floor or celestial objects other than Earth.

Review Video: Elements of a Map
Visit mometrix.com/academy and enter code: 437727

LATITUDE AND LONGITUDE

Latitude is an angular measurement expressing the angle (in degrees, minutes, and seconds) between any point and the equator (where latitude equals zero). Lines of **latitude** are the east-west lines circling the globe. All east-west lines are equidistant from each other. This means that they are all parallel to the equator and to each other. Every point on a given east-west line, therefore, is the same distance from the equator, the same distance from the North Pole, and the same distance from the South Pole. For this reason, east-west lines, or lines of latitude, are called parallels. **Longitude** is an angular measurement expressing the angle between any point and the prime meridian (where longitude equals zero). On the globe, lines of constant longitude ("meridians") extend from pole to pole, like the segment boundaries on a peeled orange. These north-south lines are of the same length, unlike the parallels of latitude, that are all parallel to the equator and whose perimeter decreases as the distance from the equator increases.

CIRCLES OF LATITUDE

Circle of latitude is simply another term for any of the parallels in the graticule. Certain of these parallels are distinguished due to their relationships with the Sun. The five main **circles of latitude** are the following:

- The **equator** (0 degrees latitude) is characterized by the fact that the Sun passes directly over this parallel twice each year, during the vernal and autumnal equinoxes.
- The **Tropic of Cancer** (23 degrees, 26 minutes, and 22 seconds North latitude) represents the northernmost area of the globe, at which the Sun may be seen directly overhead during midsummer.
- The **Tropic of Capricorn** (23 degrees, 26 minutes, and 22 seconds South latitude)represents the southernmost area of the globe, at which the Sun may be seen directly overhead during midwinter.

- The **Arctic Circle** (66 degrees, 33 minutes, and 38 seconds North latitude)represents the northernmost location that may experience days without sunrises.
- The **Antarctic Circle** (66 degrees, 33 minutes, and 38 seconds South latitude) represents the southernmost location that may experience days without sunrises.

MAP INTERPRETATION SCALES

In order to provide relatively accurate representations of Earth's surface, cartographers use specific scales in map creation. The term *map scale* refers to the size of the representation of an element on a map as compared to its actual size on Earth's surface. The smaller the area represented on a map, the larger the scale; a larger scale provides more detail about a region. Map scale is usually expressed proportionally, as a ratio of the distance on a map to that actual distance on Earth's surface. This ratio is often expressed as inches to miles. For example, 1:63,360 indicates that one inch on the map equals one mile on the surface. Knowledge of a map's scale can provide information about the intended use of that map. For instance, large-scale maps typically convey information about small, specific areas, such as planned housing developments. Smaller-scale maps, such as world land use maps, represent larger areas of the surface in less detail.

SCALES OF MEASUREMENT

NOMINAL AND ORDINAL SCALES

A nominal scale, one of four different types of numerical scales, or levels, used in scientific measurement, is a list of categories to which objects can be classified. At the **nominal** level, also referred to as the classificatory level, variable attributes are identified through the use of numbers or symbols. For example, a land use map may use green shading to identify woodland areas. Different symbols are seen as equivalent; they involve no hierarchical ordering of attributes.

An **ordinal scale**, one of four different types of numerical scales, or levels, used in scientific measurement, is one in which the numbers assigned to objects or events represent the rank order (1st, 2nd, 3rd, etc.) of the entities assessed. At the ordinal level, numbers and symbols serve both to identify objects and to express their relations to other objects. For instance, a cartographer might use dots of different sizes to convey the relative sizes of individual human settlements.

INTERVAL AND RATIO SCALES

An interval scale, one of four different types of numerical scales, or levels, used in scientific measurement, is one that represents quantity and has equal units, but for which zero represents simply an additional point of measurement. The Fahrenheit scale is a clear example of the interval scale of measurement. In **interval** measurement, the distance between objects is relevant. Variable categories are actual numbers (rather than convenient labels); the intervals between adjacent categories anywhere on the scale are equal. The ratio between any two points depends upon the unit of measurement.

A **ratio scale,** one of four different types of numerical scales, or levels, used in scientific measurement, is similar to the interval scale in that it also represents quantity and has equality of units. However, this scale also has an absolute zero (no numbers exist below zero). Very often, physical measures will represent ratio data (for example, height and weight). If one is measuring the length of a piece of wood in centimeters, there is quantity and equal units, and that measure cannot go below zero centimeters. A negative length is not possible.

SYMBOLS AND LEGENDS

Symbols are used to represent the features shown on maps. They are a vital part of any graphic representation of Earth's surface. **Symbols** may be used in cartography to signify features existing at certain points, such as buildings or dams. Generally, dots of different sizes are used to convey the relative sizes of cities and towns (larger dots for larger, more populous settlements). Linear symbols identify features like roadways and rivers on maps. For instance, major highways are typically represented by double lines. Area symbols, created through the use of patterns, color, or shading, represent land conditions, land use, or land cover. A map **legend** is a key that lists and describes the symbols used on the map.

Compass Rose, Hemisphere, and the International Date Line

A **compass rose** is a symbol on a map or navigational chart that conveys the orientation of the four cardinal directions (north, south, east, and west) and often the intermediate directions (northeast, northwest, southeast, and southwest) as well. Modern compass roses are comprised of a large circle displaying the true (geographic) cardinal directions and a smaller inner circle displaying the magnetic (geomagnetic) cardinal directions.

The term **hemisphere** literally means half sphere. The graticule divides Earth's surface into four hemispheres. The equator separates the Northern Hemisphere from the Southern Hemisphere. The prime meridian is most widely (though not universally) accepted as the dividing line between the Eastern and Western Hemispheres.

The **International Date Line** (IDL) is the meridian opposite the prime meridian; it follows the line at 180 degrees longitude. This imaginary line serves as a time zone boundary—the date to the east of the International Date Line is one day earlier than the date to the west.

Map Creation Process

In order to create a useful map, a cartographer must determine the map's target audience and make appropriate decisions about style, content, and scale. The foundation of mapmaking is observation. Cartographers make use of several different observation techniques, including aerial surveys, land surveys, and satellite imagery. **Aerial survey**, the practice of collecting information about Earth from an aircraft, supplies valuable information to mapmakers. This information is conveyed through detailed photos developed from large-format film; aerial survey is a form of remote sensing (the collection of information about an object or region from a distance). **Conventional land surveys** describe the locations and measurements of boundaries and landforms (artificial or natural). **Satellite imagery** consists of photographs of Earth taken from space. Once all relevant data has been collected, the mapmaker then plots the location of many points on a grid, which corresponds to that which will be used in the final product. Color-coded versions of the map are printed on plastic and layered to create a complete representation.

GIS

The GIS, or **Geographic Information System**, is basically a system of computers and software that collects, records, analyzes, and displays (potentially) limitless amounts of geographic information about Earth. This data is usually based on aerial surveys, existing maps and surveys, and remote sensing. Once the data is entered into the GIS, users request specific information about certain regions, and then the system analyzes the relevant data and responds. The GIS is an interactive mapping system rather than a static representation of certain aspects of the world. This technology has recently become available in certain automobiles.

Using Maps to Process Information from a Spatial Perspective

Maps are useful as **abstract representations** of physical and human aspects of Earth's surface that cannot be observed from any single point on that surface. Each human observes the world from one location at a time. Graphic depictions of large portions of the surface enable the identification of the patterns and **spatial organizations** of physical and human surface features and may be used to report information about a region's subsurface characteristics (natural or artificial). Maps illustrate how natural landmarks such as rivers and mountains are oriented in relation to one another, they show how oil resources are distributed across the surface, and they convey the arrangement of human settlements. The information provided by maps facilitates the formation of mental maps and an understanding of the layout of the world in many different respects. Depending on the intended use of a particular map, different physical and cultural characteristics of Earth's surface are reported and emphasized.

Patterns of Spatial Organization

Patterns of spatial organization are the points, lines, areas, and volumes that describe the spatial properties of objects in a geographic study. For example, a city courthouse may be considered a **point**. Points are connected by lines, usually roadways or other transportation routes. The roads around which a courthouse is situated serve to connect it to other points and areas (such as neighborhoods or parks), whereas a nearby lake can be thought of as **volume**. After identification of the components of a pattern, one may examine concepts such as location, density, direction, and arrangement to discover the relationship between elements of the pattern. It is then possible to analyze the revealed **pattern**, using concepts such as diffusion, linkage, accessibility, and movement. This analysis provides reasons for the patterns and functions of phenomena on Earth's surface.

Quantitative and Qualitative Methods of Geographic Analysis

Quantitative analysis involves the use of mathematics and statistics to explain and make predictions about geographic data. This method of study entails the synthesis of factual geographic information, such as population data. Maps, charts, and graphs are helpful in this type of analysis. The use of **quantitative** techniques allows geographers to objectively process large quantities of data and many variables. Often, geographers use quantitative inquiry to formulate hypotheses about spatial trends and patterns; they then test these theories through qualitative methods.

Qualitative analysis involves the first-hand examination of geographic phenomena in their original or natural place or site. In human geography, for example, one conducting qualitative research might interview inhabitants of an area for their perspective on a certain trend or issue. In the social sciences, qualitative analysis generally involves extensive fieldwork.

Mental Maps

A mental map is a person's internalized representation of all or part of Earth's surface in a spatial context. **Mental maps** exist on a variety of scales. They may depict regions as small as a person's kitchen or as large as the entire surface of our planet. Because they are formed through the fusion of objective knowledge (such as facts about mountain elevation, the locations of cities, and the areas of countries) and subjective knowledge (such as priorities placed on knowledge of certain areas and impressions of places), each person's mental map is unique. Mental maps are vital in understanding the world. People use their mental maps during travel or when selecting a new place to live. These individual representations of the world are constantly growing and changing with the acquisition of new information, which may be gained through personal experience or secondhand from any source. As details are added to a person's mental map, he or she becomes more knowledgeable about and comfortable in the surrounding world.

Factors Affecting Accuracy of a Person's Mental Map

Just as some people possess "natural" aptitudes for algebra or drawing, some people are more able than others to envision human activity spatially. Geographic scholars refer to this capacity as

spatial cognition. The quality of a person's **mental map** is also affected by the geographic education he or she has received. For example, when asked to sketch a map of the world, many people across the globe would orient their maps with the North Pole at the top, the South Pole at the bottom, and Europe in the center. This is so because of educational conventions held over from the colonial period in America. A person's exposure to and study of certain areas may also affect his or her mental map. Naturally, the more one knows about, for example, a state, the larger that state will seem on one's mental map. Logically, the quality and accuracy of one's mental map may be improved through geographic study.

Location and Place

The location of a point is its precise spatial situation on Earth's surface. **Locations** are often identified through the use of maps and globe. The absolute location of a point is its definitive location on Earth's surface in a specific coordinate system. At the global level, it is usually expressed using the graticule. For example, Baltimore, Maryland, is at 39.3 degrees N, 76.6 degrees W. Locally, absolute location may be expressed as a specific street address. For example, the Texas State Capitol building is located at 1100 Congress Avenue. The relative location of a point is its location in relation to something else, such as a well-known landmark. For example, in giving a friend directions, you might say that your house is "two blocks north of the market." On a global scale, one might say that Chile is west of Argentina. The term **place** refers to the human and physical qualities of a location. A place's combined array of natural and manmade characteristics distinguishes it from any other place.

Site and Situation

A location's site is defined as the physical characteristics of the place it occupies. These qualities include topography, elevation, climate, soil, and resources, as well as spatial organization. **Site** refers to a location's internal locational attributes. A place's **situation** is its relative location or regional position with regard to surrounding places; it refers to the location's external locational attributes. These include its location relative to outside areas of productive capacity, other political entities or settlements, transportation routes, and barriers to access and movement. Site and situation are especially important to geographers studying the evolution of urban areas. For example, the original site of the city of Paris was an island in a highly-trafficked area of the Seine River; eventually, the island became too densely populated, and the city grew along the river's banks. Paris's situation was conducive to growth, for the city was surrounded by fertile areas of agricultural production and many land and water routes for transportation and trade.

Map Projections

A map projection is a method of portraying all or part of the round Earth on a flat surface. Any representation of the spherical globe on a flat map entails a degree of **distortion**. However, maps are more practically useful than globes—maps are smaller and easier to transport. A given map can only accurately represent selected globular features at the expense of others. This is generally accomplished through the creation of a projection surface, which is then flattened. To create such a surface, cartographers conceptually "touch" one or more areas of the surface to the globe; the regions touched by the projection surface exhibit the least distortion in map form.

Classifying Map Projections Based on Orientations and Metric Property

The orientation of a map projection surface can be **normal** (such that the surface's axis of symmetry coincides with Earth's axis), **transverse** (at right angles to Earth's axis), or **oblique** (any angle in between).

Map projections can be classified by the metric property each preserves, as follows:

- **Conformal** map projections preserve the angles between points.
- **Equal-area** map projections preserve area.
- **Equidistant** map projections preserve distance from some standard point or line. **Gnomonic** map projections display great circles as straight lines; this type of projection is the oldest.
- **Retroazimuthal** map projections preserve direction in the transfer from a spherical to a flat surface.

Cartographic Manipulation

Cartographic manipulation is the process by which the actual sizes and shapes of areas or countries are **distorted** on maps. This manipulation may be accidental or intended. A certain degree of manipulation is inherent in the creation of map projections—Earth's surface cannot be accurately represented on a flat piece of paper. Also, unintended distortion may occur due to a lack of cartographic knowledge or poor map design; maps used by media often suffer from this type of distortion. **Intentional cartographic manipulation** may be employed to convey a certain side of an issue. For example, if a community group wishes to protest the erection of a nuclear power plant near their neighborhood, they may create a map that shortens the distance between the potential plant and surrounding homes. **Cartographic aggression** is the use of map distortion by a nation to lay claim to territory over which they have no legal authority. For instance, prior to Operation Desert Storm, Iraq's officially-sanctioned maps portrayed Kuwait as a province of Iraq.

Review Video: Map Projections
Visit mometrix.com/academy and enter code: 327303

Standard Line, Bearing, Loxodrome, Geodesics

A **standard line** is a line on a map that corresponds in scale and distance to a line on Earth; such lines are rarely straight. A map that displays a well-defined set of standard lines may be referred to as equidistant.

A **bearing**, or course, is a standard direction.

A **loxodrome** (or rhumb line) is a line of constant bearing that represents the easiest route between two points. Loxodromes are often distorted in map projections.

A **geodesic** line is the shortest line between two points on any mathematically defined surface. The shortest route between two points on a spherical surface such as a globe is part of a **geodesic** line (also called a great circle path, orthodrome, or geodetic). These lines run through the two given points and are centered on the sphere. The equator is an example of a great circle.

Cylindrical Map Projections

On a cylindrical map projection, lines of latitude are parallel to one another, equally spaced, and perpendicular to lines of longitude. Lines of travel are consistent on such a projection, while size and shape distortions increase with distance from the equator (the coordinate origin of cylindrical projections). Therefore, **cylindrical map projections** are rectangular; if such a map was rolled up, it would form a cylinder without end caps. The most famous cylindrical projection is the **Mercator projection**.

Conic Map Projections

A conic map projection is created as though the surface of a globe was wrapped around a cone with the point oriented at the **North Pole** (the coordinate origin of this type of map). On **conic map projections**, longitudinal lines (meridians) are straight and equidistant; they may or may not converge at a pole. Latitudinal lines (parallels) distorted into concentric circles. Conic projections may be equal-area (areal relationships are maintained) or conformal (local angles and scale are preserved). The **Lambert conformal projection** is a type of conic projection which is often used in the creation of aeronautical charts.

Variations of Cylindrical Map Projections

Cylindrical projections treat Earth as a cylinder on which parallels are horizontal lines and meridians appear as vertical lines. There are many variations of cylindrical projections, including the following:

- The **transverse Mercator** projection, in which the cylinder is tangent to Earth not along the Equator but along a chosen meridian, a treatment that has advantages in drawing maps that are long in the north–south direction.
- The **Robinson projection**, which is neither completely conformal nor completely equal-area; instead, it occupies a space between the two extremes.
- The **Winkel tripel projection**, which is a modified azimuthal projection that is neither conformal nor equal-area. the central meridian and equator are straight lines; other parallels and meridians are curved. The projection is obtained by averaging the coordinates of the equidistant cylindrical and Aitoff (not Hammer-Aitoff) projections. The poles map into straight lines 0.4 times the length of the equator.

Azimuthal Map Projections

Azimuthal (or planar) map projections use the **azimuth** as a reference point and often have **polar** orientations. The azimuth of a surface is the angle a person at a reference point (A) and looking at one point (B) must turn to face another point (C). On a sphere, lines AB and AC are geodesic lines. **Azimuthal projections** accurately represent direction (but not necessarily distance) from the azimuth to any other point. On any azimuthal projection (regardless of its orientation), all straight lines touching the central point are geodesics; distortion varies with distance from the center. **Azimuthal orthographic projections** portray Earth as viewed from space (at any distance); orthographic projections exhibit severe distortion around their edges. **Azimuthal stereographic projections** are conformal and preserve circles. They are most useful in the examination of one hemisphere. **Azimuthal gnomic projections** are similar to stereographic maps; however, every geodesic is mapped as a straight line, resulting in pronounced distance distortion and some direction distortion.

Pseudoconic Projections

Pseudoconic projections normally display parallels as circular arcs with common central points. Unlike "true" conic projections, **pseudoconic projections** do not represent meridians as straight lines. There are several types of pseudoconic projections, including the following:

- **Cordiform projections**, which are also called Stabius-Werner projections, produce heart-shaped maps.
- In the **normal aspect**, cordiform maps exhibit similarities. First, the prime meridian is a straight standard line; second, all other meridians are curved lines; and third, parallels are drawn in equal liner scale as circular arcs centered at a pole (usually the North Pole). All cordiform maps are equal-area and convey Earth's spherical quality.

- **Bonne projections** include parallels that are equally spaced concentric circular arcs and are all standard lines. Each Bonne map has one parallel as its center, making all such maps different. This type of map has virtually no areal distortion but does have slight shape distortion (except far from the center). Once very popular for large-scale topographic maps, the "Bonne" pseudoconic projection has generally fallen in disuse.

Tissot's Indicatrix

Tissot's indicatrix is a tool used in cartography to assess the **distortion** inherent in all flat maps. First, many small circles are drawn onto the original sphere. Then, the same circles are mapped onto the flat projection. After undergoing this process, a given circle may change in size or shape. A comparison of the circles on each surface thus reveals the distortion patterns of shape, size, and angle on the projected map. For example, the examination of indicatrices on the Mercator projection, in which the **Tissot circles** retain their shapes and parallels remain parallel to one another and perpendicular to the straight meridians, proves that this type of projection is conformal, preserving shape, angle, and scale. The sizes of the circles change when they are mapped from the sphere to the Mercator projection (on the Mercator map, the circles increase in size with distance from the equator), indicating that areas are distorted.

Projections Created to Counteract Distortion

While all map projections have some type of distortion or deformation, the following are some types that attempt to **reduce distortion**:

- An **oblique map** is one in which neither the equator nor the prime meridian is centered on or aligned with the map axes. Oblique maps generally preserve area and shape but distort properties relating to the graticule orientation of the original sphere. They are usually created to move a large area of interest from an area of high distortion to a region of lower distortion.
- An **interrupted map** is one that is "cut" at certain (arbitrary) lines. The resultant sections (called lobes or gores) then project separately from the map. Interrupted maps are used in attempts to overcome shape, area, or distance distortion on "normal" projections. Goode's interrupted projection is a notable equal-area map; it accurately portrays size and shape but distorts distance.
- A **polyhedral map** is created by projecting separate regions of the globe onto different faces of a polyhedron. The polyhedron may then be cut and disassembled into a flat map (a net or fold-out).

Classifying Maps

A map is classified primarily by its **purpose** and **content** (i.e., topographic map, weather map, road map). Maps may also be classified by **scale** or **derivation** (the source of the data represented). A **topographic or reference map** conveys general information about a geographic area, including ground elevation, natural formations (such as lakes and mountains), and structures erected by men (such as roadways and dams). **Thematic or illustrative maps** are those that represent a specific geographic theme, such as demography, geology, or land use. Such maps are created for a specific purpose. For example, land condition maps delineate surface areas that are especially susceptible to flooding, mass movements, or earthquakes; these maps are used by engineers for city planning or related activities. Land use maps, tourist maps, road maps, and mineral maps are other kinds of thematic maps. An **analytical map** represents a geographer's hypothesis about the relationship between two or more elements of Earth's surface; the ideas suggested in analytical maps are tested using mathematics.

Proportional Symbol Maps

In the creation of a proportional symbol map, a cartographer selects a particular symbol form to represent a particular **variable**. Proportionally sized symbols are oriented in specific areas to convey the relative quantity of the variable in those areas. This method of mapping may be used when data occur at points (or can be aggregated at points) and when data can be measured as absolute values. The symbol most commonly used in the creation of **proportional symbol maps** is the **circle**, because circles are easy to construct to scale. Circles are also visually stable, aiding map readers in their interpretations. Variables such as population density are often represented on this type of map. A map reader forms an image of the spatial distribution of, for example, population density through observation of the pattern created by the differently sized symbols.

Choropleth Maps

In the creation of a choropleth map, a cartographer selects a unique color, shading technique, or pattern to identify a certain variable characteristic. This symbol is then applied to the appropriate **chorogram**. A chorogram is a discrete statistical area, such as a voting district, or administrative district, such as a state or township. This method of mapping may be used when data occur in or may be attributed to a distinct spatial unit. Also, the data to be conveyed should be derived rather than "raw." For instance, a **choropleth map** may display population density but not population distribution. In other words, ratio-level data should be used. Cartographers typically use **idiographic data classification**, which involves the delimitation of intervals between variable classes based on the array of data (i.e., natural breaks, equal intervals, etc.). A map reader analyzes the use of color or shading to determine the symbol class to which a particular chorogram belongs.

Cartograms

A cartogram is a map in which some **thematic mapping variable**, such as travel time, is substituted for land area. The geometry or space of the map is distorted in order to convey the information of this alternate variable. There are two main types of cartograms: area and distance cartograms. An **area cartogram**, which is also referred to as a value-by-area map, is similar to a proportional symbol map, in that the cartographer adjusts the sizes of artificial collection units (chorograms) to convey the relative data value for each; chorograms are thus proportionally sized. This type of map is useful when there is no data generalization (as occurs in choropleth maps). Also, the data (which may be absolute or derived, and of the interval or ratio measurement level) must be aggregated in chorograms. Area cartograms are most effective when data values correlate negatively with the areas or sizes of the chorograms (when large chorograms have small values and small chorograms have large values). This method of visual representation aids in the display of spatial idiosyncrasies that could be obscured in conventional maps (due to wide variations in the sizes of the collection units). A **distance cartogram**, which may also be called a central-point cartogram, is typically used to show relative travel times and directions from vertices in a network.

Geologic Map

A geologic map describes the rocks and soils at the surface, provides information about what rocks lie at depth, describes the ages of rocks and soils, and shows where features such as earthquake faults and landslides lie. **Geologic maps** are made by studying the rocks and materials exposed at the surface and depicting information about those rocks on a map. Unlike a topography map, which represents landforms on Earth's surface, a **thematic geologic map** represents rock or mineral ore formations that exist underneath the surface. On a geologic map, common rock types (such as limestone, shale, and granite) are represented by graphic patterns or colors. Lines are used to delineate contact planes (planes separating two rock formations). Cartographers use certain symbols to indicate the presence of horizontal beds, vertical beds, axes in folded rocks, etc. These maps are extremely useful in the location and recovery of mineral resources and fossil fuels. These formations are identified through the analysis of field research data and aerial photography.

Review Video: Geographical Features
Visit mometrix.com/academy and enter code: 773539

RELIEF

The term *relief* refers to the variations in elevation across a portion of Earth's surface. The most obvious way to depict **relief** is to imitate it at scale, as in molded or sculpted solid terrain models and molded-plastic raised-relief maps. On flat paper maps, terrain can be depicted in a variety of ways, including **contour lines** showing equal elevation, which is the most common way of numerically showing elevation; **hypsometric tints**, which are a variant on contour lines that depict ranges of elevation as bands of color, usually in a graduated scheme; **shaded relief**, or hill-shading, which simulates the cast shadow thrown upon a raised relief map; and physiographic illustration, which uses generalized texture to imitate landform shapes over a large area.

GEOGRAPHIC INSTABILITY

The term *geographic instability* refers to the transitory nature of **boundaries and place names** in certain areas of the globe. Periods of geographic change often follow events such as the colonization of a new area or the fall of an empire. For example, upon the disintegration of the former Soviet Union, cartographers faced a deluge of changes. New boundaries were created, forming new countries and provinces, and certain cities were renamed. Similarly, when China switched from its old spelling system to the new Pinyin system, all maps displaying the former spellings of place names became obsolete. Because we do not live on a static Earth, boundaries and place names will continue to change. This simply means that cartographers must continue to update existing maps to keep pace with **geographic instability**.

NAUTICAL AND AVIATION CHARTS

A nautical chart, which may also be called a **hydrographic chart**, is a thematic map intended for use by sea-faring sailors in navigation. This type of map includes a latitude-longitude grid that aids marine navigators in the identification of potential hazards to a ship, such as massive coral reefs. In addition, a **nautical chart** conveys the locations of lighthouses and other artificial landforms, the relief and constituent materials of the seafloor, and the shapes of topographic features such as shorelines or islets.

An **aviation chart** (also called an aeronautical chart) is another kind of thematic map. It resembles a nautical chart but for its emphasis on airways, land topography, the heights of potential obstructions in an aircraft's path, and radio beacons.

Graphs and Charts

FEATURES OF GRAPHS AND CHARTS

A graph is a visual representation that exhibits a relationship, often functional, between two sets of numbers as a set of points having coordinates determined by the relationship. The term **chart** may be used as a synonym for graph, or it may refer to a specialized kind of map, such as a nautical chart. There are many different methods of displaying data in graphs and charts; most include the plotting of data in **two dimensions**. Many of these diagrams include several basic features. First of all, a title indicates the purpose and content of a graph or chart. Most diagrams have a **horizontal axis** (the x-axis) and a **vertical axis** (the y-axis); the intersection of these axes, where the value of each variable equals zero, is referred to as the **origin**. These axes are labeled to identify the variable being plotted and/or the range of values of that variable. Generally, independent variables (such as time) are represented on the x-axis, and dependent variables (such as temperature) are represented on the y-axis.

PIE CHARTS AND 100 PERCENT BAR CHARTS

A pie chart, also referred to as a circle graph, is a method of data representation that does not use the axes common in other kinds of graphs, and therefore does not involve the plotting of data in two dimensions. **Pie charts** are based on percentages of a total quantity; a full circle represents one hundred percent. This type of chart is useful when this quantity is known and the chart's creator wishes to convey the relative sizes of the "pieces" which add up to that total. For example, if a geographer knows the total number of people worldwide who identify themselves as having religious beliefs, he or she might create a pie chart to show what percentage of that total describes themselves as Muslims, Christians, Jews, etc. Percentages are converted to numbers of degrees and represented as sections of the circle. A **100 percent bar chart** uses represents percentages as proportional sections of a bar.

LINE GRAPHS

A line graph is a type of chart that is useful in representing relationships between sets of data. **Line graphs** are often used to show changes in a variable over time. For instance, in a graph of sale trends for a major company, a time scale (such as years or months) is laid out along the x-axis and an amount scale is oriented along the y-axis. Then, the respective sales figures corresponding to each time unit are plotted on the graph; these data points are connected with a line whose curvature conveys general tendencies about changes in sales over time. This feature of line graphs enables viewers to make educated predictions about future trends as well. In economics, a line graph may be used to show the relationship between quantity (on the x-axis) and price (on the y-axis). By connecting plotted points with lines, economists can identify changes in price as they relate to changes in the available quantities of goods.

BAR GRAPHS

A bar graph is a type of chart that is useful in **comparing quantities**. This type of chart is similar to a line graph in that each involves the placement of variables along two axes. Instead of displaying values as points on the grid, however, a **bar chart** uses rectangular bars extending from an axis and leveling off at the appropriate points. In other words, the length of a bar representing a particular variable conveys the value of that variable. Bar graphs may be vertical (in which independent variables are oriented along the x-axis and the rectangles extend vertically) or horizontal (in which independent variables are laid out along the y-axis and the rectangles extend horizontally). This type of graph aids in the observation of differences among similar things. For example, a bar chart may display the variations in population among several major cities. In a pictograph, small icons or figures relating are used in lieu of rectangles to represent values. This type of graph is eye-catching and instantly conveys the purpose of the graph.

SCATTER PLOTS

A scatter plot is a type of display that shows the values for two variables for a set of data. Like bar and line graphs, **scatter plots** use x- and y-axes to plot data points. However, their specific purpose is to display how one variable affects another. This relationship is referred to as **correlation**. Correlation between variables is identified through the examination of a large quantity of data, represented on the graph as points. The closer the points come to forming a straight line, the stronger the relationship (and the higher the correlation) between the variables. If the line formed by the points extends from a high point on the y-axis to a high value on the x-axis, the correlation is negative. Conversely, if the line extends from the origin to high x- and y-values, the correlation between the two variables is positive. One might use a scatter plot to examine the relationship between education and income by aligning education level along the x-axis of a graph and yearly income along the y-axis, and then plotting data points for a group of individuals.

Physical Geography

El Niño

El Niño refers to the unusual **warming** of surface waters near the equatorial coast of South America. This phenomenon occurs during the winter approximately every two to seven years, lasting from a few weeks to a few months. **El Niño** can cause torrential rains, violent winds, drought, and dangerously high temperatures in surrounding areas. El Niño is caused by a reversal of the atmospheric pressures on the eastern and western sides of the Pacific (normally, pressure is high on the eastern side near South America and lower on the western side near the Indonesian coast). This reversal causes a wave of warm water to flow eastward and sea levels to fall on the western side. The changes in air pressure and ocean temperature cause moisture levels in the western Pacific to rise drastically, while the region east of the Pacific experiences drought. The air pressure changes also weaken the region's trade winds, which normally serve to distribute heat and moisture.

Ecosystems

An ecosystem (an abbreviated term for ecological system) is a system in the biosphere that consists of a biotic community (a regional group of living organisms) and the surrounding environment, called a biotope. Some characteristics include:

- Ecosystems may be studied at different **scales**. For example, an ecosystem may be as small as an area within a pond or as large as the entire planet.
- Ecosystems exist in **dynamic equilibrium**, a relatively steady state maintained by various symbiotic (interactive) processes such as predation (wherein one organism, a predator, overwhelms and consumes another, the prey) and mutualism (interspecies relationships which benefit both parties).
- Ecosystems receive **energy inputs** (mainly from the Sun); this energy is transformed through the process of photosynthesis and transferred among constituents via the food web.
- Ecosystems also produce **natural resources** used by human beings, including structural materials, food, and fuel.
- Ecosystems are broadly described as **terrestrial** (those which include land animals and exist atop continents) or **aquatic** (those dominated by water and marine or freshwater life).

Ecological Succession

Ecological succession is the process that occurs after a significant disturbance or disaster has simplified an ecosystem. **Primary succession** follows a disaster that eliminates all living organisms in a region (such as a volcanic eruption). **Secondary succession** refers to the process that succeeds a disturbance in which some life survives (such as deforestation). **Ecological succession** is the change of a biotic community from a simpler state to one that is more diverse and complex. Through this process, members of an ecosystem mature and develop more intricate relationships. Though ecologists in earlier times envisioned a climax stage that represented the end point of ecosystem development, this idea is largely absent in current ecological discourse. Rather, modern ecologists believe that ecosystems are always changing and reacting to various degrees and frequencies of disturbances, making a climax community unreachable.

Review Video: Ecological Succession
Visit mometrix.com/academy and enter code: 466994

Food Web

The food web, or **food network**, is a model used to describe the transfer of energy (in the form of sustenance) between organisms in an ecosystem. Organisms feed on one another to stay alive; this process also helps to regulate the populations of species within an ecosystem. Organisms in a **food web** are generally organized into **trophic levels** that reflect their relative positions in this system. **Primary producers**, usually photosynthetic plants and algae, exist at the base of a food web. These organisms produce vital **biochemical molecules** (including carbohydrates) from light energy derived from the Sun's energy. The primary producers are consumed by **small primary consumers**, such as insects and fish. These organisms are in turn eaten and digested by **secondary consumers**, which are later preyed upon by larger organisms, and so on. **Decomposers** are soil-dwelling microorganisms that rely on detritus (decaying organic materials) for sustenance. Because energy is lost in transfer throughout the food web (due to respiration), the number of organisms and their sizes decline up the chain.

Review Video: Food Webs
Visit mometrix.com/academy and enter code: 853254

Respiration

Respiration is the process whereby energy is burned by an organism to keep it alive. It is basically the opposite of photosynthesis. This chemical process involves the decomposition of carbohydrates, which then combine with oxygen, releasing water, carbon dioxide, and heat energy into the atmosphere. Organisms' cells store the **chemical energy** produced through respiration; this energy is later used to create vital **biochemical molecules**. Respiration is thus a counterpart of photosynthesis in the cycling of elements through an ecosystem. Due to the energy loss inherent to the process of respiration, only 10-50% of the energy stored in organic matter at one level of the food web moves up to the next level.

Process of Transpiration

Transpiration is the mechanism by which water evaporates into the atmosphere from the leaves or stems of plants. Plants absorb water into their roots through osmosis. Then, as explained by **cohesion-tension theory**, water moves upward from the roots of a plant to its leaves. Some transpiration occurs directly through surface cells on the stem of a plant. More often, however, water escapes through pores in its leaves called **stomates**. Water droplets on the exterior surface of the leaves (usually on the bottom of the leaves) are consequently subjected to the process of evaporation. The process of transpiration enables **photosynthesis**, which in turn releases vital oxygen into Earth's atmosphere. Transpiration also has a cooling effect on the surface and air around the plant.

Biogeochemical Cycle

The term *biogeochemical cycle* refers to one of several chemical processes in which chemical elements are (re)cycled among **biotic** (living) and **abiotic** (nonliving) constituents of an ecosystem. The theory of relativity necessitates the presence of such cycles in nature by virtue of its supposition that energy and matter are not created or destroyed in a closed system such as Earth's ecosystem. Generally, a **biogeochemical cycle** operates as follows: Inorganic compounds are converted from water, air, and soil to organic molecules by organisms called **autotrophs**. **Heterotrophs** (organisms that cannot independently produce their own food) consume the autotrophs; some of the newly formed organic molecules are transferred. Finally, the organic molecules are broken down and processed once again into inorganic compounds by secondary and tertiary consumers and replaced within water, air, and soil. Carbon, nitrogen, and phosphorus provide examples of nutrients that are recycled in Earth's ecosystem.

BIOME

A biome is the broadest general subdivision of terrestrial ecosystems. This term is used to describe a region that exhibits the distinctive plant and animal life best adapted to an area's particular soil type and climate. This concept is associated with the interrelationships between organisms and their environment. Since vegetation is more abundant than any other species in the biosphere, **biomes** are often classified according to **climax vegetation type** (the type of vegetation that exists in mature or old-growth ecosystems). The global distribution of biomes is closely related to climate and soil variations at different latitudes. The subdivision of a biome may be further differentiated into formation classes, based upon the structural and dimensional characteristics of regional vegetation.

FOREST BIOMES

The forest biome is typified by an abundance of soil and moisture, as well as warm temperatures for at least a portion of the year. Trees are the dominant vegetation type in this biome.

SAVANNA BIOME

The savanna biome exists between forest and grassland on the spectrum of biomes. It is often situated near the boundary of an equatorial rainforest. This type of biome is commonly found in regions that experience a wet-dry tropical climate. The lack of moisture in the soil during the dry season causes trees in the savanna biome to grow in spacious patterns. This enables the growth of a dense lower layer of grasses and other plants. The trees of the **savanna biome** are similar in height and shape to those found in a monsoon forest. Though fire is a fairly common occurrence in savannas during the dry season, the vegetation in these regions tends to be quite fire-resistant. In fact, many geographers believe that such fires prevent rainforest vegetation from overrunning the savanna biome.

GRASSLAND BIOME

The grassland biome is commonly subdivided into two types: tall-grass prairie and steppe. The **tall-grass prairie subdivision** is characterized by an absence of trees and a high occurrence of tall grasses and broad-leaved herbs called forbs. This kind of biome usually forms in regions with distinct summer and winter seasons, in subtropical or midlatitude climates. The **steppe, or short-grass prairie, subdivision** is typified by sparse clumps of short grasses, existing alongside the occasional shrub or small tree. Many grass species and forbs populate this kind of region. Steppes are usually found in midlatitude areas with dry continental climates; vegetation grows in wet spring months and becomes dormant during dry summer months.

DESERT BIOME

The desert biome may be subdivided into two types: semidesert and dry desert. The **semidesert subdivision** is found at a wide range of latitudes. It is characterized by thinly-spaced xerophytic shrubs (those adapted to survival in arid climates). Steppe regions may be converted to semidesert through, for example, high levels of cattle moving through the area, treading upon and consuming regional vegetation. The thorntree semidesert is found in the tropical zone, which experiences a long, dry hot season and a short, severe rainy season. Thorny vegetation (such as cacti), called thornbush or thornwoods, populate the thorntree semidesert.

The **dry desert subdivision** is even barer than the semidesert. Only tough xerophytes, such as cacti and hard grasses, can survive under dry desert conditions. Many dry desert areas display no plant life at all, due to the unfertile sand that covers the ground.

Tundra Biome

The tundra biome may be subdivided into two types: arctic or alpine. The **arctic tundra** exists at very high latitudes near the poles. During the brief summer season in these areas, low vegetation such as herbs, mosses, and grasses are able to grow because above-freezing air temperatures enable melting of the surface layer. The type and occurrence of plant species depend upon the moisture levels in the (usually frozen) ground during the warm season. In the cold season, frost action snaps roots in the ground. Freezing wind and snow kill plants above the ground. **Alpine tundra** is located at high elevations, above the tree line and below bare mountain tops. Physically, the alpine tundra is quite similar to the arctic tundra.

Various Forets and Formation Classes

Characteristics of the Low-Latitude Rainforests

The low-latitude rainforest formation class exists in equatorial and tropical climate zones. This class is characterized by many different species of tall, densely spaced trees, normally with broad leaves. The canopy created by this vegetation casts shade on the ground below, inhibiting the growth of flora on the bottom layer.

Monsoon Forests

Monsoon forests may also be found in tropical latitude zones; however, this formation class exists in regions that experience a wet season and a dry season, during which the many tree species lose their leaves. This enables the growth of vegetation on the lower layer of the forest.

Subtropical Evergreen Forest Formation Classes

The subtropical evergreen forest may be broadleaf or needleleaf (found only in the southeastern United States). This formation class consists of fewer, shorter tree species than the low-latitude rainforest. It also includes a lush lower layer of vegetation.

Midlatitude Deciduous Forest

The midlatitude deciduous forest formation class is common in regions of the northern hemisphere with distinct seasons. During the warm summer season, the tall broadleaf trees in this type of forest form a nearly closed canopy. In the winter season, these trees lose their leaves. The lower level vegetation also varies with the season, growing in the spring and dying out with the summertime formation of a dense upper canopy.

Needleleaf Forest

A needleleaf forest is made up largely of conifers (cone-shaped trees with short branches, straight trunks, and small, thin leaves reminiscent of needles). Many trees in this type of forest (usually found at higher latitudes or regions where orogenies and/or plateaus are found) are evergreen, meaning that they shed their leaves once every several years. The spacing of the trees in this formation class may be dense, preventing the growth of vegetation on the ground.

Sclerophyll Forest

The sclerophyll forest contains widely spaced trees that are able to survive dry, hot seasons (short, with low branches; tough, thick bark; and short, thick leaves).

Earth's Rotation

Earth rotates **eastward** (from the equator) about its **rotational axis** (an imaginary line running north to south through the center of the planet). This motion exposes each section of Earth to direct sunlight for a limited period of time, thus creating the sensations of day and night. Due to minute variations in the sidereal day, which is defined as the exact amount of time it takes for a reference star to cross an imaginary north-south line above an observer (a meridian), we use the **mean sidereal day** (a period of exactly 24 hours) in timekeeping. Earth's rotation creates **diurnal** (daily) variations in air humidity, air temperature, and air motion. These patterns affect plant and animal life on the planet and also influence the **hydrosphere**, causing tidal movement and the Coriolis effect.

Earth's Revolution

Earth revolves around the Sun in an **orbit**. This process takes just over 365 days (our calendar year). The consequence of the elliptical shape of Earth's orbit is that the distance between the planet and the Sun varies over time. At **perihelion**, the minimum heliocentric distance, Earth is 147 million kilometers from the Sun. At **aphelion**, the maximum heliocentric distance, Earth is 152 million kilometers from the Sun. Earth's revolution about the Sun and the tilt of the planet's rotational axis (approximately 23.5 degrees from its orbital plane) produce the **seasons** we experience on Earth; certain areas of the surface receive different amounts of sunlight throughout the year. For example, during the portion of Earth's orbit when the Northern Hemisphere tilts toward the Sun, it is exposed to higher amounts of nearly direct sunlight than any other time of year (because days are longer and the direction of the Sun's rays striking the surface is nearly perpendicular). This time period is summer in the Northern Hemisphere and winter in the Southern Hemisphere.

Global Energy Flow System

The global energy flow system is comprised of the pathways through which energy travels between the Sun and Earth, including its storage as well as its losses in the atmosphere. A main tenet of physics is that energy, like matter, cannot be created or destroyed in a **closed system** such as Earth. This fact necessitates the **recycling of energy** from the Sun to Earth and back again. Earth receives energy from the Sun in the form of light and heat. It moves through the atmosphere as short-wave radiation and is converted to different forms, fueling nearly all of the natural physical phenomena that occur on the planet in one way or another (either directly or indirectly). **Solar energy** is also "lost" due to scattering and absorption in the atmosphere. The rate of this incoming energy, which is nearly constant, is referred to as the **solar constant**. Long-wave radiation is emitted from Earth into space, often through the release of gases such as carbon dioxide and water vapor.

Weather

Weather is the result of transfers of kinetic (heat) energy due to differences in temperature between objects as well as transfers of moisture in Earth's atmosphere. Most of the activity that produces the **weather** we experience on Earth takes place in the **troposphere**, the lowest level of the atmosphere (0-15 kilometers above Earth's surface). Atmospheric pressure, temperature, humidity, elevation, wind speed, and cloud cover are all factors in the formation of weather. A **weather system** is an organized atmospheric state, associated with a particular weather pattern such as cyclones or tornadoes. **Meteorology**, the study of weather, entails the observation of natural phenomena such as rain, fog, snow, and wind. The processes that occur at different stages in the **hydrologic cycle** form the basis of meteorological events.

Cycles of Air Temperature

The two main cycles of air temperature are **insolation** and **net radiation**. Due to Earth's rotation, **insolation** (interception of solar energy by an exposed surface) varies from location to location with the angle at which solar rays hit Earth and the length of time a particular location is exposed to direct sunlight. **Net radiation** is the difference between incoming and outgoing radiation. This quality is positive when more energy is flowing in than out, and vice versa. During daylight hours, a surface location experiences positive net radiation, causing it to gain heat; at night, the location loses heat. This pattern is the daily air temperature cycle. The annual air temperature cycle results from Earth's revolution. When a region of Earth experiences summer, the region's net radiation is positive. In wintertime, net radiation is low. Air temperature is also affected by altitude (temperature generally decreases as altitude increases), location (continental or oceanic—air temperature in maritime areas is less variable), and surface features (which may absorb or reflect heat waves). Isotherms are lines on a map connecting points with equivalent air temperatures.

Hydrologic Cycle

The hydrologic cycle, also known as the **water cycle**, is the circulation of water i Earth's hydrosphere (below the surface, on the surface, and above Earth's surface). This continuous process involves five physical actions:

- **Evaporation** entails the change of water molecules from a liquid to a gaseous state.
- **Condensation** occurs when liquid water on Earth's surface (often contained in a large body of water) becomes water vapor and enters the atmosphere when its component molecules gain enough kinetic (heat) energy to escape the liquid form. As the vapor rises, it cools and therefore loses its ability to maintain the gaseous form. It begins to condense (return to a liquid or solid state) and forms clouds.
- **Precipitation** occurs when the clouds become sufficiently dense and the water falls back to Earth.
- Water is then either trapped in **vegetation** (interception) or **infiltration** (absorption of water into the surface).
- **Runoff**, caused by gravity, physically moves water downward into oceans or other water bodies.

Review Video: Bodies of Water
Visit mometrix.com/academy and enter code: 463122

Review Video: Hydrologic Cycle
Visit mometrix.com/academy and enter code: 426578

Precipitation

Precipitation is water that falls back to Earth's surface from the atmosphere. This water may be in the form of **rain**, which is water in liquid form. Raindrops are formed in clouds due to the process of **condensation**. When the drops become too heavy to remain in the cloud (due to a decrease in their kinetic energy), gravity causes them to fall down toward Earth's surface. Extremely small raindrops are called **drizzle**. If the temperature of a layer of air through which rain passes on its way down is below the freezing point, the rain may take the form of **sleet** (partially frozen water). Precipitation may also fall in the form of **snow**, or water molecules sublimated into ice crystals. When clumps of snowflakes melt and refreeze, **hail** is formed. Hail may also be formed when liquid water accumulates on the surface of a snowflake and subsequently freezes.

TYPES OF CLOUDS

The four main types of clouds are cirrus, cumulus, nimbus, and stratus.

- A **cirrus cloud** forms high in a stable atmosphere, generally at altitudes of 6,000 meters or higher. Temperatures at these altitudes (in the troposphere) decrease with increased altitude; therefore, the precipitation in a cirrus cloud adopts the form of ice crystals. These usually thin traces of clouds may indicate an approaching weather depression.
- A **cumulus cloud** is a stereotypical white, fluffy ball. Cumulus clouds are indicators of a stable atmosphere and also of the vertical extent of convection in the atmosphere; condensation and cloud formation begin at the flat base of a cumulous cloud. The more humid the air, the lower a cumulus cloud will form.
- A **nimbus cloud** is, generally speaking, a rain cloud. Nimbus clouds are usually low, dark, and formless, sometimes spanning the entire visible sky.
- A **stratus cloud** is basically a cloud of fog that forms at a distance above Earth's surface. This type of cloud forms when weak convective currents bring moisture just high enough to initiate condensation (if the temperature is below the dew point).

Review Video: Types of Clouds
Visit mometrix.com/academy and enter code: 803166

CLOUD SUBTYPES

The four cloud subtypes are cumulonimbus, cirrostratus, altocumulus, and stratocumulus.

- A **cumulonimbus cloud** is produced by rapid convection in unstable air. This type of cloud (which is often dark) is formed as a large, tall "tower." Collections of these towers (squall lines) often signal a coming cold front. Thunderstorms often involve cumulonimbus clouds.
- A **cirrostratus cloud** is an ultrathin formation with a white tint and a transparent quality.
- An **altocumulus cloud** forms at an altitude from 1,980 to 6,100 meters. Clouds of this type, which appear to be flattened spheres, often form in clumps, waves, or lines.
- A **stratocumulus cloud** forms as a globular mass or flake. Stratocumulus clouds usually come together in layers or clumps.

ATMOSPHERIC PRESSURE

Atmospheric pressure is the pressure exerted by air in the atmosphere on the surface beneath it. This pressure subsists because the air's mass is continuously being drawn toward Earth's surface by the force of gravity. The amount of **atmospheric pressure** increases with proximity to the surface because there is more mass above the lower layers. Pressure causes air mass to compress; therefore, the layer of air nearest Earth's exterior is denser than air at higher altitudes. Atmospheric pressure is measured as force per unit area. This may be the **pascal** (Pa), which is one newton per square meter, or the **millibar** (mb); one millibar equals 100 Pa. These measurements are taken with a **barometer**. An **isobar** is a line on a map that connects all points with equal levels of atmospheric pressure.

PREVAILING WINDS AND WIND BELTS

Wind (the horizontal movement of air with respect to Earth's surface) forms due to pressure gradients (differences) in the atmosphere. Air tends to move from areas of high pressure,such as the poles to areas of low pressure, such as the tropics. **Prevailing winds**, or trade winds, are the winds (named in meteorology for the direction they come from) that blow most frequently in a particular region. For instance, the prevailing winds most common in the region from 90 to 60 degrees north latitude blow from the northeast and are generally called the Polar Easterlies. **Wind belts** are created in areas where prevailing winds converge with other prevailing winds or air masses. The Intertropical Convergence Zone (ITCZ), where air coming from tropical areas north and south of the equator come together, is an example of a wind belt.

Air Mass

An air mass is a sizeable region of air that displays consistent levels of moisture and uniform temperature throughout. The characteristics of a particular **air mass** develop in a source region, where air remains stable for a period of time long enough for said air to adopt the moisture and temperature qualities of the surface below. Air masses move due to atmospheric pressure gradients or the influence of winds. Corresponding changes in the surface environment may cause an air mass to take on new properties. These pockets of air are named for the qualities of the surface environment (**maritime** or **continental**), which determine the humidity of the mass, as well as the latitudinal position at which they form, which, in turn, determines the temperature of the mass. For example, an air mass that forms over a continent at a high latitudinal location is called a continental polar air mass (denoted as cP).

Air Stability in the Atmosphere

Air stability is the tendency for air to rise or fall through the atmosphere under its own power. Heated air rises because it is less dense than the surrounding air. As a pocket of air rises, however, it will expand and become cooler with changes in atmospheric pressure. If the ambient air into which rising air ascends does not cool as quickly with altitude as the rising air does, that air will rapidly become cooler (and heavier) than the surrounding air and descend back to its original position. The air in this situation is said to be stable. However, if the air into which the warm pocket rises becomes colder with increased altitude, the warm air will continue its ascent. In this case, the air is unstable. Unstable air conditions (such as those that exist in depressions) lead to the formation of large clouds of precipitation.

Cyclones and Anticyclones

Both cyclones and anticyclones are weather systems in which air masses move in spirals. Most such systems move across Earth's surface, affecting weather as they travel. A **cyclone** occurs when low pressure in the interior of an air mass draws air inward and upward. The risen air often forms clouds, which, in turn, produce cyclonic precipitation. A cyclone that involves large pressure disparities produces intense weather referred to as a cyclonic storm. In **anticyclones**, the movement of air is opposite to that in cyclones; air pressure in the center of an air mass is higher than the surrounding air, forcing air outward and downward. Because descending warm air does not produce precipitous clouds, anticyclones are often referred to as fair weather systems.

Weather Fronts

A front is the distinct boundary that usually forms between an air mass and the surrounding air. This boundary may be sloped or nearly vertical in orientation, depending on the relative movement of abutting air masses. There are four types of fronts:

- A **cold front** occurs when a cold air mass moves into an area inhabited by a mass of warm air. In this situation, the colder, denser air mass remains near the surface, pushing the warmer mass upward. When the ascending air is unstable, this movement may create severe weather, such as thunderstorms.

- A **warm front** is formed when a warm air mass enters an area of colder air. Again, the warmer air ascends, creating precipitation.
- An **occluded front** occurs when a cold air mass (which generally moves more quickly than a warmer mass of air due to its higher density) overtakes a moving mass of warm air near Earth's surface. As in other front systems, the coldest air remains near the ground, forcing the warmer air to rise.
- A **stationary front** forms when warm and cold air meet and neither air mass has the force to move the other. They remain stationary.

Wave Cyclones

A wave cyclone is a type of cyclone that forms at mid- to high-latitudinal regions. This kind of weather system forms at the boundary between dry polar air masses and humid tropical air masses, called a **polar front**. The cyclone forms, intensifies, and ebbs repeatedly in a low-pressure trough between the converging masses. Cyclonic motion begins with the initial contact between the two air masses; the motion of both air bodies intensifies. Then, when the colder mass overtakes and elevates the warmer one, an occluded front forms in the middle of the weather system. The polar front is then reestablished, and the process begins anew. **Wave cyclones** affect wind, temperature, cloud formation, and precipitation in the surface regions over which they occur.

Tornados

A tornado is a particularly intense cyclone, which may exhibit wind speeds of up to 400 miles per hour. **Tornadoes** often form alongside mid-latitude thunderstorms over continental North America; they are also commonly observed inside of tropical hurricanes. In fact, tornadoes are most often formed at a cold front where maritime polar air forces warm, moist tropical air upward. This type of cyclone is bred from **cumulonimbus clouds** moving ahead of a **cold front**. A dark funnel-shaped cloud extends downward from a dense cumulonimbus cloud. The funnel's base appears especially dense, due to the accumulating moisture, dust, and debris being swept up by the formation. When the base of a tornado makes landfall, it can be completely devastating.

Review Video: Tornadoes
Visit mometrix.com/academy and enter code: 540439

Tropical Cyclones

A tropical cyclone is potentially the most destructive and dangerous type of cyclone. Such a formation is referred to as a **hurricane** when it occurs over the Atlantic Ocean or as a **typhoon** when it occurs over the Pacific or Indian Oceans. **Tropical cyclones** develop at low latitudes (specifically, between 8 and 15 degrees North or South latitude) when the surface waters below reach temperatures of 81 degrees Fahrenheit or above. From their zone of origination, tropical cyclones often travel westward through the trade-wind belt; westerly winds may push the storm northward as well. This type of cyclone is associated with high wind speeds and high levels of rainfall. A tropical cyclone also displays extremely low pressure in its center, or eye, where weather conditions are fair (in contrast to the rest of the storm). These weather systems occur seasonally: in the Northern Hemisphere, cyclonic activity is highest from May to November; in the Southern Hemisphere, the cyclone season is roughly the opposite.

Tropical and Equatorial Weather System Terms

An **easterly wave** is formed in the belt of tropical trades. This formation is a trough of low pressure, which travels slowly through the belt. Easterly waves occur above oceans at latitudes of 5 to 30 degrees North or South. The influence of surface winds forces the air in an easterly wave upward, causing light rainfall and occasional thunderstorms. A **weak equatorial low** is a disturbance that occurs near the center of an equatorial trough (area of low pressure). Moist air masses meet at this point, creating precipitation. A **polar outbreak** occurs when a small region of frigid polar air reaches low latitudes near the equator. This type of air mass enters a low-latitude region as a cold front, which is followed by clear but cold weather and strong winds. While polar outbreaks are not inherently dangerous, the low temperatures involved can damage crops in low-latitude regions.

FORMATION OF LIGHTNING

Lightning is a natural electrostatic discharge that produces light and releases electromagnetic radiation. It is believed that the separation of positive and negative charge carriers within a cloud is achieved by the **polarization mechanism**. The first step of this mechanism occurs when falling precipitation particles become electrically polarized after they move through Earth's magnetic field. The second step of the polarization mechanism involves **electrostatic induction**, the process whereby electrically charged particles create charges in other particles without direct contact. Ice particles are charged through this method, and then energy-storing electric fields are formed between the charged particles. The positively charged ice crystals tend to rise to the top of the cloud, effectively polarizing the cloud with positive charges on top and negative charges at the middle and bottom. When charged clouds conglomerate, an electric discharge (a **lightning bolt**) is produced, either between clouds or between a cloud and Earth's surface.

THUNDERSTORMS

A thunderstorm is a weather phenomenon that includes lightning, thunder, and usually large amounts of precipitation and strong winds. **Thunder** is the noise made by the rapid expansion and contraction of air due to the heat energy produced by lightning bolts. A **thunderstorm** develops when heating on Earth's surface causes large amounts of air to rise into an unstable atmosphere. This results in large clouds of rain and ice crystals. The associated condensation releases high levels of heat, which, in turn, power the **growth cycle** of the cloud. The clouds created during thunderstorms are immense, sometimes reaching widths of several miles and extending to heights of 10,000 meters or more. The precipitation in such clouds eventually becomes heavy enough to fall against the updraft of unstable air; the consequent downpour is often short but intense. The differential speeds at which light and sound travel through the atmosphere enable one to estimate the distance between oneself and the storm by observing the interval between a lightning bolt and a thunderclap.

CLIMATES

Climate is usually defined as the "average weather" in a particular area on Earth. The timespan over which **climate** is measured is variable, but it is generally accepted that the climate of an area does not vary during a human life span (though climate is extremely various in geologic time). This may change, however, due to the increasing greenhouse effect. Meteorologists measure climate by averaging certain quantifiable elements such as rainfall or temperature. Climate may be studied on several different scales:

- **Local climate** refers to the climate of small geographic areas (generally up to tens of miles wide). The local climate of an area is affected by things such as its location relative to an ocean and the presence of mountains near the location.
- A **regional climate** is the climate of a larger geographic area, such as a country. A regional climate may also be delineated due to climate features that are distinctive from the surrounding climate.
- **Global climate** refers to the average weather experienced across Earth.

Climate Zones

Climate zones are areas of regional climate. These zones are created by the general circulation of the air in Earth's atmosphere. Generally, the warmest air moves from the equator (where the greatest amount of solar energy is received) toward the higher latitudes at the poles. The **latitudinal temperature gradient** produces atmospheric pressure. At the equator, solar energy heats air near the surface, causing it to rise and decreasing air pressure. The risen air is transported by winds to cooler areas at higher latitudes, where the air then descends (because cool air is heavier than warmer air), creating an area of high pressure. The descended air is then moved by surface winds, either back to the equator or up to higher latitudes, where it encounters colder air. The air then rises again in an area of low pressure. The air in polar regions is very cold, which causes it to sink, creating high pressure. Winds are thus generated to move air from warmer regions to colder ones.

The **tropical** (low-latitude) **climate zone** covers the area around the equator. This area receives a large portion of the Sun's solar energy, making average temperatures in this zone fairly high. The consistent levels of hot air in the region indicate that air is often moving upward. This convective process, in turn, produces large levels of precipitation in the area, resulting in a humid climate. Seasons in the tropical zone are delineated by the amount of rainfall, instead of by changes in temperatures. **Subtropical** (mid-latitude) **climate zones** are found about thirty degrees north and south of the equator. These zones generally consist of dry descending air, clear skies, and high atmospheric pressure. Desert climates (extreme heat during the day, cold temperatures at night, and lack of precipitation) are common in these zones. **Polar** (high-latitude) **climate zones** are found at the north and south poles. They are characterized by high air pressure (due to descending air), low temperatures (rarely above freezing), and lack of precipitation (because air cannot evaporate from frozen water).

Review Video: Climates
Visit mometrix.com/academy and enter code: 991320

Maritime, Continental, and Temperate Climates

Maritime climates are greatly affected by airflow from nearby oceans. This influence prevents extreme temperatures in such regions, which normally experience cool summers and mild winters. Also, **maritime climates** are usually quite humid, with large amounts of precipitation. **Continental climates**, unlike maritime climates, experience variations in temperature with changes in seasons (i.e., cold winters and hot summers). This is so because rock and soil have lower heat capacities than water, which serves to moderate ambient temperatures. Continental climates are usually relatively dry. A **temperate climate** is one with low variation in average temperature. Temperate climates may be maritime or continental.

Influence of Mountains on Climate

At the level of local climate, the presence of **mountains** forces air to rise in order to travel above them; this contributes to increased formation of clouds and consequently increases in levels of precipitation. **Mountain chains** can affect regional and even global climates by deflecting airflow. The **Coriolis force** causes most of Earth's atmospheric airflow to move east and west. Therefore, the presence of north-south-oriented mountain chains can forcibly alter general circulation patterns. For example, the Rocky Mountains in western North America force air to move northward; the air cools near the North Pole before blowing back down. This causes winter temperatures in Canada and parts of the United States to be very cold.

Effect of Atmosphere and Hydrosphere Interactions on Climate

The **hydrosphere** (all the water on Earth), specifically the oceans, stores much higher quantities of heat energy than the **atmosphere** is able to hold. Energy in the oceans, like energy in the atmosphere, is transferred around the globe, redistributing heat from areas of low latitudes to areas of high latitudes. Water on the surface of the ocean is driven by atmospheric wind patterns. Energy transfers between the oceans and the atmosphere effect temperatures and precipitation in regions across the globe. For example, the Gulf Stream is an ocean current that exerts an important influence on the climates of the United Kingdom and northwest Europe. This surface current originates in the Gulf of Mexico and carries warm water (about 25 degrees Celsius) northeast across the Atlantic at speeds of three miles per hour. When the ocean cools down at night, it releases warm air, regulating the temperatures of the regions mentioned above. Without the activity of the Gulf Stream, those regions would be as cold as Canada (which is at roughly the same latitude).

Earth's Ozone Layer

Earth's ozone layer is the region of the stratosphere with a high concentration of ozone (a form of oxygen) particles. These molecules are formed through the process of **photolysis**, which occurs when ultraviolet light from the Sun collides with oxygen molecules (O2) in the atmosphere. The ultraviolet radiation splits the oxygen atoms apart; when a free oxygen atom strikes an oxygen molecule, it combines with the molecule to create an ozone particle (O3). Ozone molecules may be broken down by interaction with nitrogen-, chlorine-, and hydrogen-containing compounds, or by thermal energy from the Sun. Under normal conditions, these creative and destructive processes balance the levels of ozone in the stratosphere. The concentration of ozone molecules in the atmosphere absorbs **ultraviolet radiation**, thus preventing this harmful energy from reaching Earth's surface. Ozone particles form in the region of the atmosphere over the equator, which receives the most direct sunlight. Atmospheric winds then disperse the particles throughout the rest of the stratosphere.

Divergent Plate Boundary

A divergent, or constructive, plate boundary exists when two adjacent plates move away from one another. Observation of activity at **diverging boundaries** has provided unquestionable proof of the seafloor-spreading hypothesis. At this type of plate boundary, kinetic energy generated by asthenospheric convection cells cracks the lithosphere and pushes molten magma through the space left by separating **tectonic plates**. This magma cools and hardens, creating a new piece of Earth's crust. In the oceanic lithosphere, diverging plate boundaries form a series of rifts known as the **oceanic ridge system**. The Mid-Atlantic Ridge is a consequence of undersea diverging boundaries. At divergent boundaries on the continental lithosphere, plate movement results in **rift valleys**, typified by the East African Rift Valley.

Transform Plate Boundary

A transform (conservative) plate boundary exists when two tectonic plates slide past each other laterally and in opposite directions. Due to the rocky composition of lithospheric plates, this motion causes the plates to grind against each other. **Friction** causes stress to build when the plates stick; this potential energy is finally released when the built-up pressure exceeds the slipping point of the rocks on the two plates. This sudden release of energy causes **earthquakes**. This type of plate boundary is also referred to as a **strike-slip fault**. The San Andreas fault in California is the most famous example of such a boundary.

Review Video: Plate Tectonic Theory
Visit mometrix.com/academy and enter code: 535013

Types of Geologic Faults

A geologic fault is a fracture in Earth's surface created by movement of the crust. The majority of faults are found along **tectonic plate boundaries**; however, smaller faults have been identified at locations far from these boundaries. There are three types of geologic faults, which are named for the original direction of movement along the active fault line. The landforms on either side of a fault are called the **footwall** and the **hanging wall**, respectively. In a **normal fault**, the hanging wall moves downward relative to the footwall. A **reverse fault** is the opposite of a normal fault; the hanging wall moves upward relative to the footwall. The dip of a reverse fault is usually quite steep; when the dip is less than 45 degrees, the fault is called a thrust fault. In the third type of geologic fault, the **strike-slip fault**, the dip is virtually nonexistent, and the rocks on either side move horizontally left (sinistral) or right (dextral). A transform plate boundary is a specific instance of a strike-slip fault.

Humidity and Cloud Cover

Humidity is a measure of the amount of water vapor in the air. **Specific humidity** is the expression of humidity as a ratio of aqueous vapor to dry air; it is expressed as a ratio of mass of water vapor per unit mass of natural (dry) air. **Absolute humidity** measures the mass of water vapor in a given volume of moist air or gas; it is expressed in grams per cubic foot or per cubic meter. The equilibrium (or saturated) vapor pressure of a gas is the vapor pressure (created by the movement of molecules) of water vapor when air is saturated with water vapor. **Relative humidity**, usually expressed as a percentage, is the ratio of the vapor pressure of water in air (or another gas) to the equilibrium vapor pressure. In other words, it is a ratio of the mass of water per volume of gas and the mass per volume of a saturated gas. **Cloud cover** refers to the amount of sky blocked by clouds at a given location.

Subdiscipline of Physical Geography

Physical geography is the scientific study of life environments. These environments exist in the life layer, the space where the four realms—the **atmosphere** (the layer of gases that surrounds Earth), the **hydrosphere** (the water on Earth), the **lithosphere** (the solid part of Earth), and the **biosphere** (life on Earth)—interact. The life layer encompasses the lower atmosphere and the upper lithosphere, where land and water bodies meet. The science of physical geography examines systems and cycles within the life layer; these continuous processes cause modifications in the life layer (in different areas and on different time scales), thereby creating Earth's diverse physical environments.

Systems in Physical Geography

In physical geography, the term *system* is used to refer to the processes that operate to modify and diversify various physical environments. **Physical systems** are usually natural flow systems, in which something (such as energy, water, or a chemical element) moves along one or more pathways from one place to another due to a natural power source. A system may be **open**, in which case matter enters and exits the system. All **energy systems** are open. A system may also be **closed**. Closed systems are referred to as cycles; in these systems, no matter is inputted or outputted from the system. The hydrologic (water) cycle is an example of a closed system. Feedback is the mechanism by which the flow in one pathway influences the flow in another pathway.

Positive feedback speeds up a process, while negative feedback retards a process. **Equilibrium** is the state of a system in which the flow rates on all the system's pathways are constant and nearly the same.

Earth's Layers

Earth consists of several layers. The three main layers are the core, the mantle, and the crust. The **crust** is the outermost layer of the planet Earth. It is located 0-35 kilometers below the surface. Earth's crust is composed mainly of basalt and granite. The crust is less dense, cooler, and more rigid than the planet's internal layers. This layer floats on top of the mantle. The **mantle** is located 35-2,890 kilometers below Earth's surface. It is separated from the crust by the Mohorovicic discontinuity, or Moho (which occurs at 30-70 kilometers below the continental crust and at 6-8 kilometers beneath the oceanic crust). The mantle is made up of rocks such as peridotite and eclogite; its temperature varies from 100 to 3,500 degrees Celsius. Material in the mantle cycles due to convection. The **core** is the innermost layer of Earth, which consists of two layers (a liquid outer layer and a solid inner layer). It is located 2,890-6,378 kilometers below the surface. The core is thought to be composed of iron and nickel and is the densest layer of Earth.

Earth's Sublayers

Earth also consists of several sublayers, including the lithosphere, the asthenosphere, and the mesosphere.

- The **lithosphere** consists of the crust and the uppermost portion of Earth's mantle. It is located 0-60 kilometers below the surface. The lithosphere is the cooling layer of the planet's convection cycle and thickens over time. This solid shell is fragmented into pieces called tectonic plates. The oceanic lithosphere is made up of mafic basaltic rocks and is thinner and generally denser than the continental lithosphere (composed of granite and sedimentary rock); the lithosphere floats atop Earth's mantle.
- The **asthenosphere** is the "soft," topmost layer of the mantle. It is located 100-700 kilometers below the surface. A combination of heat and pressure keeps the asthenosphere's composite material "plastic."
- The **mesosphere** is located 900-2,800 kilometers below the surface and therefore spans from the lower part of the mantle to the mantle-core boundary. The liquid outer core exists at 2,890-5,100 kilometers below surface level, and the solid inner core exists at depths of 5,100-6,378 kilometers.

Sources of Tectonic Plate Motion

The two main sources of tectonic plate motion are **gravity** and **friction**. The energy driving tectonic plate motion comes from the dissipation of heat from the mantle in the relatively weak asthenosphere. This energy is converted into gravity or friction to incite the motion of plates. Gravity is subdivided by geologists into ridge-push and slab-pull. In the phenomenon of **ridge-push**, the motion of plates is instigated by the energy that causes low-density material from the mantle to rise at an oceanic ridge. This leads to the situation of certain plates at higher elevations; gravity causes material to slide downhill. In **slab-pull**, plate motion is thought to be caused by cold, heavy plates at oceanic trenches sinking back into the mantle, providing fuel for future convection. Friction is subdivided into mantle drag and trench suction. **Mantle drag** suggests that plates move due to the friction between the lithosphere and the asthenosphere. **Trench suction** involves a downward frictional pull on oceanic plates in subduction zones due to convection currents.

Convergent Plate Boundaries

A convergent (destructive) plate boundary occurs when adjacent plates move toward one another. Earth's diameter remains constant over time. Therefore, the formation of new plate material at diverging plate boundaries necessitates the destruction of plate material elsewhere. This process occurs at **convergent** (destructive) **plate boundaries**. One plate slips underneath the other at a subduction zone. The results of converging plates vary, depending on the nature of the lithosphere in said plates. When two oceanic plates converge, they form a deep underwater trench. If each of the converging plates at a destructive boundary carries a continent, the light materials of the continental lithosphere enable both plates to float above the subduction area. They crumple and compress, creating a **mid-continent mountain range**. When a continental plate converges with an oceanic plate, the denser oceanic lithosphere slides beneath the continental lithosphere. The result of such convergence is an **oceanic trench** on one side and a **mountain range** on the other.

Fault Mechanics

Slip is a measurement of the net relative displacement of structural surfaces along a fault. **Dip** is the angle that a rock body or structural rock surface makes with the horizontal surface plane. True dip is quantified through downward measurement of the angle in the direction of greatest inclination; apparent dip is the measurement of dip in any direction. Dip is equal to zero in the direction of strike and has its maximum measurement in the direction of true dip. **Strike** is the direction of a line of intersection drawn between the horizontal surface plane and the surface of an uptilted rock structure.

Geologic Folding

A geologic fold is a region of curved or deformed stratified rocks. Folding is one process by which Earth's crust is deformed. **Rock strata** are normally formed horizontally; however, geologists have identified areas where these strata arc upward or downward. **Anticlines** are upfolded areas of rock; downfolds are called **synclines**. In anticlines, the rocks are oldest along the axis (a horizontal line drawn through the point of the fold's maximum curvature), and in synclines, the youngest rocks are at the axis. **Monoclines**, or flexures, are rock structures that slope in one direction only, and often pass into geologic fault lines. The process of folding usually occurs underneath Earth's surface, but surface erosion eventually exposes these formations. Folding is generally thought to be caused by the horizontal compression of Earth's surface, which is related to the movement of tectonic plates and fault activity.

Orogenesis

Orogenesis refers to mountain-building processes, specifically as they relate to the movement of tectonic plates. An individual **orogeny** can take millions of years. Generally, mountains are created when compressional forces push surface rock upward, resulting in a landform that is higher than the land around it. There are four broad categories of mountains (which are not mutually exclusive); these categories are based on the mountain's formative origin. **Folded mountains**, formed from the long-term deformation and metamorphosis of sedimentary and igneous rocks, usually occur in chains. This type of mountain often forms at convergent plate boundaries. **Fault-block mountains** occur at normal or reverse faults with high dips. Portions of Earth's crust are vertically displaced along the faults. **Oceanic ridges** are formed at divergent boundaries beneath the ocean. When plates move apart, material from the mantle rises and creates long mountain chains. **Volcanic mountains** form from the accumulation of products of volcanic eruptions, such as ash and lava. They often occur singularly, unlike other mountain types that usually exist in chains.

Volcanic Eruptions

A volcanic eruption generally entails a buildup of **magma** (a silicate solution formed of melted rocks) in a magma chamber. Gases present in the magma, such as water vapor, carbon dioxide, and sulfur dioxide, cause increasing pressure in the material. Often, the vent that would enable release of the built-up pressure is blocked by solidified magma. The viscosity of the magma also affects the release of gas pressure; the more viscous the magma, the more pressure will build up. A volcano **erupts** when the pressure becomes too great to be contained and the gases are suddenly and violently released. The freed gases expand, forcing magma and solid materials upward. The products of a volcanic eruption include ash, lava, and solid igneous rocks.

Volcanic Activities at Different Plate Boundaries

Volcanic activity occurs at **divergent plate boundaries** most often under the ocean. Divergent plate boundaries are also known as constructive plate boundaries because new crustal material must be formed to fill the void created by the separation of tectonic plates. As oceanic lithospheric plates pull apart, magma rises from beneath to fill the gap; the increased temperature and magma concentration breeds volcanic activity. At **convergent, or destructive, plate margins**, friction creates the heat energy necessary to melt crustal rocks into magma. Also, the subduction of one plate under another pushes crustal material into the mantle, where temperatures are higher. The presence of volatiles (such as water and carbon dioxide) at subduction zones can force magma out through vents in Earth's surface. Occasionally, volcanic activity occurs at locations far from any plate boundary. These locations, called **hotspots**, are thought to exist over particularly active mantle zones, which shoot "plumes" of molten material up toward the crust.

Earthquake

An earthquake is a sudden movement of a portion of Earth's crust. Strain energy, built up in the lithosphere, is swiftly released in the form of **seismic waves**, which, among other things, cause vibratory ground motion. The majority of these events occur at high-stress tectonic plate boundaries. The **rupture zone** is the total size of the fault that slips; the larger the rupture zone, the greater the effects of the earthquake. The **focus**, or hypocenter, of an earthquake is the location from which the seismic waves seem to emanate. The **epicenter** is the location on Earth's crust above an earthquake's hypocenter. Earthquakes are classified according to their focus depths: shallow (0-70 kilometers below the surface), intermediate (70-300 kilometers below the surface), or deep (below 300 kilometers deep).

Rock Cycle

The rock cycle is the process whereby the materials that make up Earth transition through the three types of rock: **igneous**, **sedimentary**, and **metamorphic**. Rocks, like all matter, cannot be created or destroyed; rather, they undergo a series of changes and adopt different forms through the functions of the rock cycle. **Plate tectonics** and the **water cycle** are the driving forces behind the rock cycle; they force rocks and minerals out of equilibrium and force them to adjust to different external conditions. Viewed in a generalized, cyclical fashion, the rock cycle operates as follows: Rocks beneath Earth's surface melt into magma. This magma either erupts through volcanoes or remains inside the Earth. Regardless, the magma cools, forming igneous rocks. On the surface, these rocks experience weathering and erosion, which break them down and distribute the fragments across the surface. These fragments form layers and eventually become sedimentary rocks. Sedimentary rocks are then either transformed into metamorphic rocks (which will become magma inside the Earth) or melted down into magma.

Formation of Igneous Rocks

Igneous rocks can be formed from sedimentary rocks, metamorphic rocks, or other igneous rocks. Rocks that are pushed under Earth's surface (usually due to plate subduction) are exposed to high mantle temperatures, which cause the rocks to melt into magma. The magma then rises to the surface through volcanic processes. The lower atmospheric temperature causes the magma to cool, forming grainy, extrusive igneous rocks. The creation of **extrusive**, or volcanic, rocks is quite rapid. The cooling process can occur so rapidly that crystals do not form; in this case, the result is a glass, such as obsidian. It is also possible for magma to cool down in Earth's interior; this type of igneous rock is called **intrusive**. Intrusive, or plutonic, rocks cool more slowly, resulting in a coarse-grained texture.

Formation of Sedimentary Rocks

Sedimentary rocks are formed when rocks on Earth's surface experience weathering and erosion, which break them down and distribute the fragments across the surface. Fragmented material (small pieces of rock, organic debris, and the chemical products of mineral sublimation) is deposited and accumulates in layers, with top layers burying the materials beneath. The pressure exerted by the topmost layers causes the lower layers to compact, creating solid sedimentary rock in a process called **lithification**.

Formation of Metamorphic Rocks

Metamorphic rocks are igneous or sedimentary rocks that have "morphed" into another kind of rock. In metamorphism, high temperatures and levels of pressure change preexisting rocks physically and/or chemically, which produces different species of rocks. In the rock cycle, this process generally occurs in materials that have been thrust back into Earth's mantle by plate subduction. **Regional metamorphism** refers to a large band of metamorphic activity; this often occurs near areas of high orogenic (mountain-building) activity. **Contact metamorphism** refers to metamorphism that occurs when "country rock" (that is, rock native to an area) comes into contact with high-heat igneous intrusions (magma).

Review Video: Igneous, Sedimentary, and Metamorphic Rocks
Visit mometrix.com/academy and enter code: 689294

Plate Tectonics Rock Cycle

The plate tectonics rock cycle expands the concept of the traditional rock cycle to include more specific information about the tectonic processes that propel the rock cycle, as well as an evolutionary component. Earth's materials do not cycle endlessly through the different rock forms; rather, these transitive processes cause, for example, increasing diversification of the rock types found in the crust. Also, the cycling of rock increases the masses of continents by increasing the volume of granite. Thus the **tectonic rock cycle** is a model of an evolutionary rock cycle. In this model, new oceanic lithosphere is created at divergent plate boundaries. This new crust spreads outward until it reaches a subduction zone, where it is pushed back into the mantle, becomes magma, and is thrust out into the atmosphere. It experiences erosion and becomes sedimentary rock. At convergent continental plate boundaries, this crust is involved in mountain building and the associated metamorphic pressures. It is eroded again and returns to the lithosphere.

Role of Water in Cycling of Earth Materials

Water plays an important role in the **rock cycle** through its roles in erosion and weathering: it wears down rocks, it contributes to the dissolution of rocks and minerals as acidic soil water, and it carries ions and rock fragments (sediments) to basins where they will be compressed into sedimentary rock. Water also plays a role in the **metamorphic processes** that occur underwater in newly formed igneous rock at mid-ocean ridges. The presence of water (and other volatiles) is a vital component in the melting of rocky crust into magma above subduction zones.

WEATHERING TERMS

The rocks on Earth's surface experience physical, biological, and chemical processes that are much different from the processes ambient during their formations. The operation of these processes on Earth materials is called weathering.

- **Mechanical weathering** causes disintegration of rocks and minerals. In this process, the affected rocks break apart into small fragments but retain their chemical compositions. This type of weathering occurs due to the presence of joints, or cracks, in rocks that allow the penetration of water and vegetative roots. Mechanical weathering occurs most often in cooler climates.
- **Chemical weathering** refers to the processes by which rocks experience chemical changes (such as decomposition and decay) due to the influence of organic acids. Chemical weathering occurs most often in high-temperature, high-humidity climates. The two types of weathering are not mutually exclusive; they often occur side by side.
- **Erosion** also occurs simultaneously with weathering. This term refers to the transportation of Earth materials by wind, water, gravity, and sometimes living organisms.

SUBTYPES OF MECHANICAL WEATHERING

The subtypes of mechanical weathering are pressure release, exfoliation, freeze-thaw, and salt-crystal growth.

- **Pressure release**, or surface unloading, occurs when erosion removes materials overlying rock. Decreased pressure causes the underlying rocks to expand and fracture.
- **Exfoliation** often occurs in regions with some moisture that experience substantial diurnal temperature changes. Rocks are subjected to heat during the day, which causes them to expand. At night, the much cooler temperatures cause the rocks to compact. The repeated expansion and contraction creates stress in the outer layers of the rocks, which eventually begin to "peel" off in thin layers. Exfoliation can also be caused by pressure release.
- **Freeze-thaw** operates when water, which has penetrated the joints of a rock, freezes and expands. The resultant pressure widens the joints and can even shatter the rock. If the rock does not fracture, the thawing of ice in the joints admits water further into the rock. Continuous, long-term freeze-thaw activity weakens rocks.
- In **salt-crystal growth**, the evaporation of saline solutions within rocks leaves salt crystals behind. Pressures accompanying this crystallization can be very high.

SUBTYPES OF CHEMICAL WEATHERING

The subtypes of chemical weathering are hydration, hydrolysis, oxidation, and solution.

- **Hydration** occurs when salt minerals, which are part of a rock, expand and change due to the absorption of water. For example, anhydrite changes to gypsum with the addition of water. Hydration can cause rocks to fragment mechanically.
- **Hydrolysis** involves a chemical reaction between acidic water and a rock-forming mineral. The interaction breaks the rock down into new materials. For instance, the chemical reaction between feldspar and acidic water produces quartz and clay.
- **Oxidation**, or rusting, which results in yellow, brown, or red discoloration, occurs in iron-bearing minerals when they are exposed to the atmosphere.

- **Solution** is the weathering process whereby an organic acid interacts with certain minerals in a rock, producing ions that are then washed away by erosion. Solution, therefore, is a gradual dissolving process. It produces underground channels and caverns.

Mass Movement

A mass movement (also called mass wasting) is the downward movement of large amounts of rock and debris due to gravitational forces. The speed at which the material will move and the amount of dislodged material are affected by several factors: the amount of water in the affected material, the climate, the type and extent of weathering, the steepness of the incline, the presence or absence of rooted vegetation, the type of bedrock present and its condition, and the presence or absence of seismic activity. **Mass movements** cause changes in the landscape of an area. They can also place humans and animals in the affected area in danger.

Rockfall

A rockfall is a mass movement wherein various amounts of rock material fall very rapidly (at speeds of 99 miles per hour or more) from a cliff face. This movement may involve a single rock or boulder or may spur an avalanche of tons of rock. The pile of rocks that results from a rockfall is termed a **talus**. When it occurs at a mountain base, a talus may prevent weathering of the mountain. A **rockfall** may be triggered by an earthquake, excessive rain, ice wedging (common on mountains), or human activity. Such a mass movement may, in turn, spawn an **avalanche**, a rockfall that contributes to a debris flow. The materials in motion in a rockfall often leave "scars" on the slope from which they fall.

Landslide

The term *landslide* may be used to designate several different downslope movements. Normally, a **landslide** involves the movement of soil and rock as a more or less coherent mass down a slope, although either the bedrock itself or the soil which overlays it may move independently. There are two main categories of landslides. **Glides**, or translational slides, entail a large portion of rock detached from its bedrock "gliding" outward and downward along a slope. A **slump** (or rotational slide) involves the motion of a relatively cohesive mass along a concave plane; the upper part of the sliding mass ends up below ground level, and the bottom part of the mass ends up above it.

Flow

Flow is a type of mass movement that entails viscous motion of surface materials. **Flows** are characterized by motion of the internal grains of the moving mass (unlike slides). Also, they do not include a clear barrier between the flow material and a stable surface underneath. The velocity of a flow is widely various, dependent on the slope upon which it travels and the presence or absence of water. Flows generally involve one of three types of material: earth, mud, or debris. An **earthflow** is often initiated at the end of a slump slide, when the block of sliding material breaks apart. A **mud flow** involves the motions of soil and relatively high proportions of water. Increased water content increases the velocity of the moving mass from that of an earthflow. Mudflows are common in deserts. A **debris flow** is similar to a mudflow; often, the only distinction between the two is the size of the particles in motion. The motions of both debris flows and mudflows tend to follow pre-existing channels.

Creep

Creep is another landscape-altering mass movement. It involves a shallow mass of soil material moving slowly downward. This type of movement usually occurs so slowly that no one notices it. **Creep** can be caused by freeze-thaw or wet-dry cycles, depending on the characteristics of the bedrock materials. As with other types of mass movements, the introduction of high amounts of water into creep material will cause it to move more quickly. Though creep does not pose an immediate threat to human or animal life, it can be dangerous through long-term effects on tree roots and the foundations of buildings or other structures.

Solifluction

Solifluction is an intensified form of creep. The existence of permafrost (a layer of earth that remains in a long-term state of freeze that occurs in very cold climates) prevents absorption of surface water. The excess water then enters the topmost "active" layer of soil. That layer is thus more vulnerable to the process of creep than a comparable layer of soil in a warmer climate because of its increased fluidity and the frozen surface over which it slides. **Solifluction** tends to result in a "wrinkled" landscape with smooth terrain.

Erosion Landform

An erosion landform is a landform created by the processes of weathering and erosion. For example, a cliff is an **erosion landform**. Cliffs are formed when relatively strong rocks are exposed to centuries of wind and water, weathering, and erosion. Sandstone, limestone, and basalt are examples of rocks that commonly become cliffs. A **canyon** provides the classic instance of an erosion landform. Canyons are formed from many years of weathering and erosion processes (often water-based), usually operating on a plateau (a mountain that has been eroded down to a flat but elevated surface). Strata of rocks that resisted the destructive processes remain visible in the canyon walls.

Stream Deposition

Stream deposition is the last phase in the weathering and erosion process performed by water, specifically streams. **Stream erosion** occurs when the movement of water in a stream detaches material from the sides and bottom of the channel through which it flows. This can carve out valleys and wide, meandering streams. Streams then carry the weathered material, as well as material deposited in the stream by other erosive processes, out to sea. Streams transport sediment in three ways:

- The **solid load** consists of the suspended load (sediment grains of various sizes floating in the water) and the bed load (the materials dragged along the bed of a channel by the moving water).
- The **bed load** performs much of the erosion of the sides and bottoms of the channel.
- A stream's **dissolved load** is composed of ions produced in the chemical weathering process.
- **Stream deposition** occurs when the stream drops its load of sediment. This can occur due to flooding or intersection of the stream with a larger body of water.

Landscape Evolution Terms

The movement of water in streams and rivers plays a key role in **landscape evolution**. The long-term effect of rivers and streams is to erode the land around them down to sea level, the base level of erosion. There are several theories as to how this occurs:

- **Backwasting** entails the wearing down of river valley slopes parallel to themselves. When the surface between valley slopes is worn down to the base level of erosion, the slopes retreat in parallel layers until all of the land above the widening platform is eroded to the same level.

- **Downwasting** is another theoretical process that explains landscape evolution. This process involves the diminishing of valley slopes through mass movements of soil and rock decomposition.
- A **peneplain** is the result of the erosive process of the land around streams. It is a wide, nearly flat plain of bedrock that exists just above the base level of erosion.
- A **monadnock** is an anomalous portion of especially tenacious rock that rises above a peneplain.

Coriolis Force

The Coriolis force, which gives rise to the Coriolis effect, is not really a force at all. Rather, we experience it only because Earth is a rotating frame of reference that we are observing from. In the atmosphere, air tends to move from areas of low pressure to areas of higher pressure. This air would move in a straight line, but the **Coriolis force** appears to deflect the air and cause it to swirl. Earth actually moves underneath the wind, which creates the impression of swirling air to someone standing on Earth's surface. The Coriolis force causes winds to appear to swirl to the right as they approach the Northern Hemisphere, and to the left as they approach the Southern Hemisphere.

Geomorphology

Geomorphology is a subdiscipline of physical geography. Geomorphologists study the origins and formative processes of **landforms**. Observation of weathering and erosion processes, the movement of tectonic plates, mass movements, and the effects of human activity on the environment all contribute to an understanding of the formation and evolution of landforms. Aerial photography (from within Earth's atmosphere or from space) can aid geomorphologists in their quests. Photos taken at intervals allow them to study, for example, the creative and destructive events that occur at plate boundaries. Landscape photography also enables geomorphologists to observe long-term processes of stream erosion. Geomorphology can be applied to the prediction and prevention of natural hazards such as landslides; it can also be helpful in assessing and rectifying damage to the natural environment by humans.

Human Geography

Push/Pull Factors

Push and pull factors are features of regions that cause people to want to leave or move to a particular region. **Push factors** are those that encourage residents to depart an area; they are viewed as negative aspects of a region. There are several common factors that "push" people from, for example, rural to urban areas: overpopulation and overgrazing result in scarce resources, which decreases income levels; agricultural endeavors are subject to unpredictable and sometimes harsh physical forces (such as drought or flooding); the possible lack of health and educational services so far from a downtown district; and mechanization of agricultural labor may decrease the number of available jobs. The perceived **pull factors** of urban areas also contribute to urbanization: utilities such as water and electricity may make housing more comfortable, theoretically increasing a migrant's quality of life; food sources are ostensibly more reliable in urban areas than in agricultural rural areas; there are more job opportunities in larger urban regions; and more goods and services are available for purchase in cities.

Population Density

Population density is a measurement of the population per unit (usually miles or kilometers squared). **Population density** may be an indicator of economic development; however, this is not so for many less economically developed countries. There are several factors that commonly influence population density:

- The level of **industrial activity** in an area affects the area's population; major industrial areas provide many job opportunities, which draw people into the region, increasing population density. The climate of a region also affects its population density, as people generally gravitate toward temperate climates rather than extremely cold or hot areas.
- **Urbanization** affects population density in that people often move into cities where resources, services, and employment are readily available because they no longer have to work in agriculture.
- **Natural disaster areas** influence population density as well. Although potential danger exists for residents of these regions, many large population centers are located in or near them; often, this occurs for historical or agricultural reasons. For example, the byproducts of volcanic eruptions can create extremely fertile soil.

Effect of Environmental Factors on Patterns of Human Settlement

Site factors are those taken into consideration by humans in the selection of an ideal location to create a settlement. There are several environmental characteristics weighed by settlers deciding where to place their communities. While many of these factors were more important in the pre-modern past, many of them are still relevant today. **Water supply** is an important site factor. Used for drinking, washing, cooking, and agriculture, settlements cannot thrive without a consistent, adequate supply of water. Settling in an area prone to flooding or on marshy land can also be dangerous for budding towns. Though modern settlements do not rely singularly on natural sources for water supplies, it is still important for communities to be within piping distance of a central water source. A related factor is the proximity of **rivers** to an area. In addition to drinking water, rivers provide transportation or act as natural boundaries. **Aspect** is the direction a site faces; this affects the amount of direct sunlight in an area, which affects temperature and agriculture.

Self-Governing Political Entities

A **country** is a geographical territory. Many countries are independent entities, with their own governments, constitutions, militaries, and tax regulations; however, some are non-sovereign (which means they are governed by a separate government), and some have an overseas dependency (which means that they control the government of a separate country).

A **state** is a political entity that inhabits a specific geographical territory. States have independent governments, through which they exercise internal and external sovereignty. Some social thinkers have offered alternate conceptualizations of a state. For example, Max Weber defined *state* as "a human community that (successfully) claims the monopoly of the legitimate use of physical force within a given territory."

A **nation** is a cultural entity. Historically, the term has been used to refer to a group of people who share a commonality in ethnic ancestry, descent, or parentage. The criteria used to identify members of a nation are widely variable. A state that is recognized as a nation's "homeland" is called a nation-state.

Subdiscipline of Political Geography

Political geography (sometimes referred to as geopolitics) is the branch of geographic study that focuses on the spatial implications of power relations. In other words, political geographers investigate the relationships between political and social power, and geographic location and space.

Geopolitics examines, among other things, the delineation of Earth's surface into nations, states, cities, and so on, as well as regional alliances, the locations of bases of political power, and the spatial relationships of different areas to central regions. The study of **political geography** can be useful at international, national, and metropolitan levels.

Hegemony

Hegemony is a continuous process whereby a dominant group exercises ideological control over other subordinate groups. By influencing the shared belief and value systems of others, the dominant group attempts to naturalize its own beliefs in other groups. The process of **hegemonic establishment** may or may not involve force or the threat of force; in fact, hegemony is more effective when it exists as a mixture of control (on the part of the dominant group) and consent (on the part of the subordinate group(s)). In practice, hegemony serves to empower certain religious beliefs, ethnic groups, political ideologies, economic systems, and cultural practices; this marginalizes alternative beliefs and practices. The creation of hegemony is both a method of attaining power and a means to maintain that power. Theories of hegemony attempt to explain the ways that dominant groups (referred to as **hegemons**) coerce members of non-dominant groups to accept and internalize the social, cultural, political, and economic norms of the former.

Civil War

A civil war is a conflict that occurs between antagonistic groups in the same country or empire; each faction wishes to secure control of the affairs of the state. Like any conflict, a **civil war** may take place due to differing political or religious views among members of the warring groups, an unequal distribution of wealth among citizens of a country, racial or ethnic prejudices, or the desires of revolutionary groups to change the social organization of a country. For example, the **Nigerian Civil War** (1967-1970) was bred from religious, political, and ethnic tensions between the Hausa, Yoruba, and Igbo peoples. The political boundaries of Nigeria had been created by European colonial powers with no regard for previously existent cultural boundaries, sparking conflict between the indigenous groups. The **Irish Civil War** (1922-1923) occurred between supporters and opponents of a treaty that created an Irish state (excluding the six counties of Northern Ireland). This state was described as "free" but was actually a non-sovereign dominion of the British Empire.

Causes of Historic International Wars

An international war is a violent conflict between two or more independent states. Such conflicts frequently occur as a result of competition over land, resources, and/or sovereignty. Throughout the late 19th and early 20th centuries, many of the era's great powers competed for colonial territory and trading rights in Eastern Asia. The **Russo-Japanese War** (1904-1905) was fought between Russian and Japanese forces for imperial control of Manchuria and Korea (specifically, the Liaodong Peninsula). The Japanese victory in 1905 marked the first time an Asian country had defeated a European country, and firmly established Japan as a formidable global power. The **Arab-Israeli conflict**, an extended conflict dating back to the late 1800s, is an example of international animosity based on differences in political and religious ideologies. The spectrum of points of view among members of the concerned parties problematizes any simple definition of the cause of the conflict. However, reasons cited for the conflict tend to relate to hostilities between Muslims and Jews and the dispute over Israel's right to self-determination.

Measures of Economic Development

Geographers examine several characteristics of a country in the determination of that country's level of **economic development**.

- A country's per capita **gross national product** (GNP), the total value of all final goods and services (those provided directly to consumers) produced per person in a year, is taken into account. The higher a nation's GNP, the more developed it is assumed to be.
- The annual **population growth** of a country also serves as a measure of its economic development. Generally, poorer countries have relatively rapid rates of population growth.
- The **occupational structure** of a country's labor force (the proportions of people working in the primary, secondary, and tertiary sectors of industry) is considered. In MDCs, most workers participate in tertiary activities; in LDCs, most workers participate in primary activities.
- A country's level of **urbanization** (the proportion of a country's total population living in urban areas) is seen as progress in the process of economic development, as urban areas often provide specialized job opportunities and services.

Subdiscipline of Human Geography

Human geography is the subdiscipline of geography that involves the identification and analysis of the ways humans interact with the physical Earth. It focuses particularly on the causes and effects of the **spatial distributions of humans and human activity** on the planet's surface. **Human geography** draws upon cultural, economic, political, and social data about particular regions to reveal patterns about the ways human beings interact with their environments. This field of study includes several subdisciplines that focus on certain aspects of human life, such as medical geography, feminist geography, military geography, and religion geography. While the focal point of human geography is human activity, it is impossible to discuss such activity without knowledge of the physical landscape upon which it occurs.

Population and Demography

Population refers to the conglomeration of people or organisms of a certain species in a particular area. This variable is especially important in the study of human geography, which deals with (among other things) changes in the **population** of a region and why those changes occur.

Demography is the study of human populations. This field examines the characteristics of a population, such as its size and distribution, the way it changes over time, and the religions, ethnicities, and languages of members of the population. The term *demographic* refers to specific population attributes, especially as used in marketing or opinion research.

Terms

- A **standard of living** is a quantitative and qualitative assessment of the material goods and services available to members of a society. It is often measured through observation of the average yearly income per person (adjusted for inflation); however, variables such as the literacy rate and cultural resources of a society may also be taken into account in the estimation of that society's standard of living.
- The **gross national product** (GNP) of a country is defined as the aggregate value of all goods and services generated by a society in a particular year. When the GNP is divided by the population of the country, the per-capita GNP is revealed.
- The **literacy rate** of a society is the percentage of people in that society who can read and write.
- **Population density** is defined as the number of people per specified unit of area.

- The **life expectancy** of a society is the average lifespan of people living in that society.
- The **birth rate** of a society refers to the number of births per 1,000 people in that society. This figure, usually expressed as the crude birth rate (CBR), is calculated without consideration of the sex or age of the population.
- The **death rate** of a society is figured in the same manner but with regard to deaths rather than births and is expressed as the crude death rate (CDR).
- The **fertility rate** of a society is the average number of children which would be born by a woman during her "childbearing" years. Replacement fertility is the fertility level at which women on the average are birthing just enough children to "replace" themselves and their partners in the population.
- **Population momentum** is the phenomenon whereby a society's population persists after the attainment of replacement fertility. This occurs at the end of Stage 3 in the demographic transition model, due to the relatively high concentration of people of the same age in their "childbearing" years.

Delineation of the Developed/Developing World

The terms *developed world* and *developing world*, when used in human geography and related fields, have a few different definitions. One common delineator is based on education and technology levels in a given country.

The **developed world** refers to those regions of the planet where people were able to cultivate natural and human resources using technology made available by the Scientific Revolution. Developed countries had direct access to the tools and information discovered in this era. These regions share several characteristics. For one, people living in developed countries are generally well-educated and highly literate. Public education systems are relatively sophisticated, and young people spend many years in a structured school environment. Education of a developed society's youth is often seen as a precious human resource. Countries of the developed world also display low rates of population growth; some are experiencing negative growth. Another characteristic of the developed world is that most people work in the service or manufacturing industries (as opposed to the agricultural industry).

The **developing world** refers to regions in which the advancements offered by the Scientific Revolution were either slow to arrive or ignored by the inhabitants. Today, many countries are attempting to **modernize**; however, the process is very expensive and people in developing regions have relatively little money. Several characteristics distinguish this part of the world from the developed countries. For example, many people in developing societies have not had time to receive thorough educations because they must work from a very young age. This means that literacy rates are often much lower in developing countries than in developed countries.

Malthusian Catastrophe

The Malthusian Catastrophe (also referred to as the Malthusian Disaster, Dilemma, or Crisis) is the prediction by English political scientist and demographer **Thomas Malthus** (1766-1834) that the **world population** would eventually surpass the **global food supply**. Malthus's relatively pessimistic views were developed as a rebuttal to the hopeful theorizing of his peers. For one, Malthus believed that the global population would increase exponentially unless methods to check such growth were implemented. He felt that after a certain point, society would return to subsistence-level food production (the level at which people consume only enough food to survive), due to a decrease in the amount of available nourishment per person. Obviously, this catastrophe has not yet come to pass. Malthus underestimated the rate at which agricultural and economic production would increase with technological, scientific, and industrial advancements in those fields. Also, the rate of global population expansion has not undergone continuous growth, as evidenced by the demographic transition model.

Phases of the Demographic Transition Model

The demographic transition model is a representation of changes in population in industrial societies, created by demographer Warren Thompson. This model describes variations (transitions) in birth and death rates in developed nations over the past 200 years. The **demographic transition model** encompasses four transitional phases.

- **Stage 1** is associated with premodern (that is, preindustrialized) society; it characterizes most regions of the world through the 17th century. In this stage (the high stationary stage), birth and death rates are high and nearly equivalent, indicating that population growth is slow. The second stage in the demographic transition model is differentiated by a sharp increase in a society's population due to a dramatic decrease in the death rate. This transition occurred in the late 18th century in Western Europe and spread outward.
- **Stage 2** is associated with advances in public health such as the creation of food handling regulations and sewage disposal, as well as advances in agricultural practices (including crop rotation) that helped to create a stable food source.
- **Stage 3** of the demographic transition model involves a decrease in a society's birth rate (following the rapid population growth in Stage 2). Most developed nations entered this phase late in the 19th century. Many hypotheses have been advanced to explain this phenomenon. For example, some have suggested that the decline in birth rates observed in developed societies is related to urbanization, which dilutes the high value traditionally placed on fertility; also, the costs attendant to urbanization make it less financially desirable for a family to have many children. The decline in birth rates has also been said to relate to medical advancements that decreased the rate of childhood mortality, or to improvements in contraceptive technology (though this occurred later, in the second half of the 20th century).
- In **Stage 4** of the demographic transition model, the populations of societies are either stable or declining. After the decline in birth rates, the general population grows older. If the fertility rate dips below replacement, the population experiences a rapid decline.

Developed vs. Less-Developed Societies

An alternate demographic transition model exists that applies demographic analysis to less-developed nations. There are several differences between the transitions observed in more-developed countries and those observed in less-developed countries, two of which include the following:

- Less-developed societies experienced a more pronounced **decrease in death rates** (about 50 years, as compared to 150 years in more-developed societies) in Stage 2 of the transition model. This is so because of medical advancements as well as increases in the female literacy rate (behavioral changes) due to exposure to more-developed countries. Rather than being "(re)discovered," this type of information was imported by less-developed countries and quickly applied.
- Less-developed societies experienced a **later** (20th century) **Stage 3 transition** (decline in birth rates). This difference stems from the fact that the technological advancements which accompanied the decline of birth rates in more-developed societies were unavailable in less-developed societies at the time.

Human Settlements

A human settlement is defined as any area inhabited by humans. The term may refer to a newly established region of residency for a group of people, or it may refer to a single home. Settlements are described as **nucleated** if residents live very closely together; settlements are described as **dispersed** when people live separately. A village is an example of an agglomerated rural settlement, in which people reside together in small groups. There are several different general types of settlements. The **temporary residences** set up by nomadic peoples (those constantly traveling due to their pastoral responsibilities, or in search of employment or food) constitute a type of settlement. There are also several types of **permanent settlements**.

Rural, Urban, and Suburban Communities

Permanent human settlements are classified by their economic activities and layouts, as follows:

- **Rural settlements** are those in which a majority of land is used for agricultural purposes. Inhabitants of rural areas often work in the agricultural industry, serving their own community.
- An **urban settlement** is typified by many nucleated buildings. Most residents of urban areas work outside of the agricultural industry, serving outside communities. Cities and larger towns are examples of urban areas.
- A **suburban community** is one that exists just outside a large urban area; it is generally smaller and less nucleated than the major urban community it abuts. Often, city workers reside in a suburban area and commute to work, aiming to avoid unsavory elements of urban life, such as crowding and pollution.

Central Place Theory

Central Place Theory is also referred to as Christaller's Theory for its formulator, **Walter Christaller**. This theory describes the typical size and spacing of human settlements. It rests on the idea that centralization is a natural principle of order that manifests itself in human settlement patterns. Christaller's Theory predicts that a large central market will have several smaller towns around it at equal distances; the smaller towns purchase goods and services from the central hub. From several assumptions, Christaller derived laws for the determination of the size, number, and distribution of towns. These assumptions include the even distribution of population and resources; similar purchasing power among all consumers; a flat, expansive surface; and providers of goods and services who cannot earn excess profits. There are three principal laws of **Central Place Theory**:

- The number of settlements is inversely proportional to the size of the settlements.
- The larger the settlements, the greater the distances between them will be.
- As settlements increase in size, services become increasingly specialized.

Order of Settlements

Following Central Place Theory, the goods and services available for purchase in settlements vary depending on a settlement's size. Settlements may thus be classified by these factors. **Settlement order** may be displayed in a hierarchical pyramid, in which lowest-order settlements make up the bottom level (they are most plentiful) and highest-order settlements are at the top of the pyramid (they are fewest). In a **high-order settlement**, such as a conurbation (a large urban city or capital), one might expect to find the following services: government buildings, museums and theaters, churches of various religions, multiple medical centers, transportation terminals, and large shopping complexes. A **middle-order settlement** (a city or town) might house a hospital, multiple retail stores, a few specialized medical practices, a high school football team, and a cathedral. In

low-order settlements, such as hamlets and villages, one may find a single church, a main store, a tavern, and a small junior high school. The **lowest-order settlements** offer no services whatsoever.

Common Settlement Forms

Study of the shape (form) of a settlement can reveal information about its origins and development.

- An **isolated settlement** is a single structure, such as a farmhouse. This settlement form is often found in areas where physical conditions make survival difficult or uncomfortable. Historically, isolated settlements were common in the early stages of pioneer settlement.
- A **dispersed settlement** consists of two to three buildings that are two kilometers or farther from the next dispersed settlement, possibly forming a hamlet.
- A **nucleated settlement** includes many buildings grouped together for a social, economic, and/or defensive purpose; they often form around crossroads.
- A **loose-knit settlement** is similar to a nucleated settlement, but the buildings are spaced farther apart.
- **Lineated settlements** consist of buildings spread out in lines along a river, canal, or dike, allowing all residents access to the waterway.
- **Planned settlements**, usually made up of crescent-shaped estates housing several small buildings, are typically constructed near one or more major cities that support the workforce.

Human Migration

Human migration is simply the movement of people from one location to another. **Human migration** may be international or internal:

- **International migration** is movement from one country of residence to another. This kind of migration generally covers permanent movements, thus excluding such transitory activities as migrant labor, nomadism, tourism, and commuting. When leaving a country, migrating peoples are referred to as emigrants; when they arrive in a new country, they are called immigrants.
- **Internal migration** occurs when citizens move within a country, such as in the United States when people moved west from adjacent areas in the east.

Migration may also be voluntary or forced:

- **Voluntary migration** (movement based on uncoerced personal decisions) occurs for many reasons: proximity to family and friends, expansion of territory, a search for employment and economic opportunity, an attempt to improve one's quality of life, and the settlement of undeveloped territory.
- **Forced migration** occurs when a person or group of people is compelled to move regardless of their individual preferences. This type of migration has many possible causes: slavery; overcrowding; racial, religious, or political persecution and/or discrimination; natural disaster (such as hurricanes or flooding); and war.

Population Transfer

The term *population transfer* refers to actions taken by a political authority in a state or country to drive large groups of people out of a particular region (forced migration). Historically, **population transfer** has been used to force groups of people with ethnicities and/or religious beliefs different from the dominant norm into isolated regions. This **forced migration** is often detrimental to the well-being of the ousted people, as no consideration is made for the suitability of the new region to the group's way of life. The "Indian Removal" that occurred in the United States in the 1830s is a classic example of population transfer. Native Americans were forced off of their homelands onto isolated, federally owned reservations. The mass expulsions of Jews, Muslims, and Gypsies that took place in various European countries numerous times throughout history are also instances of population transfer. Though these discriminatory practices were considered "humane" resolutions to religious, ethical, and cultural conflicts for centuries, they are considered violations of international law in modern times.

Internal Migration

Internal human migration is the movement of people within a country; this type of migration may be permanent or temporary. **Permanent internal migrations** include urbanization (the migration of people from less developed rural areas to more developed urban areas, which often occurs when people seek access to the wide variety of services usually available in urban areas), urban depopulation (the opposite of urbanization, which occurs when people seek residencies in quieter, less polluted, less crowded areas), and regional migration (a general trend of movement within a country, such as from northern areas to southern areas). Temporary internal movements such as commuting to work or school are referred to as **daily migrations**. **Seasonal migration** is that practiced by transhumant nomads and farmworkers. The movement of people from one region to another for a significant period of time (but with the intent of returning to the original region) is referred to as **semipermanent migration**. Workers on ships and oil rigs engage in this type of movement.

Early Human Migrations

The early human migrations helped to shape the path of human development throughout history. The first anatomically modern Homo sapiens evolved in **Africa** between 100,000 and 150,000 years ago. These prehistoric beings probably practiced hunting and gathering, meaning that they moved constantly in search of food. These communities became more organized, developing more sophisticated tools and cooperative predation tactics. The population grew as they quickly migrated to other regions, inhabiting each of the continents but Antarctica within 50,000 years. Hunting alone could not sustain the increasing population, spurring the transition from hunting and gathering to migratory slash-and-burn agriculture; crops spread across the globe. People began to settle in permanent, stable agricultural communities. The innovation of sailing vessels encouraged human migration, resulting in new settlements bred from colonization and/or conquest. Seafarers and nomadic pastoralists aided in the distribution of new technologies to various regions. The sharing of increasingly specialized knowledge enabled the rise of several early empires. New social circumstances then bred new (increasingly violent) forms of human migration.

Modern Human Migrations

Due to increases in the population, as well as advancements in technology, **modern human migrations** have surpassed earlier movements in terms of size and scope. The many technological innovations associated with the Industrial Revolution facilitated, among other things, transportation over long distances. This factor, combined with economic, cultural, environmental, and political forces, led to many massive migratory movements. The **Great Atlantic Migration**, which involved the relocation of many people from Europe to North America in the mid- to late-1800s, was the largest such migration. This period of mobility began with the immigration of many Irish and German people to the United States; these migrants left their countries in search of ample food after failure of the potato crop in Ireland and southern Rhineland led to famine in those areas. The mass movement of residents of developing countries to more industrialized nations is another major migration that has taken place in modern times.

Population Structure

The population structure of a society is a description of that society in terms of the ages and sexes of its members. The study of **demographic structure** includes, by extension, analysis of crude birth and death rates and infant mortality rates (the number of infants in a society who die before they reach one year of age divided by the number of live births per year). Practitioners in this field also examine **natural increase**, which is the rate at which a society's population grows due to a difference between the birth rate and the death rate. A society's **population structure** is usually represented by a population pyramid. This type of diagram is created through the placement of two bar graphs (one denoting females and one denoting males) side by side. The x-axis shows the percentage of people of each sex who fall into a certain age group as shown on the y-axis.

Population Pyramid of a Developing Country

The population pyramids of developing countries tend to be wide at their bases and increasingly narrow toward the tops of the diagrams, indicating that a sizeable portion of developing countries' populations is made up of young people, due to high birth and death rates. Improvements in the living conditions of many developing nations may decrease the **CDR**, resulting in a youthful population (one in which the majority of the population is teenaged or younger) and a large gap between the **CBR** and **CDR** (a high rate of natural increase). Developing countries often exhibit high birth rates for several reasons, some of which may become less applicable as a society's standard of living improves. For instance, high infant mortality rates in some societies impel parents to bear many children in the expectation of losing some of them. In agricultural societies, members of large families can share farming and household duties. High death rates in developing nations result from insufficient access to medical services and from unsanitary and/or insufficient food and water supplies.

Population Pyramid of a Developed Nation

Generally, the population pyramid of a developed country is slightly narrow at the base, consistently wide through the middle, and narrower at the very top. A **population pyramid** of this shape indicates relatively low birth and death rates—the number of babies born is less than the number of adults, and a majority of children reach late adulthood. The small discrepancy between the **CBR** and **CDR** implies a low rate of natural increase. Decreasing birth rates can result in an aging population, in which a large number of people are over age 65. Developed nations often exhibit low birth rates because women are likely to have access to reproductive and family planning services, which gives them control of their own fertility. Also, it can be expensive to raise a large family in a developed country. Death rates (including infant mortality rates) in developed countries are usually lower than those observed in developing countries because of better access to medical services, clean water, food, and adequate housing in the former.

Study of Population Structure

The study of population structure supplies geographers with useful information about social trends and patterns. On a **national scale**, the examination of **population structure** provides clues as to the economic status and standard of living of a nation, as evidenced by the patterns observed in the population pyramids of developed and developing nations. On a **regional scale**, variations in population structure may result from migratory processes or from the presence of institutions that attract and concentrate people of a certain age in a given area. For example, the existence of a large university in an urban area will decrease the average age of the area's residents. The study of a region's population structure and changes in that structure is helpful in **city planning**, as different age groups have different physical and social needs and engage in different sorts of leisure activities. Also, examination of the number of males and females in each age group can aid in the **prediction of future variations** in population structure.

Culture

Culture is the acquired knowledge that people use to interpret the world around them and to guide them in social behavior. Therefore, **culture** is not behavior itself; rather, it is a body of shared knowledge that causes people to act and interact with others in certain ways. Also, culture is not genetic. From a young age, members of a group learn about the (arbitrary) aspects of that group's culture from observation of and participation in social activity. Culture may be **tacit**, meaning that its transmission occurs unconsciously (for instance, certain linguistic conventions), or **explicit**, meaning that its transmission is purposeful and articulated (for example, religious education). Culture is a complex system of interrelated parts. While some aspects of culture are shared by all members of a particular society, each person in that society is a member of multiple groups with their own cultural knowledge. For example, one is likely to behave differently in the presence of his or her family than in the presence of friends.

Ethnicity

Ethnicity refers to the classification of a group by its distinctive cultural traits; these traits form a comprehensive cultural entity. Members of an **ethnic group** feel strong ties to the group's cultural traditions and knowledge and identify themselves as a "people" rather than simply a statistical population. **Ethnicity** may be expressed through music, dance, dress, kinship patterns, moral and value systems, food, religious beliefs and activities, language, and literature. In an ethnic group, these cultural qualities are common throughout the society and are seen as unique with respect to other ethnic groups. Often, an ethnic group will share a common history and territorial "homeland." The concept of ethnicity differs from that of race, which divides people into arbitrary categories based on perceived differences in people's physical and biogenetic characteristics. The labeling of a group as a race group versus an ethnic group is thus determined by the criteria used to define it.

Ethnocentrism

Ethnocentrism is the belief that one's own cultural norms are "natural" and therefore superior to other belief systems. Historically, dominant groups have been wary of ethnic diversity, and ethnocentrism tends to occur in less enlightened societies. **Ethnocentric beliefs** have led to the discriminatory and hostile treatment of minority groups throughout history. The actions taken by Nazis against Jews in World War II Germany provide an extreme example of the attempted elimination of a particular ethnic group.

Pluralism

Pluralism is a doctrine that advocates the autonomous participation of differing ethnic, racial, religious, and/or social groups in a common civilization.

Cultural Relativism

Cultural relativism is a theory that suggests it is possible to observe other cultures without making value-based judgments. This can be achieved only through complete detachment from one's own cultural beliefs. **Cultural relativism** proposes that each group's cultural "reality" is equally valid and worth preserving, and that aspects of a particular culture can only be fairly evaluated in terms of that culture as a whole.

Assimilation

Assimilation is the process whereby individuals of a minority ethnic group are absorbed into and internalize cultural characteristics of a dominant group. **Assimilation** may be voluntary or forced.

Voluntary assimilation often occurs when immigrants arrive in a new country. As they learn about the dominant culture through contact with and participation in their new societies, many immigrants gradually begin to abandon their previously held cultural beliefs and practices in favor of those predominant in those societies; this helps them to thrive in a new culture. For example, learning the dominant language is extremely important in the creation of economic and educational opportunities. **Forced assimilation** occurs when one group invades and conquers the territory of another group. The conquering group forcibly impels the native group to forsake their ethnic beliefs and practices in favor of those of the newly dominant group. Forced assimilation constitutes an attempt to create artificial unity, which may help the invaders retain control of the region.

Amalgamation

Amalgamation, in cultural studies, is the process whereby a society becomes **ethnically mixed**. This process is also known as **hybridization**. Though assimilation is common among new members of a society different from their own, it is rarely complete. More often, assimilating peoples adopt certain useful characteristics of the dominant culture while retaining certain important aspects of their culture. Examination of Mexican culture reveals that nation's amalgamated society. Throughout centuries of contact, certain aspects of Native American cultures and Spanish cultures have been extracted, modified, and synthesized to create a new society. The hybrid nature of this society may be observed in, for example, spoken dialects, religious beliefs and practices, and architectural styles.

Language

A language is a conventionalized system of sounds, gestures, and signs used for communication. It is an important and distinctive aspect of any culture. Human language relies heavily (though not exclusively) on **vocalizations**. The activities that produce vocal sounds are referred to as speech; speech is generated and interpreted through language. In language, words act as **symbols** that refer to something else. We learn to associate particular words with particular referents. For example, the symbol "wall" refers to a barrier between spaces. Symbology in language simplifies the task of communication; it enables us to communicate about things that are not present. Symbols in language may also be **nonlinguistic**. Posture, eye contact, clothing, and material goods are symbols through which information may be communicated. **Sociolinguistic rules** are cultural conventions that govern the ways humans communicate in different social situations. For example, a person is likely to speak differently during a job interview than he or she would among peers at a social gathering.

Subsystems of Language

The subsystems of language are phonology, grammar, morphology, syntax, and semantics.

- **Phonology** deals with the formation and ordering of sounds. Sounds are classified as phonemes, the basic units used in word construction. Phonemic categories are culturally defined. For example, in English, the "t" sound is treated as a single phoneme; in Hindi, the same sound is divided into four distinct phonemes.
- **Grammar** provides categories and rules regarding the combination of vocal symbols.
- **Morphology** combines units of meaning to make words or modify word meaning. Morphemes are categories of the smallest vocal units intrinsic to meaning. They may be words (categorized, for example, as nouns or verbs) or parts of words. For example, "s" is a morpheme when used to pluralize a word.
- **Syntax** provides rules for organizing words into phrases.

- **Semantics** deals with the categories and rules for relating vocal symbols (words) to their referents. Semantic rules tell us how to combine words with what they stand for. For example, the semantics of the English language instruct us to associate the word "chair" with an object upon which we sit.

Sapir-Whorf Hypothesis

The Sapir-Whorf Hypothesis, developed by the linguists **Benjamin Whorf** and **Edward Sapir**, directly contradicts the belief that language mirrors reality, that words are simply symbols for what already exists. One's **native language** is completely embedded in one's consciousness; we use our languages to formulate thoughts and to identify and classify things that we encounter in nature. Also, certain words and concepts cannot be directly translated from one language to another. Whorf believed that humans are only capable of conceptualizing ideas that may be articulated and expressed through language. Therefore, we cannot think about something we do not have the words or structures to express. The Sapir-Whorf hypothesis states that humans dissect and interpret the multitude of stimuli provided by the outside world using the linguistic systems in our minds. Consequently, people's native languages govern their views of reality and determine their perceptions of the world.

Modified Whorfism

"Modified Whorfism," which suggests that language affects but does not dictate the reality experienced by humans, is accepted by many social and linguistic thinkers. The nature of language itself problematizes any attempt to prove the Sapir-Whorf Hypothesis. Since language is such an integral part of human consciousness, it is fruitless to ask a person how the language he or she speaks has affected his or her view of the world; no one could answer such a question objectively. **Euphemistic language**, the use of words that are seen as less offensive in place of more unpleasant, direct, or harsh synonyms, lends credence to the idea that language has some effect on one's perceived reality. Though different languages may not create exclusive worldviews for their speakers, they do influence the thought patterns of native speakers in distinctive ways.

Industrial Location Factors

Industrial location factors are the various issues that industry owners and managers must take into consideration during the selection of an ideal physical location for their businesses. **Human or economic factors** include the availability of a labor source (the proximity of potential workers to the location), the location of leisure facilities for workers, the market (the capital required to keep a business in operation, which depends on the wage demands of laborers in a particular area, the cost of the transportation of goods, and the size of the business's sphere of influence), the relative location of transportation routes (such as seaports, railways, and highways), the government (which may impose laws, restrictions, and/or incentives in a particular area), access to technology (such as manufacturing robots), and geographical inertia (which refers to traditions of producing particular goods in particular areas). **Physical location factors** include the relative locations of natural transportation routes (such as rivers), the relative locations of raw material sources (the primary industrial location factor), and the size and relief of the prospective business site.

Scientific Revolution

The Scientific Revolution was the second period of major change in human history. This period (approximately 1500-1750 AD) involved intellectual and geographic explorations that produced many scientific and industrial advances in human civilization. Geographic expeditions, such as the ones undertaken by Christopher Columbus, were enabled by **technological developments** in the fields of cartography, shipbuilding, and navigation. Such explorations taught Europeans about the physical and human geography of different regions and about the layout of land on Earth's surface.

Scientific exploration, practiced by noted thinkers such as Isaac Newton and Galileo Galilei, was enabled by inventions such as the microscope and the telescope. With these and other new tools, people made discoveries about our world and its function that are considered fundamental today. The Scientific Transformation eventually gave rise to the **Industrial Revolution**, which produced a plethora of new inventions, factories, and opportunities for the attainment of wealth. It also produced inequalities (still observable today) between societies with these technological capabilities and those without.

Characteristics Defining Independent Countries

An independent country shares four defining characteristics:

- Any independent country inhabits a specific territory (land and water) defined by **boundaries**. The sizes and shapes of countries differ widely.
- Each country has a **population** that occupies its territory. The sizes and constitutions of each country are also extremely variable.
- Any independent country possesses **sovereignty**, which is the freedom to control and protect its territory, population, and foreign interactions without outside influence. The geographic location and landscape of a country's territory may affect its ability to defend its sovereignty. For example, the high mountains surrounding Switzerland have served to protect the country against foreign invasion for centuries.
- Every independent country has a **government**, an institution that creates and enforces laws and policies and acts to further the public good (through protection, the maintenance of order, and provision of certain services). There are several types of government structures and governmental authority.

Types of Government Structures

Governments may be classified by the nature of the relationship between the central governing body and the smaller units (states, provinces, etc.) that make up a country. Three types of government structures include the following:

- A **unitary system** exists when a central governmental body exerts sole control over an entire country. The principal government formulates policies applicable at all levels of government; smaller units exert power only if the central government grants it to them.
- A **federation** exists when certain powers are allocated to a central government and certain powers are given to regional or local governmental units. In a federation (such as the United States), federal, state, and local governments share political power.
- A **confederation** exists when smaller governmental units retain their sovereignties and allow the central government only specific, limited powers (usually regarding national defense or international trade). In this type of structure, states and provinces retain a large degree of independence but still ally to address common concerns.

Type of Government Authority

A government may be classified by the source of its authority. Different kinds of governments are run with various degrees of public participation. In an **anarchy**, every citizen in the population is seen as a qualified participant in decision-making that will affect the country. There is no central governing body; people govern themselves. A **democracy** also involves rule by the people. However, unlike an anarchy, a democracy includes a central government that aims to serve the people. In a representative democracy, citizens exercise their political franchise or suffrage (the right to vote) in the selection of leaders, who, in turn, participate in governmental proceedings and make political decisions. Citizens of a democratic nation also express their opinions about certain issues by voting. In an **oligarchy**, political power is concentrated in the hands of a small group, usually made up of wealthy people with strong military influence and/or familial traditions of power. Often, the most influential participants in an oligarchic government operate outside the public eye in the economic realm.

Types of Authoritarian Governments

An authoritarian government is one in which the country's leaders possess all (or a majority of) political power. Until fairly recently, most countries across the world had authoritarian governments. Today, various forms of democracy are more common. There are different degrees of authoritarianism. A **monarchy** is a type of authoritarian government in which monarchs (for example, queens, shahs, and pharaohs) inherit political power simply by being born into a ruling family. Monarchs may serve as symbols of national unity, or they may rule as dictators. A **dictatorship** (the most common type of authoritarian government) is a system in which political power is held by a small group or even a unitary individual. The dictator exerts control through military force and intimidation, and he or she attempts to control the behavior of their subordinates. **Totalitarianism** is the most extreme form of authoritarianism. In this kind of system, the ruling body tries to control every aspect of society in its territory, from economic activity to people's personal lives.

Boundaries and Frontiers

A boundary is functional though a hypothetical structure that delineates territories of differing political entities or legal domains, such as countries, provinces, and states. Prior to modernized conceptions of territory, nations defined their territories as the area over which they could exert authority. Today, territories are demarcated by **boundaries** that are effectively material and officially designated. A map whose sole purpose is to convey the sizes and shapes of various governmental units is termed a political map. Though boundaries may run alongside physical features of Earth's surface, such as mountains, they are contrived by humans to segregate one area from another. The areas on either side of a boundary are often referred to as borders. A **frontier** is an area of undeveloped land, the edge of civilization; frontiers exist outside of certain boundaries. Throughout history, competition for the control of boundaries and frontiers has been the cause of much military and ideological conflict.

Phases of Boundary Formation

The processes of boundary formation and implementation occurs in four general phases:

- During the **historical precedent phase**, boundaries are established and maintained based on the cultural characteristics (such as religion, language, or ethnicity) of people in an area. Different cultural groups form communities that inhabit particular areas. The recognition of boundaries in this stage may also be based on previous attempts to establish a dividing line.
- The **political definition or delimitation phase** entails the official establishment of boundary lines through the use of legal documents such as treaties. These lines are drawn on official maps. Often, the placement of a boundary is negotiated by representatives from the concerned regions.
- During the **technical demarcation phase**, the boundaries agreed upon during the previous phase are practically implemented. Demarcators analyze the relevant terrain and material markers, or monuments are constructed to display the location of the officially defined boundary.
- Finally, the **characterization phase** entails modification of the demarcated boundary to accommodate population growth in the border areas.

Boundary Terms

A **natural boundary** is a boundary arbitrarily formed by landscape evolution. This type of boundary may be hydrologic (formed by a waterway such as a river) or orthographic (formed by a land formation such as a mountain chain). An **artificial boundary** is an abstract line formulated by humans to aid in identifying specific locations. Geodesic lines and the lines that constitute the graticule are examples of artificial boundaries. A **separation barrier** is a physical construction (for instance, a wall or fence) intended to separate disparate populations or to inhibit movement between two areas. The Great Wall of China, which spans nearly 4,000 miles, provides a classic example of a separation barrier. It was initially built to protect citizens against raids by conquering tribes. Another example is the border of the United States with Mexico, which was created to prevent the free entry of immigrants into the US

Cultural Boundaries

As displayed on maps, boundaries may appear as straight lines, as lines that follow natural landscape features, or as wiggles that seem to twist and turn for no reason. The last of these boundary types is known as a **cultural boundary** and may be attributed to many (perhaps continuous) boundary disputes between cultural and/or ethnic groups on either side of the separating line. For example, the border region between Belgium and the Netherlands is sprinkled with tiny, hamlet-sized areas "belonging" to one country on the other's side of the boundary. This type of boundary is sometimes referred to as a cultural boundary. When conflict along a cultural border ebbs, the formal process of boundary formation often begins, resulting in the wiggles observed along borders across the world.

International Power Relations

International power refers to the ability of one state to exert control or influence over other states. Power is generally defined as the capacity of an individual or group to impose their wills on others. This may be achieved through hegemonies (soft power) or through the use of brute force (hard power). Today, states may be classified by the degree of their influences, especially in relation to the power of other states. **Middle powers** are those states that cannot dominate other states but still possess degrees of international influence. Such states often ally themselves with groups but do not lead them. Canada is an example of a middle power. A **regional power** is a state that exerts control over other states in its region but not necessarily around the globe. **Great powers**, **global powers**, and **superpowers** are terms for strong states that share power with a few other influential states. A **hyperpower** is a singular dominating state in a unipolar world. Many consider the modern United States a hyperpower.

Spheres of Influence

In international politics, the term *sphere of influence* refers to the claim of a powerful state to exclusive or predominant control over foreign territory, often in the surrounding region; this claim may or may not be recognized as legitimate by other entities. States within a powerful state's sphere of influence often function as **satellite states** (states that are officially independent but influenced by the more powerful state in practice). For instance, during its prime, the Japanese Empire exerted much political power over events in the nearby states of Korea, Vietnam, and Manchuria. Historically, the term *sphere of influence* has been used to refer to the respective **colonial territories** of two or more powers in a region. For example, in the 1880s, Great Britain and Germany signed an agreement stating that neither would interfere in the other's (predefined) sphere of influence in the Gulf of Guinea. In regional geography, a major urban area may exert economic influence over the surrounding area; this is also referred to as a sphere of influence.

Monroe Doctrine

In 1823, President James Monroe formulated a foreign policy which is known today as the **Monroe Doctrine**. In his annual address to Congress, Monroe indicated that the Old World (namely Europe) and the New World (namely the United States) were distinct entities with distinct systems, and should therefore exist as separate spheres. His statement included four main points:

- the United States would not participate in conflicts inside or between European nations;
- the United States officially recognized and would not interfere with existing colonies in the New World;
- the Western Hemisphere was off-limits for future colonization; and
- any endeavor by a European power to influence any nation in the Western Hemisphere would be considered a hostile act against the United States.

Though the Monroe Doctrine was militarily unsustainable at the time of its formulation, as the US emerged as a global power in the 1870s, the Monroe Doctrine came to be viewed as a geopolitical definition of the country's **sphere of influence** as the entire Western Hemisphere.

Review Video: The Monroe Doctrine
Visit mometrix.com/academy and enter code: 953021

Cooperation

Cooperation is the practice whereby individuals and groups work together (possibly with common methods) to achieve a **shared goal**. Often, those working in concert accomplish more than those acting independently or against one another (competition), though the impetus to compete against others is often a motivation for individual behavior. In fact, individuals or nation-states may cooperate with a larger group in order to be part of a larger, more competitive entity. There are potentially infinite reasons for collaboration between people and nation-states. For instance, at the local level, a group of citizens may form a group to protest the planned construction of a large shopping center in a rural neighborhood. At the regional and national levels, organizations such as Mothers Against Drunk Driving (MADD) collaborate in attempts to change public policy and spur the passage of legislation aimed at making society safer. Internationally, the governments of nation-states and/or their citizens may join together to promote humanitarian activities such as the International Federation of Red Cross and Red Crescent Societies (IFRCS).

Home Market Effect

The home market effect is a model that exemplifies one type of international governmental cooperation. Trade, the voluntary exchange of goods and/or services, is a vital mechanism by which nation-states that do not have and cannot feasibly produce a particular good can obtain it. In the **home market effect** situation, it is assumed that it is impractical and/or impossible for a single country to produce all of the resources it needs in sufficient quantities. Therefore, it becomes desirable for each country in a system to specialize in the efficient production of **one resource** and trade a surplus of that resource for another material. This process requires **cooperation** among the participating nation-states in discussions of costs and quantities. For example, Arabic countries control a large portion of the world's oil reserves. Western countries in need of that particular resource often share technological information with Arabic countries in exchange for oil. In this manner, each country has the potential to obtain the resources it needs.

Economic Interdependence

Economic interdependence is a situation in which two or more countries depend on one other for any or all of the following: energy, food, manufactured goods, minerals, or labor. Resources (including natural resources, such as minerals and land, as well as human resources), fuel sources, and information are distributed **unevenly** across the globe; no single country possesses all the resources it needs to subsist and thrive. Therefore, each must **trade** its surplus goods and services for those it lacks. The **North American Free Trade Agreement (NAFTA)** was formed among three economically interdependent countries (Canada, the United States, and Mexico) in an attempt to ease trade restrictions on vital imports and exports in the member states.

Burgess's Concentric Zone Model

Burgess's Concentric Zone Model was developed in 1925 by **Ernest Burgess**, based on his observations of Chicago and other American cities. This model of land use and urban development suggested that towns grow outward from a central "downtown" area, creating **concentric circles** (zones) of building and activity; this indicates that the age of structures decreases with distance from the central hub. Burgess's model also implies that inner zones have tendencies to expand into the outer regions. This characterizes **urban growth** as a process of expansion and reconversion of land uses. While this model is less complex than actual cities existing in the twenty-first century, it is still useful as a theoretical approximation of urban growth patterns. The descriptions given of the zones in Burgess's model are based upon observation and analysis of modern city growth.

Inner Zones

The inner zones of the Burgess Concentric Zone Model are Zones A, B, and C.

- **Zone A**, the central zone in the Burgess Concentric Zone Model, is the **central business district (CBD)**. Land in the CBD is more expensive than in any other zone. As the area accessible to the largest number of people, the CBD houses retail shops, banks, health care facilities, and office buildings. This zone tends to be densely developed, with high levels of traffic and a lack of vegetation.
- **Zone B** is referred to as the **Transition Zone** or the **Twilight Zone**. This area may be subdivided into a declining industrial sector and a section of low-class residential housing (older buildings arranged in tight grids with no yard space). In a continually developing city, Zone A's growth, coupled with attempts to renovate older areas of the region, creates constant activity in Zone B, characterizing it as a transition zone.
- **Zone C**, called the **Council Estates**, houses middle-class residencies; there are fewer apartment buildings with more yard space than in Zone B.

Outer Zones

The outer zones of the Burgess Concentric Zone Model are Zones D and E.

- **Zone D** is the region often referred to as the **suburbs** or the **commuter zone**. The suburbs are typified by high-class (expensive) residential buildings. Houses abut garages and other outbuildings; nearly every residency has a yard. Theoretically, the most affluent members of a community are able to reside at a distance from the CBD because they have the means to procure transportation into the downtown area to work and purchase goods and services.
- The **countryside zone (Zone E)** was not present in Burgess's original formulation of his model. Rather, it has been added to represent the residents of an area who wish to live as far as possible from the busy CBD while retaining the ability to use the employment opportunities and services available in the innermost zone of the city. The countryside zone is a rural area with large areas of natural vegetation and a less nucleated form than that of zones closer to the CBD.

Hoyt's Sector Model

The Hoyt Sector Model, formulated by **Homer Hoyt** in 1939, is essentially a modification of Burgess's Concentric Zone Model. Based on observations of the development patterns of many American cities, Hoyt deduced that most large urban areas centered around major **transportation routes**, such as railways and seaports. Commercial entities and industrial facilities were often erected around high-access thoroughfares, and low-income housing was often found near railroad lines. Hoyt updated Burgess's model to account for these patterns. He suggested that cities grow outward from the Central Business District in wedged sectors along major transportation routes. In the **Sector Model**, commercial businesses remain in the CBD, while manufacturing and warehousing interests (a portion of Burgess's Zone B) form in a wedge around major paths of transportation. The low-income housing in Burgess's Zone B abuts the wedge of industrial activity (pollution and noise affect the quality of life in this region, decreasing the land value). As in Burgess's model, middle- and high-income housing in Hoyt's model are situated away from the CBD.

Multiple Nuclei Model

The Multiple Nuclei Model was developed by **Edward Ullman** and **Chauncy Harris** in 1945 to explain urban growth patterns that did not fit the somewhat outdated Concentric and Sector Models. By this point in the development of American cities, many suburbs were growing rapidly and operating as small business districts. Ullman and Harris found that land-use patterns formed around these **nuclei** or **nodes of economic activity**, which were specialized to the needs of residents with certain levels of incomes and certain leisure patterns. The **Multiple Nuclei Model** retains the Central Business District as the main commercial region, from which retail and manufacturing companies spanned outward along transportation routes. In this model, heavy industry is located near the outskirts of a city, possibly near areas of low-income housing. The small communities surrounding suburban nuclei filled the urban periphery.

Exerting Control over Resources Using Boundaries

Though boundaries appear as lines along Earth's surface on two-dimensional maps and globes, they do more than separate terrestrial territories. Theoretically, **boundaries** exist as vertical planes, extending below the surface and into the air, effectively separating **underground resources** and **airspace**. For example, disputes about the "ownership" of an underground oil field (inconveniently located beneath the Iraq-Kuwait border and extending into both countries) contributed to the development of a conflict that culminated in the Gulf War. Disputes over the exploitation of other underground resources, such as coal and natural gas, have been and continue to be sources of international conflict. International boundaries also extend above the surface, creating divisions of airspace (the zone above a state's territory where the rights of other states may be limited). Often, commercial aircraft may fly through another state's airspace only with official agreement. During the communist period, for example, Soviets shot down a commercial Korean aircraft that strayed outside the narrow corridor the USSR had delimited for flights over its territory.

Maritime Boundaries

Maritime boundaries were created by seafaring peoples to claim certain fishing grounds or trading ports for themselves. The concept of territorial control of portions of the seas originated centuries ago. The delimitations of these boundaries have become more and more specific as time passes. A critical action by President **Harry Truman** in 1945 hastened the rush to claim **oceanic territory**. Truman claimed all of the potential natural resources located on the continental shelf for the United States. After Truman's declaration, countries across the world scrambled to lay claim to their own oceanic territories. Today, the following conventions exist regarding maritime law: states may claim up to twelve nautical miles of oceanic territory; states may claim up to 200 nautical miles as their **Exclusive Economic Zones**—coastal states have the sole rights to manage and exploit natural resources within these zones; and coastal states possess exclusive rights over the natural resources on and beneath the continental shelf of their respective continents.

Religion

Religion is culturally shared knowledge and beliefs about the **supernatural realm** (that which exists beyond human experience) that people use to explain the relationship between human life and the universe. People tend to feel most at ease when they are sure of themselves and the order of the world around them. When a particularly traumatic or incongruous event cannot be explained intellectually or experientially, people often turn to **religion** for answers. Religion can provide people with worldviews (sets of beliefs and assumptions about the origin of life and the way things work). An important aspect of religion is the **emotional nature** of the dilemmas it addresses. Consequently, religion can unify disparate peoples with similar beliefs or create unbridgeable divisions between different groups. In human geography, the term is often used to refer to **organized religion** (a structured organization of people supporting a particular religion) rather than an individual's belief system. Organized religion may be public (state-supported) or private (funded by donations from those who attend religious functions).

Governmental Policies Regarding Religion

There are three general attitudes taken by governments regarding religion.

- A **secular government** is one that neither advocates nor discourages religious practices and beliefs. Theoretically, in a secular state, a legal separation exists between religious affairs and political affairs. The "separation of church and state" in the government of the United States of America exemplifies a secular standpoint.
- An **atheistic state** is one in which the government attempts to suppress or even prevent religious practices. North Korea is an example of an officially atheistic state, while China allows people to participate in religious practices under state supervision.
- A **religious government** is one with official links to a particular religion or branch of religion. For example, Sweden is considered Evangelical Lutheran, and Nepal is officially Hindu.

Monism, Dualism, and Pluralism

- **Monism** holds that the universe is created of one single substance, energy, essence, or principle. Substantive monism is the belief in one substance; attributive monism is the belief that while there is only one kind of thing, that category is made up of many individual objects or beings; and absolute monism is the belief that there is but one being created of one substance. Monism may also be broadly subdivided into idealistic monism (which holds that only the mind is real), neutral monism (which states that both mental and physical phenomena can be reduced to a third energetic substance), and materialism (which claims that physical reality is the only reality).
- **Dualism** may refer to the belief in two opposing universal forces that are often personified as deities, to the perceived division between mind and matter, or to the belief that the entire world may be divided into two categories.
- **Pluralism** holds that the universe is made up of many different substances.

Monotheism and Polytheism

Theism is the belief in a divine being.

- **Monotheism** is the belief in a single, all-powerful, universal deity. Zoroastrianism, Islam, and Judaism are examples of monotheistic religions. Deism, a subtype of monotheism, is the belief that although there is one God, this deity does not intervene in human affairs and may be understood only through observation of nature. Monistic theism is a type of monotheism that includes monistic and pantheistic elements as well as the belief in a universal divine being. Substance monotheism, an aspect of some indigenous African religions, claims that the many gods are manifestations of a single God. Inclusive monotheism holds that all polytheistic deities are simply alternate names for the one Supreme Being, while exclusive monotheism asserts that there is one true God and that all others are false.
- **Polytheism** holds that there are many deities; these gods are believed to exist in a pantheon (a set of divine beings with complex, human-like personalities and varying degrees of power in different realms).

Pantheism vs. Panentheism

Pantheism, in its original Greek translation, literally means "all is God and God is all." It is thus a type of monotheism that holds the single divine being and the universe are one. In classical pantheism, God personifies natural order and natural law. Natural pantheism, on the other hand, equates nature with a non-sentient divinity.

Panentheism is the belief that the universe was created by a single immanent God; unlike pantheism, panentheism does not view God and the universe as one. Rather, God is seen as more powerful than and outside of the universe.

Generally, faiths that are considered classically pantheistic may also be described as panentheistic. However, natural pantheism and panentheism are not equivalent concepts—natural pantheists do not believe in the existence of a conscious being that is more powerful than nature.

Largest Religious Bodies in India

Hinduism is the oldest religion practiced in India in modern times, dating to approximately 4,000 years ago. Those who adhere to the principles of Hinduism are referred to as Hindus. Today, each of the several sects of Hinduism relies on the **Vedas** (sacred hymns and verses) as the absolute authority on fundamental truths about the universe. Also, the majority of Hindus believe in **Brahman**, the ultimate universal power. Reincarnation, karma, and the caste system are ideas prevalent in Hinduism. Different branches of Hinduism espouse belief systems that may be described as monistic, dualistic, or pantheistic. In principle, Hindus support religious tolerance and consider different doctrines inadequate rather than wrong.

Buddhism, which grew out of Hinduism during a period of social change in India, was founded by **Siddhartha Gautama** (Gautama Buddha). The goal of Buddhists is to attain the blissful state of **nirvana**. This can be accomplished through the purification of one's thoughts via strictly defined behavior. Buddhism may be described as a polytheistic faith, though any otherworldly powers of Buddhist deities are de-emphasized.

Largest Religious Bodies in Eastern Asia

Confucianism was founded by Confucius (551–479 BC), who lived around the same time as Buddha. This faith was designed to relieve conflict in all arenas, from that which existed among families to that between Heaven and Earth. Confucius defined "appropriate" social roles for people of different ages, sexes, and social ranks; by assuming these roles, Confucians attempt to create a more peaceful world.

Taoism originated in China at approximately the same time as Confucianism. Taoism strives to create harmony between humans and the natural world. Unlike Confucianism, which has a significant political aspect and is largely monistic, Taoism values natural goodness and expressiveness over social order and is largely dualistic.

Note that both Confucianism and Taoism are considered traditional Chinese religions. In fact, most adherents to Chinese religious tradition build their faiths upon a fusion of Confucianism, Taoism, and Buddhism.

Shinto is an ancient Japanese religion. A polytheistic belief system, Shinto espouses a belief in many spirits of nature called **kami**. **Animism**, the belief that all things possess consciousness, is another tenet of Shintoism.

Largest Religious Bodies in Western Asia

Judaism, Christianity, and Islam, all of which originated in Western Asia, are the largest monotheistic religions practiced today.

- **Judaism** is nearly as old as Hinduism. This religion centers on the belief that faithfulness to God and the Ten Commandments will ensure blessings for His followers. The **Torah** is the Jewish religious text, though the **Talmud** in practice is their main authority.
- **Christianity** has its roots in Judaism; like Judaism, Christianity claims the existence of a single, omnipresent, omniscient God. Unlike Jews, however, Christians believe that **Jesus Christ** was the son of God. Christian doctrine asserts that Jesus was crucified to atone for the sins of humanity and rose again three days later to ascend to Heaven. Currently, Christianity has more followers worldwide than any other religion. The **Bible** is the Christian religious text.
- **Islam**, practiced by Muslims, is based upon the guidance of the Prophet **Muhammad**, who advocated the existence of one all-powerful God (**Allah**). The **Koran**, the Islamic religious text, calls for daily prayer, an annual month of fasting, and almsgiving. Islam, like Christianity, has roots in Judaism.

Methods of Religious Diffusion

As evidenced by, for example, the existence of Buddhism in the United States and the presence of Christianity in Africa, all bodies of religious thought have been **diffused** across the globe. As different belief systems come into contact, religious ideas are discarded, changed, and fused, branching existing religions into sects and creating new religions altogether. Some of the factors that influence religious diffusion include the following:

- **Military campaigns** have been an important vehicle in religious diffusion. The Crusades (11th to 13th centuries), a series of military forays by Catholics striving to "recapture" Jerusalem from Muslims, provide an example of religious imperialism (an approach to spreading religion to different people through the use of warfare, oppression, and persecution).
- **Colonization** has often involved religious imperialism.

- **Trade routes** have played a key role in the diffusion of religions. Missionaries, those who attempt to convert others to their faith, often traveled along these routes with traders and explorers.
- **Migration** has also served to bring groups with different religious beliefs together; in fact, religious persecution has spurred many mass human migrations throughout history.

Non-Governmental Organizations

A non-governmental organization, or **NGO** (sometimes referred to as a private voluntary organization) is, as its title suggests, a cooperative group formed independently of any state government. Usually, a group of this type forms for reasons other than commercial gain, such as the advocation of social or environmental policy; non-governmental organizations are often non-profit. There are two general types of NGOs:

1. **Advocacy non-governmental organizations** are formed to promote awareness of and/or support for a certain issue, which they accomplish through lobbying activities, orchestration of awareness-raising events, and press work.
2. **Operational NGOs** participate in the organization and execution of relief-oriented or development-oriented projects. Most development-related groups evolve in three stages: first, the group concentrates on relief and welfare activities; next, on the development of self-reliant activity in affected areas; and lastly, on the implementation of sustainable development activities at local, state, and national levels.

United Nations

The United Nations (**UN**) is a group of nation-states (including nearly every independent country) that defines itself as a "global association of governments facilitating cooperation in international law, international security, economic development, and social equity." This organization was founded after World War II in 1945 by the victorious countries, which possessed the shared aim of **preventing future conflicts and wars** between nations through the establishment of a situation of **collective security**. This means that any aggression against any of the member states is viewed as an attack on the entire organization, which will respond as a whole. Today, the United Nations consists of several specialized agencies that deal with issues such as human rights, arms control, global health, economic development, and humanitarian assistance. As a large organization made up of nearly 200 member states, the UN does not always function perfectly. However, the group has achieved more through international cooperation than any single nation-state could accomplish alone.

Sustainable Development and Agenda 21

Sustainable development is a developmental process that satisfies the needs of those living in the present without impairing the abilities of those in future generations to attain the same degree of comfort; it is development that does not exhaust the global supply of natural resources. In other words, sustainable development refers to a balance achieved between economic development, social development, and environmental protection.

Agenda 21 is a UN program that strives to reach sustainable development. It consists of four sections:

- The **social and economic dimensions section**, which stresses the importance of addressing global poverty in developing nations through health education, promotion of sustainable settlement patterns, and altering destructive consumption patterns;

- The **conservation and management of resources development section**, which includes information on environmental protection and the preservation of biodiversity;
- The **section on strengthening the role of major groups**, which aims to empower groups at the individual and local levels; and
- The **means of implementation section**, which describes educational, technological, financial, and international procedures for the attainment of the program's goals.

Conflict

Conflict is a situation of discord and/or opposition between two or more individuals or groups. In political science, **conflict** is defined as a continuing state of hostility between groups of people, which often involves physical violence. Conflict must be distinguished from **competition**, which involves two or more groups possessing mutually exclusive goals, meaning that attempts by one party to achieve its goal compromises the ability of the other group to attain its goal. Competition (and occasionally cooperation) may lead to conflict. Individuals and nation-states may become involved in conflicts for a variety of reasons at a variety of scales. For example, two local groups may have conflicting views on a proposed tax increase. At the regional level, different religious or ethnic groups may exist in a state of conflict. Internationally, competition for scarce resources or ideological disagreements may lead to a war between countries.

Class Conflict

Class conflict refers to discord that usually exists between members of different classes. **Social classes** may be defined and differentiated using various criteria. An individual's membership in a particular class may be based on his or her income, education level, possessions, reputation, manners, relationship to a means of production, or any combination of these and other factors. **Class conflict** may be overtly manifested through, for instance, physical violence, worker strikes, or protests. Class conflict may also be expressed more subtly, through, for example, informal "slowdowns" in production or prejudicial treatment of members of an oppositional class. Ironically, conflict between different classes may increase the level of cooperation within a single class, as members ally to lobby public policy makers.

Indigenous Peoples, Colonialism, and Imperialism

Indigenous peoples is a term that describes distinctive cultural groups whose historical associations with an area or region predate that area's colonization, annexation, or integration into a nation-state. **Indigenous societies** are often non-urbanized and are frequently based on agricultural, pastoral, or hunting and gathering production methods.

Colonialism is the practice whereby a nation-state asserts sovereignty over territories outside of its boundaries, usually in order to gain control of an area's resources (natural and human) and potential markets. Colonization may occur violently, through the forcible suppression and domination of indigenous peoples, or it may occur relatively peacefully, through the hegemonic promotion of ideologies designed to imply that the colonizers are spreading superior (and thus beneficial) values and systems to colonized areas.

Imperialism is similar to colonialism in that each practice involves the extension of a nation's control over foreign territories. However, imperialism refers more specifically to the creation and/or maintenance of an empire, a set of regions officially ruled by a single emperor.

Factors of Production

Classical economics identifies three main factors in the production of consumable goods and services:

- **Land** refers to the physical location at which production occurs, as well as material goods (including natural fuel resources, such as coal, as well as materials such as minerals and soil that are used in production). Rent is the monetary compensation paid for the use of land owned by a separate party.
- **Labor** refers to the work executed by humans in the production of goods and the performance of services. The quality of labor is affected by education and training levels.
- **Capital goods** are manmade goods that are used, in turn, to produce other goods and services. Capital goods are also referred to as means of production. This factor includes tools, buildings, and machinery.

Types of Economic Systems

The term *economic system* refers to the way in which goods and services are produced, distributed, and consumed in a society. Three types of **economic systems** are traditional, market, and command.

- In a **traditional economy**, determinations of the types and amounts of goods produced, methods of production, and distribution of goods are based on long-established customs and habits. Such economies are sometimes referred to as subsistence economies because little surplus is produced, which negates the need for markets.
- In a **market economy**, producers of goods and services are free to trade them as they see fit. The types and amounts of goods and services produced (and their prices) are determined by the laws of supply and demand, and by private individuals and organizations.
- In a **command economy**, nearly every aspect is controlled by a central government. The government often makes economic decisions based on social and political goals; for instance, a government may set the price of a gallon of milk at 25 cents, even if it costs one dollar to produce, so that everyone can afford to purchase it.

Industry

The term *industry* refers to a method of economic production, namely manufacturing, that involves the investment of large amounts of capital prior to production. An **industry** may also be defined as a group of businesses that produce similar products; for example, all of the businesses that participate in film production constitute the "film industry." Industries in general may be classified into four sectors based on the resources needed for production and the type of goods produced.

- The **primary sector of industry** is made up of businesses that transform natural resources into raw materials used in other industries. Agriculture, mining, and forestry are examples of activities related to the primary sector of industries.
- The **secondary sector of industry** involves the manufacture of goods suitable for sale to consumers and other businesses. Businesses in this sector often make use of the materials produced in the primary sector. The clothing, tobacco, and energy industries are considered to be in the secondary sector.

- The **tertiary sector of industry** is also referred to as the service industry or sector. Businesses in this industrial category provide services to consumers and other businesses. Hair salons, hospitals, and restaurants are examples of tertiary businesses that provide services directly to consumers. Members of the tertiary industry may also provide services to other businesses, such as the transportation, distribution, wholesale, or retail of goods produced by businesses in the secondary sector. While the provision of services may involve the alteration of the secondary product (like the preparation of raw foods in the restaurant industry), the focus of the tertiary sector is on interaction with consumers.
- The **quaternary sector of industry** is a relatively new categorization, having been recently distinguished from the tertiary sector. The quaternary sector involves the provision of specialized "intellectual" services, such as education, scientific research, and the distribution of information technology.

Labels Classifying Levels of Development

Economic geographers use different terms to classify countries by their levels of economic development. Most broadly, countries may be classified as either **more developed countries (MDCs)** or **less developed countries (LDCs)**. In this system of classification, distinctions are made often made based on political factors as well as economic factors. Geographers may also categorize the level of a country's economic development as **First World** (capitalist), **Second World** (communist or socialist), **Third World** (underdeveloped), **Fourth World** (severely underdeveloped), or **Fifth World** (poorest). Currently, the **World Bank** (an international organization that monitors the economic status of countries) classifies countries as high income, upper-middle income, lower-middle income, or low income. Any of these categorizations may be misleading when applied to an entire country. Most of the world's countries exhibit highly developed cores as well as peripheral regions stricken by poverty. Therefore, averages of national economic statistics have lost some of their meaning. It is useful to consider the relative advantages (geographic location, resources, political stability, etc.) of certain countries over others.

Measures of Economic Development

A country's **consumption per capita** is observed as a measure of the country's level of economic development. Naturally, the higher a nation's level of economic development, the wealthier its citizens will be and, therefore, the more they can afford to consume. A country's **infrastructure** is studied in the assessment of its economic status. Transportation systems, urban centers, distribution mechanisms, industrial businesses, communication systems, and service facilities such as hospitals and police stations are all considered aspects of a country's infrastructure. A country's **social conditions** are also used as measures of economic development. These conditions include the literacy rate, the infant mortality rate, and the availability of health care. The United Nations Development Program has developed a **human development index** based on the national averages of three figures: life expectancy, education (assessed through examination of the adult literacy rate and the combined rates of enrollment in secondary and tertiary schools), and per capita income. A higher human development index is seen as an indicator of a higher level of economic development.

Environment and Society

Environmental Effects of Burning Fossil Fuels

Burning fossil fuels (naturally-occurring hydrocarbon compounds that may be used by humans for fuel), especially coal, releases harmful elements into the atmosphere. The chemical reaction of coal combustion produces, for example, large amounts of carbon dioxide. When these gases reach the atmosphere, they inhibit the release of infrared photons into space, as carbon dioxide molecules absorb the photons and may reflect them inward, back toward Earth. This phenomenon is called the **greenhouse effect**. While the greenhouse effect is desirable, to a certain degree, to maintain a comfortable climate on the planet, increased levels of carbon dioxide can change the balance of energy in the atmosphere. This is termed **global warming**. Coal burning can also cause acid rain. Sulfur dioxide, a byproduct of burning coal, rises to the atmosphere and combines with water molecules to form sulfuric acid. This **acid rain** falls back to Earth, where it can cause harm to plants, animals, water bodies, and exposed structures. Burning gasoline can also contribute to the formation of acid rain.

Ozone Depletion

Ozone depletion occurs when the balance between creation and destruction of ozone particles in the stratosphere is tipped toward destruction. **Chlorofluorocarbons** (or CFCs) are chemicals created by humans for use in, for example, refrigeration, aerosol cans, and cleaners. When these chemicals interact with sunlight in the atmosphere, chlorine atoms are released; these free atoms participate in processes that destroy ozone particles. **Ozone holes** (areas of severe ozone depletion) have been identified over Antarctica and various other areas, where spring sunlight contributes to the chlorine-ozone reactions that destroy the latter molecule. There are numerous reports that show that these ozone holes are able to repair themselves given the correct weather and atmospheric conditions.

Environmental Regulations and the Factor of Uncertainty

Environmental regulation frequently encounters the unknown. In many cases, it is not scientifically proven whether environmental damage exists or will occur, and if so, whether certain human activities have caused or will cause it. For example, in the past, it took much time to clarify whether sulfur dioxide emissions caused acid rain damage to forests. Currently, regarding global warming induced by greenhouse gas emissions, it is not clear whether counter-effects such as increased carbon dioxide emissions, which cause increased growth of vegetation, which in turn produces cooling effects, can reverse that global warming or not. In today's world, many nations adhere to the **precaution principle**. This principle demands that even in situations with no certainty of damage but with a risk of damage, preventative safeguards are used. It is easier thus to change or reverse decisions to allow risky endeavors if new information reveals hitherto unknown dangers.

Interactions Between Scientists, the Public, and Politics

The environmental issues of climate change and the loss of biodiversity are of great concern among both scientists and the public. Scientists have only recently begun to realize the weight of their potential influence on policymaking. They are thus learning how to communicate their research findings and theories to make impressions on the public. A side effect of this interaction is that scientists are becoming increasingly used for political purposes. Previously, a media network would use a scientist to further clarify or explain a technical or scientific phenomenon, however it is often the case now that a scientist is intentionally interviewed when they reject the seemingly more mainstream interpretation of data. Whether this is done specifically by the media to generate controversy, and thus, publicity, or is instead the concentrated effort of parties or businesses that stand to gain or suffer monetarily by bolstering or diminishing such data interpretations remains to be determined. Perhaps the only certain outcome of such controversies is that this type of opposition delays action in terms of policymaking.

Human-Induced Global Climate Change and Further Climate Change

Today, the climate change debate mostly focuses on whether it is specifically **human activities** that have wrought **changes in our world climate**; in other words, is mankind directly responsible for causing the change in global temperature and thus directly responsible for implementing choices to counteract the impact of its actions. For example, the United Nations Intergovernmental Panel on Climate Change, a multinational group of the world's leading environmental scientists, has documented increases in the average tidal levels, increasing temperatures at ground level, concentrations of greenhouse gases in the atmosphere, glaciers whose ice is melting, explorations of the Arctic ice core, and so forth. Based on this data, this panel has made predictions of variations in patterns of weather and temperatures in the near future. They believe these variations to be directly caused by emissions from human use of fossil fuels. These foremost scientists state that the climate likely will change dramatically within 50-100 years, almost completely due to human actions and their impact on the natural environment.

Example of Human Activity Destroying a Place where a Society of People Lives

A common argument presented by climate change advocates is melting **polar ice**, resulting in "sea-rise." This means that the sea level is becoming higher as the melted ice adds to the total volume of water in the oceans. A concrete example of the effects of sea-rise is that some **atolls** and/or islands in the tropical Pacific which are low-lying are threatened by the rising sea level. The encroaching salt water is destroying the people's crops and killing the trees that they use to build their homes. The tribal society of people living on these atolls will have to relocate to another island that has higher ground before their own land actually sinks beneath the ocean. While some people deny the reality or import of climate change, such concrete evidence—that an entire population's native habitat can simply vanish in short order—confirms that the environment is, at least, changing in ways previously unseen, and it is important for mankind to determine how it will respond to these changes as they come.

Recent Environmental Disasters

In 2010, the BP Oil company's Deepwater Horizon oil rig exploded, causing a massive **oil spill** that spread for miles and had far-reaching effects of environmental devastation that evidence suggests are still causing ramifications to this day. Fish, seals, and all forms of marine life were destroyed, fishermen's livelihoods were ruined, people lost their homes, and there were many more grave consequences. Despite public outcry, oil companies continue to pressure the government to allow unsafe drilling. On the one-year anniversary of the devastating explosion, another incident occurred. A gas-well used for **fracking**—the popular name for hydraulic fracturing to release natural gas underground—in Pennsylvania blew out, spilling toxic chemicals. (Fracking fluid contains 596 such chemicals.) These contaminated a local stream and farmland and required home evacuations. While the amount of oil spills and fracking related incidents does seem to be on a downward trend in recent years, there are still numerous occurrences each year that have devastating effects.

Managing Natural Resources for Our Benefit

Human enterprises, such as diverting water to provide farming irrigation and domestic water supplies, can be important for human well-being yet environmentally undesirable. For example, an irrigation company proposed to rebuild its dam inside a protected wilderness to meet federal safety standards. Environmental groups argued that the company should find alternatives using "traditional skills" including non-motorized, non-mechanized methods instead of the helicopters and heavy machinery it proposed to use, which would significantly damage the character of the wilderness. The groups pointed out that the dam was built without machines, and updated safety standards would not prohibit non-mechanized methods. They called for an **Environmental Assessment** and an **Environmental Impact Statement**, including minimum safety requirements, addressing the law regarding water storage capacity, clarifying the dam's hazard rating, etc. The environmental organizations have also offered help to the owner company in finding and applying alternatives.

Conflicting Efforts to Preserve Environmental Systems

One way to supply renewable energy is to use **wind power** rather than only fossil fuels. However, when large, powerful wind turbines are proposed to be built too close to wilderness, their noise, vibrations, and appearance directly interfere with objectives for preserving and maintaining natural areas, threatening public and wildlife health. For example, in 2012, a large-scale wind turbine project proposed in a national forest was protested by an environmental group because it would affect a protected wilderness area and set a negative precedent. The group supported its protest by showing that information given by the US Forest Service was outdated and not based on complete, objective information, because the preparer was not independent as regulations mandate and had a conflict of interest. They also found the project would not meet Forest Service regulations' goals and would not comply with federal and state regulations for water quality standards and dam safety or the national forest's land management plan.

Enacting Legislation to Protect and Restore Environmental and Public Health

While the US federal government has passed laws **regulating** our treatment of the environment and setting standards, our individual states can also do much to regulate activities affecting the environment. This not only helps the natural environment and public health within each state, but also influences the whole country to follow suit. For example, the state of California recently passed a new law that will require utility companies to derive 100% of their energy from clean and renewable sources, like sun and wind, by the year 2045. This requirement will reduce harmful emissions, slow the progression of climate change, make the air cleaner, and create new jobs to help workers and the economy. The law constitutes one of the most aggressive renewable energy requirements in the country. It establishes a precedent for other states and the federal government to follow.

Environmentalist Groups' Opposition of Coal Technology for Energy

Environmental groups are opposed to the use of **coal technology** because it releases many toxins into our air and water, including mercury. Environmental protection agencies find that thousands of babies are born annually with elevated mercury levels, which have been correlated with increased incidences of developmental disabilities in children. Many energy utility companies are currently interested in updating existing coal plants and/or building new ones. However, environmental organizations find through research that the millions of dollars this would cost are not a worthwhile expenditure, due to the long-term financial commitment and costs to our environment, our public health, and our economy caused by this outdated technology. Their analyses find that by increasing **energy efficiency** and using more **renewable sources** such as solar and wind energy, nearly all coal plants could be replaced within twenty years. This would save lives, slow down climate change, and decrease consumers' energy costs.

US Power Plant Emissions

Power plants in America source half of their energy from **coal**. The emissions from coal-fired power plants include arsenic, lead, mercury, and many other poisonous air pollutants. Death, respiratory illnesses like asthma, and developmental disabilities in children are all attributed to this **air**

pollution. Historically, there have not been any legal regulations in the US to control power plants' emissions. However, the **EPA** has developed such regulation with laws such as the Disposal of Coal Combustion Residuals (CCR) that is continually updated and amended. The EPA holds public hearings in key cities, allowing people to voice their concerns. Environmental organizations enlist members' support by informing them of and encouraging their attendance at these hearings, where they can testify and submit comments supporting the EPA's proposal.

Using Factual Data to Fight Industrial Destruction of the Environment

Environmental organizations can not only cite predicted environmental damage by an industrial project, but moreover can conduct **research** demonstrating whether such activity is even justified. For example, when environmental authorities approved plans for a giant hydroelectric facility on two of the wildest rivers in Chile, an environmental organization reported this project would flood thousands of acres of wilderness, endangering many complex ecosystems, and that its power line would cut through national parks, protected areas, and more than a thousand private communities. They moreover conducted a technical study proving that projects already approved would supply more than enough energy for future needs. The majority of the public opposed and has protested voting for such construction. By exposing shortcomings in the project's environmental review, activists delayed the vote for years before it was finally rejected in 2014.

Effect of Federal Legislation and Mining Activities on Drinking Water Quality

The growing **mining industry** in America had caused so much water pollution in the past that by the 1970s, many lakes and rivers were closed to swimming, fishing, and drinking. In response, Congress passed the **Clean Water Act** in 1972 by an overwhelming majority, prohibiting mining and other industries from dumping waste directly into bodies of water. In 2002, lawmakers invented a different definition of "fill material," allowing coal miners to dump waste from blowing up mountaintops into streams. In 2004, they enlarged this loophole, later referred to as the Halliburton loophole, to include dumping toxic wastewater (from chemically extracting metals from ores) into streams, lakes, and wetlands. Recent high prices for gold and other metals have stimulated a mining boom, exacerbating the problem. Environmental groups are campaigning for stronger mining regulations to protect the world's fresh water. Legislation has been and continues to be proposed and ratified to attempt to further regulate toxic waste disposal, with the FRAC Act being one of the most recent.

Green Revolution

The Green Revolution began in 1945 with the development of **agricultural technologies** that aimed to improve the agricultural output of Mexico; these techniques were eventually diffused to regions all over the globe. The technologies that spawned the **Green Revolution** involved the breeding of new plant varieties and the application of modern farming practices, which included the heavy use of pesticides and fertilizers, irrigation methods, and machines to increase crop output. The techniques introduced during the Green Revolution did produce higher yields and decrease dependence on human labor in agriculture. However, the disadvantages of these techniques include decreased biodiversity (as fewer varieties of crops are produced), decreased crop quality (including health value), and the detrimental health effects of agricultural chemicals on plant, animal, and human life.

Influence of Topography on Climate

The **physical features** of a landmass have a significant influence on the climate. For instance, there are distinct climate patterns on the alternate sides of a mountain range. The windward side of a mountain, which in the United States is typically the western side, will have more precipitation. The leeward side, on the other hand, is arid and less cloudy. The dry valleys that extend out from the eastern side of mountain ranges in the United States are often said to have a rain shadow. The formation of clouds is affected by mountains as well. As air is forced up by mountains, it cools and forms clouds. This is why the tops of mountain ranges are frequently misty or cloudy. Bodies of water also affect climate. Water heats and cools more slowly than land, so places where air arrives from over a body of water will also have less-extreme variations in temperature.

Effect of Human Behavior on the Climate

Leaving aside the debate over whether climate change is a direct result of fossil-fuel combustion, there are numerous other ways in which **human behavior influences the climate**. Urban areas are warmer and drier than nearby areas, because the asphalt absorbs heat. Also, sewer and storm water drainage systems remove standing water from the terrain, so heat that otherwise would be evaporating water instead is absorbed by the land. Industrial facilities and large numbers of automobiles also affect the climate. Smokestacks and exhaust pipes emit tiny particulates and water vapor, which encourage the development of clouds downwind. This phenomenon is assisted by the natural heat of cities. It is typical for the area immediately downwind from a large city to have more cloud coverage and precipitation than would otherwise be expected.

Natural Resources

A **resource** is something valued by humans for its role in survival. A **natural resource** is a naturally occurring material (such as water, soil, minerals, or animals) that humans use to maintain their existences. Such resources are unevenly distributed across the globe; their monetary values vary with scarcity, technology, and specific human needs. For example, petroleum became much more valuable after the invention of automobiles, which require the substance to operate. Some natural resources are renewable, meaning that they are constantly being replenished in nature. Energy from the Sun, water, and soil are all renewable resources. **Nonrenewable resources** are those of which Earth has a limited supply. Fossil fuels such as coal and oil take millions of years to form in Earth's crust; therefore, once humans exhaust the current supply of these resources, no more will be naturally available in our lifetimes. Most natural resources (renewable or nonrenewable) are used to provide energy to fuel modern industry.

Distribution of Resources

Resources are not evenly distributed across the globe. Fossil fuels, for example, form over millions of years (under specific natural conditions) from the remains of fossilized plants and animals. Even renewable resources such as water are not equally distributed. Certain global regions experience droughts while others withstand deluges of rain. The **uneven distribution of natural resources** affects the locations and sizes of human settlements, the quality of life in those settlements, and the economic activities in which certain people can participate. A lack of resources in an area may lead to mass migration to an area with a larger supply or to the formation of trade networks with countries possessing higher quantities of a particular resource.

Earth's Physical Systems and Human Involvement in Those Systems

Each of the people who live on Earth has several basic needs, including food, water, and shelter. The planet's **physical systems** provide many natural resources (those that may be used by humans to meet a need), such as timber for building shelter, rainwater to drink, and plants and animals that may be consumed by humans. However, **human involvement** in these systems may be detrimental to their function. For example, high levels of human activity (including logging and the clearing of land for agricultural purposes, such as crop cultivation and animal grazing) are threatening rainforest ecosystems in low-latitude areas. When humans eliminate portions of a rainforest for their own purposes, the delicate balance between native plants and animals is damaged, sometimes irreparably. With increasing awareness of the threat to Earth's natural resources, some nations have created restrictions on their acceptable use. If the harvesting of natural resources for human use is practiced in small amounts with minimal use of dangerous chemicals, a balance may be achieved between Earth's physical and human systems.

Neolithic Revolution

The Neolithic Revolution, one of two eras of change that altered human life and its relationship with the environment, began approximately 10,000 years ago. Prior to this time, humans subsisted by hunting animals and gathering native plants for food. With the onset of the **Neolithic Revolution** (which probably began in the Middle East), people began to domesticate plants and animals. They started practicing agriculture (cultivating and storing certain plants for food) and herding (taming and raising animals specifically for human use). These developments allowed groups of people to settle in one area, rather than roaming the land in search of their basic needs. They irrigated lands and built stable, permanent shelters of wood. With stable sources of food, shelter, and clothing, populations began to expand. People had more time to practice other activities, which often bred technological advancements. Individual members of societies began to specialize in, for example, pottery creation or leatherwork. Increasing specialization eventually produced vast civilizations, which influenced the world as humans know it today.

Altering Average Surface Temperatures Through Human Activity

Humans change Earth's surface for reasons other than those which are agriculturally motivated. For example, the building of cities involves the elimination of native vegetation as well as the pavement of large sections of land (which effectively covers natural, usually moist soils). This, in turn, prevents naturally occurring plants from practicing transpiration. It also concentrates solar heat at the surface, since there are no leafy trees to intercept and diffuse the energy. Materials such as concrete and stone repel rainwater and absorb and trap heat. Thus, the net effect of city building is the production of an **urban heat island**. Air temperatures in a city are often several degrees higher than the temperatures of surrounding suburban or rural areas. The absence of heat-mediating plants and soils, taken with the high instance of heat-absorbing materials, creates an area in which air temperatures do not drop immediately with the sunset; heat collected during the day remains in the region after nightfall.

Water, Fisheries, and Forests

The United States contains abundant **water resources**. There are massive freshwater lakes, rivers and streams, and underground water tables to supply all the water needed for industry, agriculture, and consumption. Americans use about 450 billion gallons of water every day. The majority of this water is used for irrigation or steam power plants. There are also plentiful supplies of fish in the nation's waterways, though these supplies are being threatened by overfishing. The species most commonly drawn from the Pacific are cod, halibut, tuna, and salmon. The Atlantic Ocean supplies abundant cod, flounder, herring, lobsters, and other shellfish. The Gulf of Mexico is known for its abundant supplies of oysters and shrimp.

Mining

The United States ranks only behind Saudi Arabia and Russia in the production of **petroleum**, and only behind China in the extraction of **coal**. The largest deposits of petroleum are in Alaska, California, Louisiana, New Mexico, Oklahoma, and Texas. The most productive coal mines are in the Appalachian Mountains, particularly in Pennsylvania, Kentucky, and West Virginia. Some of the other products that are lucratively mined in the United States are copper, gold, cement, clay, granite, iron ore, zinc, salt, and sand. There are mining operations in virtually every state, though mountainous regions remain the most heavily mined.

Agriculture

Massive improvements in **agricultural technology** have reduced the energy and manpower required for American agriculture, even while increasing the overall yields. American farms grow enough to feed every American with some left over for the rest of the world. Indeed, about a quarter of American farm income comes from exports. The most lucrative product of American farms is beef cattle. These profitable animals are primarily raised on massive ranches in the West. Dairy cattle operations are more likely to be found in the northern states, primarily in a strip extending from New York to Minnesota. The other major crops and livestock in the United States are milk, chickens, eggs, corn, soybeans, wheat, hogs, and cotton.

Mineral Resources and Soil

The rise of the United States to global prominence was due in large part to the abundance of natural resources. With regard to **minerals**, the United States has significant deposits of coal, iron ore, natural gas, and petroleum. However, the enormous energy needs of the nation require it to import still more petroleum and iron. There are also large mining operations based on the extraction of gold, lead, sulfur, zinc, and silver. The **soil** of the United States is for the most part exceptionally fertile, particularly in the Midwest and South. There is a nutrient-rich, thin soil called **loess** that makes farming possible in Washington State. The Mississippi River brings a rich soil known as **alluvium** to the region around the Gulf of Mexico.

Modes of Transportation in the United States

The United States has one of the highest per-capita rates of **automobile ownership** in the world, as well as a vast network of roads and highways to accommodate all those drivers. For every four Americans, there are three automobiles. There are also approximately 50,000 miles of federal interstate highway, many of them built during the Eisenhower administration. A little more than a quarter of all commercial freight moves in trucks. The leading freight carrier, however, remains the **rail system**. Though only about 1% of passenger traffic takes place on the rails, close to 40% of commercial shipping is done on railroads. Another 15% of freight moves over **water**, whether across Great Lakes or along rivers like the Mississippi, Arkansas, and Ohio. Boats can reach the inner parts of the United States from the Atlantic Ocean by means of the Saint Lawrence Seaway. The busiest ports in the United States are New Orleans, Houston, and New York.

Environmental Ethics vs. Frontier Ethics

In contrast to the frontier ethic, which assumes unlimited resources for unlimited growth potential, an **environmental ethic** is becoming more popular. It assumes that Earth's resources are limited, and that rather than being managers of their natural environment, humans are a part of it. Thus, human activities such as uncontrolled use of natural resources can harm the natural world, and such activities are restricted under the environmental ethic. A **sustainable ethic** is a type of environmental ethic. It proposes that humans need to utilize and conserve our planet's natural resources to enable their future ongoing use. Also, the sustainable ethic maintains that if a natural ecosystem is harmed, human beings will in turn suffer from harm, because they are viewed as being a part of the natural environment.

Anthropocentric and Biocentric Approaches to Sustainable Environment

Anthropocentric approaches are human-centered and consider only human needs. **Biocentric approaches** are life-centered and consider ecological needs. Since sustainable ethics consider human populations part of their ecosystems, practices causing ecological damage must also cause damage to the humans inhabiting them. Sustainable ethics may be anthropocentric or biocentric. For example, relative to an oil shortage, an anthropocentric sustainable ethic would regard oil as human property and focus on the conservation and wise use of oil to further its availability to posterity. Conversely, a biocentric sustainable ethic would be more likely to seek alternative, renewable energy sources, such as solar energy, wind energy, water energy, and biomass energy instead of depleting the limited oil. A main difference is that anthropocentric sustainable ethics concentrate on extending the future access to a limited natural resource, while biocentric sustainable ethics concentrate on controlling the use of limited natural resources to prevent environmental damage and hence, human damage.

VARYING ETHICAL CODES AFFECTING THE ENVIRONMENT

Ethical codes are based on standards of conduct that differentiate between right and wrong behaviors. However, these vary across people and situations; there is no universally agreed upon code of ethics. For example, an impoverished small farmer might be considered justified by some in clearing a portion of rainforest land for planting crops to support his family; others more concerned with the effects of deforestation on climate change and soil erosion would consider his action unjustified. A society's ethics are typically based on the ethics of the majority of the society's individuals. The **frontier ethic** is anthropocentric, considering only human needs, assuming resources are unlimited and/or depleted resources can be replaced or substituted. Historically, European settlers exhausted natural resources in eastern America and then expanded westward to fresh resources. Currently, proponents of the frontier ethic believe outer space is the next frontier. Opponents find this unrealistic, as terrestrial population growth would exceed extraterrestrial colonization rates. However, additional resources could be obtained from space.

PRINCIPLES OF A SUSTAINABLE ENVIRONMENTAL ETHICS

Sustainable ethics espouse principles including the following: The planet Earth's natural resources are limited in their amounts. Human beings must conserve our finite natural resources. Humans also have to share Earth's natural resources with the planet's other living things. Human beings are a part of nature. Human beings are also subject to natural laws. Growth is a process that is not sustainable. Moreover, a key guiding principle of the sustainable environmental ethic is that human beings and their endeavors are the most successful when they cooperate with nature, work in harmony with nature, and protect and preserve the integrity of natural environmental processes.

LAND ETHIC

The land ethic is an environmental ethic that is sustainable and **biocentric** (life-centered) rather than **anthropocentric** (human-centered). Human beings are seen as one part of an ethical framework. Including the land in this ethical framework constitutes the land ethic. This was originated by **Aldo Leopold**, the American philosopher and wildlife natural historian. Leopold proposed that humans have always viewed land as property, comparable to the ancient Greeks viewing slaves as property. Leopold found mistreating the land, like mistreating slaves, economically and morally irrational. He wrote: "The land ethic simply enlarges the boundary of the community to include soils, waters, plants, and animals; or collectively, the land. In short, a land ethic changes the role of Homo sapiens from conqueror of the land-community to plain member and citizen of it. It implies respect for his fellow members, and also respect for the community as such." (Aldo Leopold, *A Sand County Almanac*, 1949)

TYPES OF CONSERVATIONISTS

According to Aldo Leopold, who first proposed the land ethic, conservationists of one type see the soil as a **commodity**, while the other type sees the soil as **biota** with diverse functions. For example, in forestry terms, conservationists, seeing soil as a commodity, would plant as many trees as possible; conservationists, seeing soil as biota, would work instead to preserve the natural ecosystem as much as possible. In the **land ethic**, all components of the natural environment are respected regardless of utility/lack thereof. Many species with no human economic worth are vital parts of working ecosystems. Removing them would unbalance and could destroy ecosystems. Leopold insisted that economic necessity was an insufficient basis for the conservation movement. Land-ethic-based decisions promote **biological stability**. As Leopold wrote, "Anything is right when it tends to preserve the integrity, stability, and beauty of the biotic community. It is wrong when it tends to do otherwise." (*A Sand County Almanac*, 1949)

UTILITARIAN CONSERVATION VS. PRESERVATION

Utilitarian conservationists believe in conserving natural resources for the public good, while **preservationists** believe in saving the wilderness for its own value. For example, California's Yosemite is a protected National Park. However, after the 1906 San Francisco earthquakes caused fires destroying much of the city, many residents were in favor of damming the Hetch Hetchy Valley in Yosemite to create a dependable water supply. President Teddy Roosevelt and his Chief Forester, Gifford Pinchot, advocated the dam. John Muir, founder of the Sierra Club, opposed it. Though the preservationists lost the conflict when Congress voted in 1913 to dam the valley, they nevertheless influenced America to rethink its traditional values: by 1916, Congress had passed the National Park System Organic Act, decreeing that our public parks must be preserved undamaged for posterity.

SHARED BELIEFS IN THE EARLY 20TH CENTURY

Conservationists in general believed in conserving our natural resources, regarding them as finite. As such, both utilitarian and preservationist conservationists rejected the first belief of the frontier ethic, that our natural resources and our growth potential were unlimited. However, **utilitarian conservationists** accepted other principles of frontier ethics, including using natural resources for human purposes without regard for consequences. **Preservationists** rejected these; since humans were part of the ecology, ecological harm would cause human harm. Each view is reflected in two quotations: "The fundamental principle of the whole conservation policy is that of use, to take every part of the land and its resources and put it to that use in which it will serve the most people," (US Chief Forester Gifford Pinchot, 1913) and "These temple destroyers, devotees of ravaging commercialism, seem to have a perfect contempt for Nature, and instead of lifting their eyes to the God of the Mountains, lift them to the Almighty Dollar," (John Muir, Sierra Club founder, 1912).

REGULATORY INSTRUMENTS AND ECONOMIC INSTRUMENTS

Regulatory instruments for environmental protection include specific standards, such as emissions limits, quality standards for products, and goals for environmental quality; regulatory powers to order measures for adjustment; license requirements; and obligations of the administration and the industry to monitor environmental outcomes. Many economists find **regulatory instruments** inefficient for not taking into account the varying costs of reducing pollution to various entities, costing more for all without commensurate protective results. They propose using **economic instruments** instead, such as pollution charges and tradable pollution rights. They find these more efficient by allowing businesses the choice of polluting and paying for it, or investing in abating pollution and not paying. However, research finds that administrative agencies are flexible regarding their investment requirements. Research also finds that enforcement agencies have a bargaining advantage through stringent and uniform standards. Additionally, research shows that both regulatory and economic instruments require close monitoring to be effective.

DIFFICULTIES IN ENFORCING LEGAL PROTECTION AGAINST ENVIRONMENTAL RISKS

While there are civil and public laws to protect against environmental risk, one problem inherent in litigating environmental risk is that when a third party is affected by environmental damage, such damage may extend **beyond** the individual. For example, damage could be caused on land that is someone's property, but also involves destroying a biotope that could lead to a whole species' extinction. Another difficulty is when a third party is affected only **indirectly** or **morally**. For example, an area could be deforested and the third parties affected are birdwatchers losing this field. Or pesticide use could contaminate groundwater, and the affected third parties are those who would have used it as a source of drinking water. Legal systems can address these challenges by extending arguments in scope to encompass group issues, and/or permitting groups as well as individuals to defend collective interests. US law requires plaintiffs to be affected in a factual interest and that said interest is protected or regulated by the pertinent law.

Environmental Education

Educational theorists frequently describe **Environmental Education (EE)** with three divisions: in, for, and about the environment. Many subjects in higher education, such as environmental engineering (e.g., dam construction or forestry), recycling education, and environmental politics and management, relate to the study of EE for the environment. Studied separately, this is informative, but it may not influence student beliefs or values or be relevant to real-life issues. EE about the environment is common in secondary schools, exemplified by subjects like geology, biology, physics, etc. While this content is relevant, and its application could forge great connections among students, it is typically taught in isolation. Considering EE's ultimate purpose as developing politically informed, involved persons, all three categories must be taught together. Students must be given environmental knowledge, critical thinking skills, democratic skills, and experience with environmental politics in its daily and long-term processes. Scholars believe teaching the interdisciplinary concept of the "earth system" gives a perspective of humanity within our environment, removing walls between nature and society.

Environmental Issues Becoming Political Issues

Such matters as toxic emissions, global climate change, and the availability of clean water may be considered the concerns of individuals when their effects are limited. However, as their impacts increase to encompass common regional and global spheres, the concern extends to governments and becomes **political**. **Public education** is in a singularly powerful position to teach awareness of environmental impact issues and our capacity as citizens to effect democratic changes to address those issues. Teaching students critical thinking skills is essential generally and will gain specific importance relative to the environment as its problems increase, and both our government and our culture will need to make serious interventions to perpetuate the quality of all life on our planet. Education thus must address not only content knowledge, but the skills of logic and argumentation that allow citizens to make adaptive responses to political demands.

Japanese Events Illustrating Interaction with Unexpected Natural Events

Japan suffered its biggest earthquake ever recorded in 2011, triggering an equally devastating tsunami. Although Japan leads the world in earthquake preparedness and management, the scope of these disasters was so great that it damaged the country's **infrastructure**, compromising **nuclear reactors** at the Fukushima Daiichi nuclear power plant. While scientists were aware of the dangers inherent in nuclear power plants during their construction, the current situation was not likely anticipated. Environmental groups condemned the energy company for not controlling massive radiation emissions and for keeping information secret from authorities and the public for weeks. Some groups also asked the US government to help. The energy company admitted dumping hundreds of tons of radioactive wastewater into the ocean. A Japanese senior nuclear advisor resigned when the Japanese government allowed local elementary school children to be exposed to high radiation levels, for which it also received much public criticism.

New Developments Presenting Additional Threats to the Environment

One of the most common methods of obtaining natural gas from the earth, **hydraulic fracturing**—more commonly known as **fracking**—involves injecting millions of gallons of fracking fluids made up of water, sand, and chemicals into gas wells. The pressure cracks open underground rocks to release natural gas. This procedure is highly controversial for its dangers, including explosions, radioactive wastewater, and contamination of drinking water. Natural gas providers have found a legal loophole to avoid disclosing the numerous fracking chemicals they use. Environmentalist groups, such as Save Our Environment's Food and Water Watch, have asked the public to urge Congress to pass the **FRAC Act**, a law that would close the loophole and enforce compliance with the **Clean Water Act**, which includes requiring energy companies to disclose the chemicals they are pumping into the ground.

Conflicts of Commercial Industrial Activities and the Environmental Damage

In addition to causing explosions, purposefully or accidentally contaminating the supply of drinking water, and generating radioactive wastewater, the process of fracking also appears to be associated with increased **earthquake activity**. Seismologists have been studying the effects of injection wells and the process of fracking in respect to the generation of earthquakes. Studies suggest that not only are earthquakes becoming more frequent as fracking processes increase, but the earthquakes themselves are growing more potent as well. Whereas it was traditionally believed that wastewater injections seemed to be the major culprit in terms of generated seismic activity, studies from various scientists in geologically diverse areas have shown much more direct correlations between earthquakes and the fracking process. Shale gas firms in the Sichuan province of Rongxian, China were instructed to temporarily suspend their operations in response to three earthquakes striking the region in 2019, which killed two people and injured twelve. Despite these incidences, it is unlikely that major reductions of operations are likely to occur.

Example of a Non-Sustainable Energy Damaging the Environment

In May 2011, the Dakota Access **pipeline** spilled thousands of gallons of oil in southeastern North Dakota and had to be shut down. The ruptured pipeline created a gusher of oil six stories high at a pumping station. The oil spray contaminated a neighboring field's soil and water before the gusher could be contained. In only its first year of operation, the pipeline sustained twelve oil spills. Despite this dismal accident rate, an even larger pipeline to move tar sands oil across the US was founded by the same company. The Keystone XL pipeline would transport close to a million barrels of oil a day from Canada to Texas. It would cross several major rivers, a great deal of farmland, and the Ogallala, the country's biggest aquifer. It has been a major point of contention throughout three presidential terms over the course of a decade—having been vetoed twice and reinstated once with about 8% total completion to date.

General Measures Protecting the Environment and Citizens

New offshore oil drilling and development is an activity that demands new **safety requirements** in order to meet the demands of a growing but dangerous industry. Members of the oil industry are known to fight against safety inspections, which are obviously necessary considering the dangerous nature of the operations and the industry's accident records. The Bureau of Safety and Environmental Enforcement issued rules in 2016 that firmly regulated offshore drilling, but were revised in 2019 in order to,"...[correct] errors and [reduce] certain unnecessary regulatory burdens imposed under the existing regulations." When lawmakers try to enable royalties to give public taxpayers fair value in return for the oil industry's use of public lands, industry forces block such endeavors.

Political Conflicts in the USA Over Commercial Oil Interests

One of the frequently recurring battles within legislation is how **subsidies**—financial aid provided to industries by US tax dollars in the form of cash payments or tax incentives or reductions—are to be implemented or restricted when the oil sector is involved. The oil industry accounts for nearly a tenth of the overall Gross Domestic Product of the US. Because of how lucrative and influential these companies are, the idea of how much the government should be involved in helping them maintain such a dominant position in the economic sector is highly contested. Many claim that the government hands out money to "big oil" well beyond anything necessary or fair to keep commodities and services at reasonable rates. Major proponents and lobbyists for the industry claim they pay more than their fair share of the taxes, and that to continually force them to pay more and more will pressure these industries to leave for other countries that would be glad to receive their lucrative industry.

Legislative Proposal to End America's Subsidy of Corn Ethanol

Corn ethanol was introduced as a potential alternative to fossil fuels. However, ethanol production not only causes pollution, it also diverts corn from the food supply, increases food prices, and seems to create more problems than it solves. The Environmental Working Group found ethanol cultivation adds chemicals, depletes soil, contaminates water, and was ineffective at lessening our oil dependence because blends of gasoline with too much ethanol are wholly inefficient. This was all compounded by the fact that our government subsidized ethanol, at taxpayer expense, including a mandate, an import tariff, and refundable tax credits for blending ethanol into gasoline. Congress allowed the subsidies given to the ethanol industry to officially expire in 2012, but the remaining initiatives of the Renewable Fuel Standard (RFS) still remain in effect. Ethanol is still required to be blended with gasoline in order to meet EPA guidelines and the RFS, but the hope is that these policy changes have helped address hunger in a growing world population as well as promote continual research into renewable and clean energy.

Federal Laws Protecting the Natural Quiet in National Parks

When we think of protected national parks, we usually think of protecting concrete features like land, vegetation, water, and wildlife. However, **noise** is also considered a type of pollution that destroys **natural quiet**—an integral part of the national park experience. In 2000, Congress passed the **National Parks Air Tour Management Act** that is still in effect to this day. While commercial air tours allow aerial views of national parks, aircraft noise ruins enjoyment below for visitors in the parks. This law requires tour planes to use quiet-aircraft technology as well as requires the FAA and NPS to maintain and develop Air Tour Management Plans (ATMPs) in order to effectively mitigate adverse effects of commercial air tour operations. The related **1987 Overflight Act** regulates flight of other/non-tour airplanes over national parks. The Grand Canyon, Hawai'i Volcanoes, and Mount Rainier National Parks prepare **environmental impact statements (EIS)** for managing air tours. The National Park Service has an EIS with flight rules for the area around Grand Canyon National Park, and works with the FAA to enforce the Overflight Act and reduce air tours.

Environmental Groups Addressing the Need for Protection of Wildlife

There are some instances where the Fish, Wildlife, and Parks (FWP) Departments want permission from the US Fish and Wildlife Service (FWS) to hunt **endangered animal species** in an area of federally protected public land. Montana is one such state, where the balance between the population of wolves and elk is continuously being shifted because of human action. Conservationists find the elk population is being reduced more by human hunters than natural predation. However, Montana's FWP has continually raised its maximum elk population goals and even implemented wolf bounties to stimulate even more wolf hunting. Its wolf-killing project is regarded as motivated by state hostility against wolves and not in line with objective data by many professional wildlife biologists and former employees of the FWP. These members of the Montana Wildlife Federation have joined together to oppose various policies they believe will ultimately tarnish the image of hunters and hunting in Montana, as well as disturb and damage the **ecosystem**.

Backfiring of Human Conservation Efforts Protecting Wildlife

Sometimes human efforts are well-intentioned, such as conserving a critically endangered wildlife species. Yet these efforts may not foresee the possible unintended **negative environmental impacts** in the methods they use to accomplish their goal. For example, the monarch butterfly population has been steadily decreasing over the past few decades. In an attempt to try and help the population rebound, well-meaning butterfly lovers began planting milkweed—a weed butterflies eat and rely on to breed that has been increasingly eradicated by farmers. What these people did not know, was that the type of milkweed they were planting was actually a non-native species that significantly increased the likelihood that the monarch butterflies would become infected with a deadly parasite. This type of tropical milkweed does not die as easily in the winter as the traditional native species, which means that this milkweed lasts long enough for multiple generations of monarchs to be born on the same plants. This ultimately results in an increase of parasitic spores on the milkweed leaves which then get transferred to caterpillars.

Opinions, Beliefs, or Attitudes on Decisions Affecting the Environment

It is no secret that the **leadership** within a business has the greatest impact on overall business enterprises. When the leaders change, so can the directions of their businesses. Consequently, when major business leaders begin producing more efficient and environmentally conscious products, the industry as a whole can be impacted as well. For example, Tesla, Inc. produced and promoted its solar roof panel technology to mixed reactions from the greater community. However, it continues to innovate and upgrade its technology with great success in a variety of areas. When a major company and its leaders begin establishing a presence of commitment to futurizing energy production or meeting some particular niche, many other companies begin to start advancing and developing products and research to stay relevant and competitive.

Nature Outings

One of the largest environmental organizations in the United States, the **Sierra Club**, is known for originating the idea of "eco-travel" or nature outings. Such outings range from longer trips farther away to local day hikes. Outings are led by trained volunteers. These trips not only afford participants the enjoyment and exploration of nature, and educate them about natural history, wildlife, and conservation; they give them experiences that make them better environmentalists and/or create new environmentalists. For example, the experience of witnessing a giant leatherback sea turtle dig a nest to lay her eggs on a beach in the moonlight creates real motivation to take action against commercial developers who would build on such coastal land, destroying the habitat of endangered species. Actually experiencing nature that could be lost is a more powerful motivator than only learning facts and figures or hearing/reading reports.

Importance of National Forests

America's **public lands** constitute an area the size of Texas (193 million acres). These areas are keeping 20% of federally protected threatened and endangered species alive. Our country's **national forests** include rivers, streams, and lakes that supply clean drinking water to over 20% of American citizens. They also support a great diversity of ecosystems, plants, and wildlife. Many groups, such as the Wilderness Society and Save Our Environment, find the Forest Service's current plan inadequate to protect these resources. They call for strengthening it by the following:

expanding wildlife safeguards; maintaining healthy, sustainable fish and wildlife populations; removing discretion from individual forest managers to abandon the protection of endangered species without public accountability; setting enforceable clean water and healthy watershed standards in national forests; making forest plans congruent with the best science; and maintaining public accountability by keeping the existing 90-day standard for public review and appeal of forest plans.

Importance of Biodiversity

The majority of scientists concur that **biodiversity** is important in terms of several specific aspects. Many recreational activities and tourism industries heavily rely on unique biodiversity. It is important in terms of niche complementarity; the greater the variety of species living in an ecosystem, the more efficiently each of them occupies a niche, job, or function in the system, with fewer or no vacancies. Biodiversity is important in production of crop biomass because greater variety avoids depleting soil of nutrients and provides a more varied diet to consumers, promoting public health. Despite their consensus on the value of these aspects, scientists find it difficult to identify which one is most important in biological management.

Types of Value Attributed to Biodiversity

Biodiversity affords a functional value to natural ecosystems because it sustains **biological, geological, and chemical cycles** (and/or cycles combining all three elements) and keeps these systems stable, protecting them from invasions. It confers a utilitarian value in crop production by making the most efficient use of the resources of land and time. It has a serendipitous value in conferring unexpected salutary benefits, such as the discoveries of medicinal properties in rare plant species as one example. **Biodiversity** also has an intrinsic value in that many traditional cultures regard it as necessary and valuable. Biological and land management are valued by both politicians and public citizens. Public lands offer many physical, psychological, and social benefits to human beings. Additionally, because public lands are publicly managed, they represent a significant investment of taxpayers' dollars. Environmental educators find that because the different values of biodiversity can conflict, managers must strive to achieve a balance among all of them.

Degree of Political Participation in American Society

Public comments and testimony are allowed during open periods between the proposal and the voting on many proposed government bills affecting the environment. Environmental organizations also encourage their members to engage in such **participation**. However, even while members of these groups have influenced legislation with their responses, in general the American public is not that invested in participating in their government, as evidenced by eligible voter percentages in election years. The principles that underlie citizen democracy and "citizen science" are actually quite similar in many respects. Both processes are social, based on some kind of consensus; both demand strong evidence to back them up; both employ models that appear universal, but really are bound by local contexts; and both call for critical thinking skills, especially those related to persuasion and argumentation. Therefore, teaching either citizen democracy or citizen science can significantly inform the other and vice versa.

Rare Earth Elements

For environmentally responsible or green economies to succeed in the United States and globally, we need more access to **rare earth elements (REEs)**. These are minerals used in many of today's technologies, including cell phones, laptop PCs, and military weapons systems and radar, the world's most powerful magnets; and in "green" alternative energy sources, such as wind turbines and electric cars. The USA has been mining and processing only a small fraction of these minerals, while the vast majority of this industry is in China. To supply its own national revolution in "green" technology, **China** is stockpiling its REEs. This allows the Chinese greater control of international prices for these elements, which have risen dramatically over the years. China's monopoly on REEs is a competitive disadvantage to America in the areas of clean energy and defense. American leaders find it also threatens the USA's national security by causing strategic vulnerability.

Responding to Trends and Supporting Environmental Literacy

Too much natural biodiversity has already been lost through the destruction and extinction of plant and animal species. Trends in our societal practices can lead to losing our connections to nature; losing the experiences of addressing natural challenges, which have evolved qualities of leadership and cooperation; and our children losing comprehension of natural cycles of growth and death so we cannot teach them about the origins of their foods. More wilderness and nature will always be needed in our classrooms. Meanwhile, educators can teach students to become engaged with and excited about our environment, teach them information about and care for it, and encourage passion for its cause. Constructing **environmental literacy** builds communities and creates learning opportunities.

Economic Geography

Subdiscipline of Regional Geography

Regional geography is the subdiscipline of geography that involves the study of how human and physical characteristics combine to form **geographic regions**. Geographers use a regional concept to organize Earth's surface into sections based on the presence of at least one shared characteristic. The classification of groups of places into regions enables geographers to examine the associations between historical, cultural, organizational, economic, and environmental factors within a particular region. Geographers then investigate the effects of these associations on that region's development and interrelationships with other regions. Regions may be studied at many levels, from the local to the international.

Review Video: Regional Geography
Visit mometrix.com/academy and enter code: 350378

Impact of Oil Production and Sale on Oil-Exporting Countries

The production of oil and its sale have had significant effects on the countries of the North Africa/Southwest Asia realm that export it. These effects illustrate the impact of trade patterns on participating regions in a number of ways:

- The high demand for oil across the globe creates higher incomes among the populations of oil-exporting countries, which tend to place these countries among those in the upper-middle income category (in contrast to those in peripheral regions of the realm).
- Large oil revenues have led to increased modernization in certain countries.
- Oil-exporting countries have experienced increased industrialization as an effect of oil production and sale.
- Many workers from peripheral areas of the realm migrate to core countries; thus intra-realm migration is an effect of oil.
- Oil-exporting countries also experience inter-realm migration.
- Concentrated oil production in the realm has heightened regional disparities, both economic and cultural.
- Oil-exporting countries of the realm have begun to receive foreign investment, which creates further international relationships.

Geographic Regions

A geographic region is a demarcated area of the Earth. The classification of areas into **geographic regions** is more refined than the classification of realms. A region is a smaller spatial unit than a realm; each realm is subdivided into one or more regions. There are several properties that all regions have in common:

- All regions have **area**. While they are indeed theoretical constructions, regions are materially present in the real world, occupying space on the surface of the globe.
- All regions have **boundaries** that delineate their spatial territories. Like the boundaries of nation-states, regions' boundaries are defined by a synthesis of natural and human factors. They are occasionally rather sharp but generally function more like transition zones. Regional geographers may make use of political boundaries to aid in the designation of regions within realms.
- All regions also have **location**, both absolute and relative. The names of some regions (for example, Equatorial Africa) convey information about their locations.

Formal Geographic Region

A formal geographic region is one that is identified based on physical and/or human characteristics shared throughout the area. In other words, **formal regions** exhibit a high degree of homogeneity or similitude. Formal regions may be based on political or cultural characteristics or physical homogeneity:

- A **political region** is defined by shared governmental/legal systems, as in the cases of states, countries, and cities.
- A **cultural region** is based on population information (including factors such as typical industrial or agricultural production techniques, ethnic heritage, per capita income, or density and distribution). For example, several large American cities include cultural regions characterized by high concentrations of people of Chinese descent practicing their cultural and social traditions, referred to as "Chinatowns."
- **Physical homogeneity** defines a formal region in, for instance, the areas of climate, topology, and vegetation. For instance, the steppe region of Northern Eurasia is typified by temperate grasslands with rich soils.

Functional Geographic Region

A functional geographic region consists of a central node and the surrounding areas affected by it. Often, the focal point and the proximate areas are linked by economic activities such as manufacturing, retail trading, and transportation and communication systems. However, like formal geographic regions, **functional regions** may be identified through the application of several different criteria. The New York metropolitan area provides an example of a functional region. This region includes parts of four states (New York, New Jersey, Connecticut, and Pennsylvania), associated by common media distribution, commuting patterns, and trade flows.

Balance of Trade

The term *balance of trade* refers to the relationship between the values of imported goods and services and exported goods and services. The exchange of raw materials, manufactured goods, agricultural goods, transportation, and travel are all considered in the determination of a country's **balance of trade**. If the value of a country's imports exceeds that of its exports, the balance of trade (the trade deficit) is said to be **negative**. Conversely, if the value of a country's exports is higher than that of its imports, the balance of trade (the trade surplus) is considered **positive**. A nation's balance of trade must be distinguished from its balance of payments; this term covers any international flow of money, including investment income and transfer payments.

TRADE PACTS

A trade pact is a broad agreement between two or more nations that specifies which forms of production and consumption are ideal and which are undesirable. This type of agreement attempts to increase productive efficiency through the facilitation of free trade (the international exchange of goods and services without tariffs or trade barriers, such as import quotas). **Trade pacts** often come under political scrutiny for their roles in increasing economic interdependence between entities or altering traditional economic customs. There are several different types of trade pacts.

TYPES OF TRADE PACTS

Four types of trade pact are the following:

1. A **Trade and Investment Framework Agreement (TIFA)** institutes an agenda aimed at the resolution of conflicts and expansion of trade between two or more nations.
2. A **Bilateral Investment Treaty (BIT)** establishes the requisites for the foreign direct investment of nationals/companies of one state in another.
3. A **preferential trade area** is a group of nations that gives preferential access to particular goods from other countries in the area. A trade pact that identifies this type of agreement usually reduces tariffs without eliminating them.
4. A **free trade area** is a zone whose component states have agreed to do away with trade barriers such as quotas and preferences on most goods exchanged between them.

TRADE BLOCS

A trade bloc is a large free trade area delimited by one or more trade pacts. **Trade blocs** are usually regionally based. Occasionally, a state may act as a member in more than one bloc. For instance, Venezuela is a part of both the Andean Community and the Mercosur trading blocs. Generally, such pacts name formal adjudication panels, such as NAFTA's, which may allow differing degrees of member participation. The European Union, for instance, includes a democratically elected parliament, which acts as a decision-making body. A trade bloc may decide to eliminate visa requirements and (at least theoretically) borders between its member states, enabling free travel in the region. NAFTA and the EU are two of the most active trade blocs on the globe. The Caribbean Community and Common Market (CARICOM) is another active group with a state-like governing structure. There are currently 15 full members of CARICOM. The Economic Community of West African States (ECOWAS) is a regional trade bloc aimed at furthering economic integration among its member states.

STAGES OF ECONOMIC INTEGRATION

The six stages of economic integration are the following:

1. The first stage is the existence of a **preferential trading area**, which is the weakest form of economic integration between economies.
2. The second stage of economic integration is a **free trade area**.
3. The third stage, a **customs union**, is a free trade area whose participating states have agreed upon a common external tariff, which involves the application of the same customs duties, quotas, and preferences on all goods entering the union.

4. The fourth stage of economic integration may be referred to as a **common market** or a single market. A single market exists when all states in a customs union share common policies on product regulation, and when all factors of production (goods, services, labor, and capital) move freely between them.
5. The fifth stage is the creation of an **economic and monetary union**, a single market with a common currency.
6. **Complete economic integration** is reached when integrated units have no individual control over economic policy. Complete economic integration is more common within countries than in supranational organizations.

Intensive and Extensive Agriculture

Intensive agriculture or **intensive farming** is a type of agricultural production system that involves the use of high levels of chemical inputs, such as fertilizers, pesticides, and growth regulators, on relatively small plots of land to maximize the output of that land. This method of agricultural production is associated with modern farming techniques, including mechanization. While the use of intensive farming techniques can assist in the maintenance of a stable food supply, it often occurs at the expense of the environment. For example, the clearing of land eliminates local vegetation and therefore the natural habitat of the area's fauna, and can lead to soil erosion. Also, the use of chemicals creates pollution, which may affect the local ecosystem and the area's water supply.

Extensive agriculture, in contrast, involves the production of crops over large areas of low-cost land without the use of pesticides and fertilizers. While this type of agricultural production is not harmful to the environment, it cannot produce crops at the same volume as intensive agriculture.

Agrarian Revolution

The term *agrarian revolution* is used to refer to the period of transformation of agricultural production methods in Europe from the 16th to mid-19th centuries. These improvements enabled European farmers to sustain a rapidly growing population during this time. The resultant increase in urbanization and growing markets served as impetuses for improved organization of land ownership and agrarian activities, in the forms of land enclosure and consolidated farmland; higher crop prices encouraged farmers to move from subsistence levels of agricultural production to production for a capitalist market. Other advancements included the introduction of new crops (such as potatoes from the Americas) in the realm, crop rotation (which increased the variety and amount of crops produced and also improved the quality of the soil), and the improvement of storage and distribution systems. The products of the later **Industrial Revolution** contributed to the ongoing process of agricultural advancement. Ultimately, the agrarian revolution marked the development of improved agricultural practices that eventually diffused throughout the realm and world.

Geographic Realm of Europe

The geographic realm of Europe is made up of five geographic regions: Western Europe, the British Isles, Northern Europe, Southern (Mediterranean) Europe, and Eastern Europe. It is home to one of the largest population clusters in the world. Despite the relatively small size of its territory, Europe's people and their actions have affected (and continue to affect) all the world's realms. Technological innovations, political revolutions, and vast empires have influenced the behaviors of people on each continent. European colonial endeavors have established communities and impacted the formation of ideologies the world over. Europe's natural and human resources have helped the realm to survive and grow throughout the years. For approximately the last 50 years, Europe has been engaged in a unification program known as the **European Union**. Currently, 27 of the realm's 48 nation-states are members of the Union.

General Economic Geography of Europe

The **economy of Europe** is dominated by the **European Union**, which, if considered as a whole, has the largest economy in the world. Though the functional region of Western Europe has historically been the hub of economic activity in the realm, this situation is changing with the development of other core regions, productive complementarities, and interregional/international trade markets. Levels of economic development tend to decline as one moves from west to east across the realm; this too is changing with the growth of the economies of former member countries of the Soviet Union and their increasing interactions with other regions and realms. Europe's agricultural and fishing sectors are highly developed and still center on Western Europe. Europe's manufacturing sector is also quite developed. While many of the realm's industries are concentrated in Western Europe, deindustrialization in the region has resulted in the outsourcing of labor to areas such as Eastern Europe and China. Financial activity in the realm is concentrated in several cities, with London as the largest.

Geographic Realm of Russia

Russia, the largest territorial state on Earth, is an example of a geographic realm that has undergone tremendous amounts of change throughout its existence. Tsars conquered and dominated Russian territory, which was subsequently inhabited by Soviets, who then shaped the domain and its peoples into the Soviet Union. Though World War II tested the empire, it also validated the USSR's status as a global superpower, which it retained until the late 1980s. Internal factors (such as mismanagement of a communist government) and external factors (including the Second World War, pressure from anti-communist leaders, and the global decline of colonialism) eventually led to the dissolution of the Soviet Union in 1991. Consequent cultural, economic, and social diversity have given rise to the establishment of **four geographical regions** (each of which contains subregions): the Russian Core, the Eastern Frontier, Siberia, and the Far East.

General Economic Geography of Russia

The economic geography of Russia is highly varied and is characterized by discrete core and peripheral regions of **economic activity**. Despite the presence of substantial natural resources (such as gas and oil) and a well-educated labor force, the effects of the transition from a failed centrally planned economy during the Soviet Era to a free market continue to hinder the development of the economies in certain regions. In the agricultural sector, production has decreased drastically with attempts at the privatization of collective farms and restructuring of the economy. Also, the harsh climate in the realm has had an effect on agricultural production. The levels of meat, milk, vegetables, and grains have decreased yearly since 1989. This has had negative ramifications in a country that is largely dependent on its own food production. The inefficiencies and inadequacies held over from the Soviet Union continue to disturb Russia's industrial sector, particularly in the extraction of raw materials and the distribution of goods. Still, Russia is the most industrialized of all the former Soviet republics.

Geographic Realm of North America

The geographic realm of North America is home to two countries, Canada and the United States (which is currently considered a global superpower). This realm is characterized by **pluralistic (diverse) societies** which, unfortunately, are often plagued by **social inequalities**. It is also a **postindustrial realm**, which means that the economies of Canada and the United States each experienced increases in the amount of available information technology and rapid expansions of the tertiary (service) sector of industry after the industrialization processes in those countries. The eight regions of North America (many of which stretch across the US-Canada boundary) are largely differentiated by differences in the various economic activities practiced in different areas. These regions include the Continental Core, the South, the Southwest, the West Coast, the Agricultural Heartland, French Canada, the New England/Maritime Provinces, and the Marginal Interior.

General Economic Geography of Canada

As one of the world's wealthiest nations, **Canada** has a largely **postindustrial economy**, with employment concentrated in the **service sector** (particularly retail). However, unlike many developed countries, primary economic activities (specifically logging and oil production) are important aspects of the country's economy. Canada has a large and varied (though regionally variable) supply of natural resources, such as oil, nickel, and lead. Canadian agricultural products (especially wheat and grains) are exported in high levels to the United States, Europe, and East Asia. Another unusual aspect of Canada's economy (as compared to those of other highly developed nations) is the historical secondary status of the manufacturing sector of industry. Though it is certainly not unimportant, manufacturing has never been as vital to the nation's economy as primary or tertiary activities. Many of Canada's industrial firms are branches of US companies. Regional disparities in wealth and economy strength have increased regionalism throughout the region.

General Economic Geography of the United States

As a current superpower, the **United States** has one of the most advanced economies in the world. Like Canada, the United States contains many deposits of **natural resources**. For instance, the North American realm has more coal reserves than any other. The spatial organization of regional agricultural production in the United States exists within the framework of a modified Von Thunen model, with the "megalopolis" of New England at its center and belts of specialized activity extending westward. Though the **manufacturing** sector is less important in a postindustrial economy, this type of activity is still practiced in the United States and tends to cluster around several urban-industrial nodes, especially within the Manufacturing Belt (located in the Northeast United States). Increased mechanization and advancements in technology have eliminated many "blue-collar" jobs in this region. Most laborers in the US workforce are employed in **quaternary economic activity**. States offering noneconomic amenities (such as weather and proximity to urban centers and universities) have experienced higher levels of growth than other regions.

Geographic Realm of Central America

The geographic realm of Central America, which is sometimes referred to as **Middle America**, covers the territory between southern North America and the boundary between Panama and Colombia. The exact demarcations of the realm vary from source to source; however, the economic subregion recognized by the United Nations includes all mainland states of North America south of the US-Mexico border in the realm. Basically, this definition counts Mexico and Belize as members of the Central America realm, while other definitions assign these countries to the North American realm. Due to the influence of Spanish and Portuguese colonialism in Central America, this realm and South America are often jointly referred to as **Latin America**. Central America is divided into four regions: Mexico, the seven states of Central America (Belize, Costa Rica, El Salvador, Guatemala, Honduras, Nicaragua, and Panama), the larger islands of the Caribbean (the Greater Antilles), and the smaller islands of the Caribbean (the Lesser Antilles).

General Economic Geography of Central America

The economic geography of Central America includes the least developed territories in the Americas, with the exception of Mexico. Under the **Mainland-Rimland framework**, Central America is divided into a **Euro-Amerindian Mainland** (made up of mainland Middle America from Mexico to Panama, excluding parts of the Caribbean coast) and a **Euro-African rimland** (consisting of the coastal zone and the Caribbean islands). Economic activity on the Mainland has historically been oriented around **haciendas** (privately owned estates maintained more for prestige and self-sufficiency than maximum production), and is therefore less dependent on trade with other nations. Governmental and social pressures have led to the forced specialization of productive activity in or the parceling out of haciendas in this area. The Rimland's economy has traditionally focused on **plantation production**, characterized by efficient production of one crop specifically for export and the importation of labor. The Rimland's economy is thus more dependent on the fluctuating global market. Plantation systems, like hacienda systems, continue to metamorphose under internal and external pressures; still, their effects remain visible in the region.

Geographic Realm of South America

The geographic realm of South America is made up of four regions: Brazil, the Northeastern countries, the West, and the Southern Cone. South America and Central America are often collectively referred to as **Latin America**, due to the enduring cultural and social influences of former Spanish and Portuguese colonial presences in these areas. These influences are most visible in the languages, architecture, music, and visual arts of the peoples of South America. Roman Catholicism and traditional systems relating to land ownership, also transmitted from European countries, continue to be major factors in the evolution of South American societies. In addition, the cultural practices and beliefs of Native Americans have been and continue to be vital shaping forces in the realm.

General Economic Geography of South America

The economic geography of South America is characterized by high levels of regional disparity. In many of the realm's countries (such as Brazil, Bolivia, and Venezuela), the richest 20% of the population may control over 60% of the nation's wealth, while the poorest 20% may own less than 5% of that wealth. Although several South American nations have become involved in the mining of oil, coal, and valuable minerals in high amounts, the realm's main economic focus is **agriculture**. The South American realm is unusual, because subsistence farming and commercial farming exist side by side; generally, a geographic realm is dominated by one or the other. **Commercial farmers** in this area tend to be involved in cattle ranching, wheat farming, grain farming (in a "Corn Belt" zone similar to that in the United States), or plantation-type agriculture. Commercial agricultural endeavors tend to be located near the coasts of the South American continent, with small pockets of activity in the interior. **Subsistence-level farming** takes place on all other arable land.

Geographic Realm of North Africa/Southwest Asia

The size and geographic diversity of the geographic realm of North Africa/Southwest Asia have spawned a number of different labels for the region, none of which are completely satisfactory. These labels include the Islamic realm, the Arab World, the dry world, and Afrasia. Though Islam and aridity do dominate the religious and climatic aspects of the realm, that domination is not complete, and the heterogeneity within these groups alone problematizes the notion of referring to the realm by a single characteristic. The use of relative location is seen as less divisive. The **North Africa realm** is composed of three regions (Egypt, North Africa, and the Southwest), and **Southwest Asia** is composed of four (the Middle East [this label is also disputed, due to what some see as the pejorative connotations of the term], the Arabian Peninsula, the North, and the East).

Mesopotamia

Mesopotamia, a major historic culture hearth, is located in the Tigris-Euphrates lowland, from the northern edge of the Persian Gulf to present-day Turkey. **Mesopotamia** (literally the "land between the rivers") was an area of fertile alluvial soils and plentiful sunshine and water. This zone saw the development of **advanced farming techniques**, such as planned sowing and harvesting, irrigation, and the distribution of surplus crops for later consumption. Unfortunately for residents of the realm, much of the area's land is now **desert**; this climate change is thought to be related to glacial recession in the late Pleistocene era. However, this realm is still home to the Nile and the fertile Tell Atlas mountain range area (the northern coast of Morocco, Algeria, and Tunisia).

General Economic Geography of North Africa/Southwest Asia

The economic geography of the realm of North Africa/Southwest Asia is primarily **agricultural**. Though much of the fertile farmland associated with Mesopotamia and the Fertile Crescent (another ancient culture hearth characterized by its advanced agricultural activity) has dried up, many residents of this realm continue to produce resilient crops (particularly cereals), mostly at subsistence levels. Another important aspect of the economic geography of this realm is the vast **oil reserves** located on the southern Arabian Peninsula, in North Africa, and near the Caspian Sea. While oil is considered one of the most important natural resources on our planet, its presence in North Africa/Southwest Asia has improved the quality of life for only a small portion of the population. This realm exhibits a large gap between the rich and the poor.

Geographic Realm of Sub-Saharan Africa

The geographic realm of Sub-Saharan Africa is composed of the territory between the southern border of the Sahara Desert and the southernmost coast of the country of South Africa. The boundary between the North Africa realm and the Sub-Saharan realm is a prime example of a **transition zone**; several states straddle this hypothetical divide. This area of the globe constitutes a fairly distinctive cultural realm, due to a fusion of traditional African beliefs and cultures with the influences of European colonialism. Many countries in this realm exhibit export-oriented transport systems and European concepts of political geography while retaining their traditional languages, religions, and social practices. The realm of Sub-Saharan Africa is the least developed realm in the world, and the majority of its residents engage in agricultural production. This realm is made up of four regions: West Africa, East Africa, Equatorial Africa, and Southern Africa.

General Economic Geography of Sub-Saharan Africa

The **economic geography of the realm of Sub-Saharan Africa** is primarily **agricultural**. Though many raw materials useful to industrialized countries (such as oil and diamonds) are located within this realm, most residents of Sub-Saharan Africa have little or no access to the technology needed to extract these resources, or to the world economy. Agriculturalists in this realm generally produce at the subsistence level (partially due to the harsh physical conditions—hot, dry weather—of the realm). Grain crops are produced more easily in drier areas, while root crops are grown in relatively wetter areas. Peoples in Sub-Saharan Africa also depend on **pastoralism** (especially the raising of goats, cattle, and chicken) and fishing for their livelihoods. Though this realm is the least developed in the world, farmers are attempting to better their situations by introducing cash crops to their land. Still, many in the area (which has the highest rate of population growth in the world) remain malnourished.

Geographic Realm of South Asia

The geographic realm of South Asia, which is one of the world's largest population agglomerations, has **India** at its center. This realm is delineated by **natural boundaries**: the Himalayan Mountains to the north and east, and the Arabian Sea and the Bay of Bengal to the south. India was once the cornerstone of civilization, and later a key part of the British colonial empire. Violent conflicts over the control of territory within South Asia have culminated in the creation of six states. This realm, with its many languages and variety of religious affiliations, contains deep cultural divisions. It contains five regions: the Ganges Plain, Pakistan, the mountainous North, Bangladesh, and the Dravidian South (including the island of Sri Lanka).

General Economic Geography of South Asia

The economic geography of South Asia is **low-income**, as the area continues to experience the effects of former British colonialization. When they came to South Asia, European powers changed trade patterns in the realm; Europe replaced India as the provider of manufactured goods for the realm. This caused a decrease in South Asian industry. Colonialists also exploited raw materials in the realm. Today, each of the states in South Asia has a low-income economy, due largely to the fact that these economies tend to center on inefficient and relatively less productive agricultural methods. Most residents of this region live in villages and survive directly on their parcels of land (often measuring less than an acre). Low-technology production methods keep crop yields (both per acre and per worker) at the **subsistence level**. Also, local traditions of inheritance often subdivide already undersized plots, preventing the organization of progressive measures, such as cooperative farming and shared irrigation in many states. The lack of a strong official agricultural development policy at the state and federal levels also inhibits the maturation of agricultural production.

Geographic Realm of East Asia

The geographic realm of East Asia has **China** at its center; this realm houses the largest concentration of human population in the world. Culturally, the 1.4 billion Chinese people dominate this realm, while the Japanese dominate economically. In fact, the economic activity and success of Japan have recently led to the tentative identification of the **Pacific Rim region**, a functional region with Japan as its anchor. The conceptualization of this region, as well as its practical development in the real world, continues to affect several realms and regions facing the Pacific Ocean. East Asia contains five regions: China Proper (eastern and northeastern China), which includes (somewhat precariously) North Korea, the mountains and plateaus of Xizang (the former Tibet), the deserts of Xinjiang, Mongolia, and the Pacific Rim (including Japan, Taiwan, South Korea, Thailand, and sometimes Malaysia), most of which was formerly referred to as the **Jakota Triangle**.

General Economic Geography of East Asia

The economic geography of East Asia is highly variable: Japan is one of the **most developed** countries on the globe, while Mongolia is one of the **least developed**. The wide inter- and intraregional variations in this realm's development level, therefore, demonstrate that it is inappropriate to label entire realms as "developed" or "underdeveloped." **Agriculturalists** in the realm tend to inhabit the fertile basins of the great rivers of the east, and produce grains such as wheat. East Asia is also home to large deposits of **raw materials** such as coal and natural gas. Economic development in the nations of the Jakota Triangle (Japan, South Korea, and Taiwan) is thought to presage the future growth and modernization of the other political entities in the region. Japan, in particular, has experienced rapid growth in all **industrial** sectors and possesses long-established trading relationships with nations across the globe. China, the other giant of the realm, has developed a mixed-market economy that displays both capitalistic and communistic characteristics.

Geographic Realm of Southeast Asia

The geographic realm of Southeast Asia contains ethnic and linguistic groups that are particularly diverse. The high occurrence of conflicts for territory and/or power in this realm throughout history has led some to refer to the realm as "the Eastern Europe of Asia." Some use the term **Indochina** synonymously with Southeast Asia, which is appropriate because it conveys the identities of the two major cultural contributors to the realm. The ethnic affinities of those in this realm tend to lie with China, while cultural influences (specifically religious) arrived in the region from India. The two major regions of Southeast Asia are differentiated by their spatial separation.

Indochina is the eastern, mainland part of the region; the archipelagoes of the **Philippines** and **Indonesia** make up the other region.

General Economic Geography of Southeast Asia

The economic geography of Southeast Asia resembles that of East Asia. It is a study in **economic contrasts**; like Eastern Europe, this realm is a shatter belt. Singapore, for example, has the second-busiest port in the world and is a major banking and financial center. Indonesia, Thailand, and the Philippines have grown from foreign direct investments (a manner of transferring capital across political boundaries, in which the investor exercises control over the acquired asset) in local industries. Also, the islands of Southeast Asia contain large petroleum reserves. Countries such as Vietnam and Cambodia, on the other hand, are some of the least developed countries in the world. This is partially due to the effects of the transition from a planned economy to a market economy. Levels of unemployment tend to be high in both urban and rural areas, as masses of people leave their farmlands (typically rice and/or grains) for crowded cities with limited job opportunities. The lack of a cohesive infrastructure, coupled with political instability, continues to problematize economic growth in these countries.

Geographic Realm of Australia

The geographic realm of Australia is formed by the regions of **Australia** and **New Zealand**. This realm is distinguished from other areas of the world by its **continental isolation** and the strong influence of Western culture among its peoples, who are demographically unique. Today, the furthest northwestern points of Australia may be considered part of the Pacific Rim region of East Asia. Australia is anomalous alongside Southeast Asia and the regions of the Pacific, due to its relatively high level of economic development. Still, some of the peoples of New Zealand remain traditional societies. The realm of Australia is made up of four regions. Australia the state is divided into an urbanized core and an arid interior, and New Zealand is made up of two large islands that are physically and culturally distinct.

General Economic Geography of Australia

The economic geography of Australia, as well as New Zealand, relies principally on the exportation of **livestock products**; Australia also participates in farming (especially wheat) and mining activities. Dependence on a constantly fluctuating world market places this realm's economy in a **precarious** position. Despite the plethora of advantages enjoyed by residents of the realm (plentiful farmlands, diverse mineral deposits, access to waterways, and underground water resources, as well as political stability), the Australian economy's growth has declined. Though it is considered one of the most developed realms in the world, Australia must now compete with the emerging Pacific Rim for trade opportunities. Australia has attempted to integrate itself into the Pacific Rim by exporting raw materials to countries in that region. Agriculturalists in this realm produce grains, rice, and certain fruits, while pastoralists produce wool and meat raising sheep. Manufacturing in Australia remains oriented to local domestic markets, partially due to the high costs of shipping and transportation to and from the relatively isolated realm.

Geographic Realm of the Pacific

The geographic realm of the Pacific is made up of the thousands of islands (large and small) that are situated in the Pacific Ocean, between Asia and Australia to the west and the Americas to the east. This geographic realm is more fragmented than any other; it is also culturally heterogeneous. The Pacific Realm is traditionally subdivided into three regions: **Melanesia** (the most populous Pacific region), which is associated with New Guinea; **Micronesia** (so named for the small sizes of this region's constituent islands), which is located to the north; and **Polynesia**, which extends from the Hawaiian archipelago southward to Easter Island and southwestward to New Zealand. The regions of Melanesia and Polynesia meet in New Zealand (the residents of which are descended from Polynesian peoples) and Australia (whose indigenous population is Melanesian).

General Economic Geography of the Pacific Realm

The economic geography of the Pacific Realm is based on **tourism**. Though this realm covers a larger total area than any other, it possesses the least land area. Coral atolls, ancient volcanoes, open sea, and tropical vegetation offer travelers one spectacular view after another. The region of Melanesia produces valuable export items such as palm oil, coffee, and cocoa, in addition to the subsistence-level production of root crops and bananas. Melanesia also houses large mineral deposits. Micronesia is also involved in agriculture; fertile soils in this region help to diversify crop production. Polynesia, the region that includes the Hawaiian Islands, has a highly developed tourism economy. Most states in the Pacific Realm have high or upper-middle-income economies.

Place

In geography, a place is a space on Earth's surface that has been given particular meaning by humans. A **place** may be as small as a room or as large as a continent. Places are differentiated by the unique combination of human and physical properties exhibited by each and are often bounded and named. The human characteristics of a place include political systems, economic systems, languages, population statistics, and cultural norms. A place's physical characteristics include climate, vegetation types and distributions, landforms, animal life, and soils. Constant changes in these qualities affect entire places; therefore, places never stay the same for long. They may thrive or ebb, become simpler or more complex, or become altered in organization.

Enclaves

An enclave is a piece of territory that is completely surrounded by another political territory of which the former is not a part. For example, the sovereign country of Vatican City is enclaved within Italy. There are several kinds of enclaves:

- A **true enclave** is one that can be entered only via another country.
- A **practical enclave** is one that may be more easily accessed through another country, even though it is not completely detached from the "mother" country, due to, for example, its topography or available transportation routes.
- A **subnational enclave** is a territory that belongs to one political subdivision of land, yet is attached to another. For instance, Long Island is considered part of the city of Boston, but is road-accessible only from Quincy, Massachusetts.
- An **ethnic enclave** is a community of members of a minority ethnic group that is situated in the midst of a larger ethnic group (such as a Chinatown).

Exclaves

An exclave is a territory belonging to, yet detached from, one political entity and surrounded by other political entities. The term is similar in meaning to enclave. However, the two are not synonymous; an **exclave** is not necessarily an enclave. For instance, if area C, whose motherland is country B, is located in the center of country A, area C may be referred to as B's exclave and A's enclave. If, however, area C is located along the boundary between country B and another foreign country (D), it is no longer referred to as an enclave, but it is still appropriate to describe it as B's exclave. Like enclaves, exclaves may be subnational, true, or practical.

Irredentism

Irredentism refers to any nationalist policy that seeks to extend cultures and possibly expand political territories through the incorporation of territories ruled by foreign entities. Originally, the term referred to the nationalist Italian movement that advocated the annexation of certain territories (which were officially held by Austria but populated by a majority of Italians) to Italy. An example of **irredentism** can be found in Hungary. While the population of Hungary proper is close to 10 million, there are large concentrations of Hungarians living in Romania, Slovakia, Croatia, Serbia, and Slovenia (holdovers from a time when Hungary was more powerful and held more territory on the Balkan Peninsula). The Hungarian government appeals to these "ethnic cohorts" and seeks to protect them, if needed, from the government of the states in which they live; this behavior is referred to as irredentism.

GLOBALIZATION

Globalization is the process whereby regional differences are reduced due to the increased exchange of cultural, economic, and political ideas and practices among traditionally isolated nations. Advancements in technology have bred increased interdependency among the world's countries and enabled people to interact with others on a global scale. Time-space convergence is the increasing nearness of people and places due to the technological reduction of the travel/communication times and distances between them. Social theoriest Arjun Appaduri has identified five categories of **global connectivity**:

1. **Ethnoscapes** are the movements of people from one region to another.
2. **Financescapes** are the movements of money around the world.
3. **Ideoscapes** are the global movements of ideas and belief systems.
4. **Mediascapes** are the mass distributions of images through the media.
5. **Technoscapes** are the movements of technologies around the globe.

Some view the changes associated with globalization as positive steps toward the development of a fully multicultural global society. Others see globalization as a synonym for **imperialism**.

PROCESSES OF SPATIAL DIFFUSION

Spatial diffusion is the mechanism whereby ideas, practices, and innovations spread through a population over time and space. Study of the processes through which **spatial diffusion** takes place allows geographers to hypothesize the dispersal of cultural and economic ideas in the past and future. There are four processes associated with spatial diffusion:

1. **Expansion diffusion** is the type of diffusion in which a strong central source area emanates propagation waves in all directions. These waves affect ever-growing populations and places.
2. **Contagious diffusion** is a method of expansion diffusion that relies on local proximity to spread phenomena.
3. **Hierarchical diffusion** involves the diffusion of phenomena from a high leader such as a king or chief.
4. **Relocation diffusion** occurs when a phenomenon spreads after the movement and resettlement of a source population; expansion from the relocated source area typically follows.

ECONOMIC GEOGRAPHY

Economic geography is the subfield of geography that investigates the ways in which people support themselves and their families, and the ways in which the goods and services they produce are spatially organized. For example, the types of goods produced in a particular geographic region may be influenced by the region's climate, political and/or social organization, infrastructure, and geology. Scholars of **economic geography** seek to explain how the interaction of these and other factors creates the patterns of **diverse economic activity** observed across the surface of the globe. Recognition of these relationships can help geographers make predictions about past and future events and to postulate solutions to the problems of **unequal economic development** among the nations of the world.

Medical Geography

Medical geography is the subfield of geography that studies the **health** of the global population in a spatial context. Most diseases that affect human beings originate in the natural environment. Certain environmental qualities facilitate the spread of **disease**. Tropical Africa, for instance, with its hot, humid climate, is the ideal habitat for carriers such as mosquitoes and flies. Cultural factors, such as personal hygiene, sexual behaviors, and food preparation techniques, can also contribute to disease diffusion. One virus that has its roots in the environment is the Ebola virus, which periodically breaks out randomly and violently in the region of Equatorial Africa. These viruses are born in **source (core) areas** and diffuse throughout the surrounding population through **hosts**. Analysis of the spatial patterns of diseases and the geographic characteristics of the affected regions can provide vital information about the nature, prevention, and cure of diseases.

Cultural Landscapes

A cultural landscape is a geographic area that includes cultural and natural resources associated with a historic event, activity, person, or group of people. People of every cultural group transform the lands upon which they live. They erect buildings, create transportation routes, till soil, and subdivide their territories into smaller parcels. The ways in which humans interact with the natural environment often differ from culture to culture. For example, industrialized societies may ignore the presence of certain vegetation or even see it as an obstacle to development, while traditional societies may view the same vegetation as an important natural resource. **Carl Sauer**, a geographer who focused his cultural studies on the concept of **cultural landscapes** provides a straightforward definition: cultural landscapes are "the forms superimposed on the physical landscape by the activities of man." The term *sequent occupance* refers to the stages of evolution undergone by an area when different cultural groups successively occupy that particular landscape. The presence of a distinctive cultural landscape is a major criterion in the delineation of a cultural region.

Epochs of Metropolitan Evolution in North America

Analysis of advancements in transportation technology and industrial energy reveals five epochs of metropolitan evolution in North America:

1. The **Sail-Wagon Epoch** (1790-1830) was characterized by basic overland and waterway methods of transportation. North America depended on overseas trade, which was more plausible than trade with the largely inaccessible western periphery.
2. The **Iron Horse Epoch** (1830-1870) was dominated by railways. The completion of the transcontinental railroad near the close of this epoch heralded the start of the creation of national urban systems.
3. The **Steel-Rail Epoch** (1870-1920) was greatly affected by the US Industrial Revolution, with the associated increases in production levels and railway efficiency.
4. The **Auto-Air-Amenity Epoch** (1920-1970) saw the invention of the gasoline-powered internal combustion engine and a consequent rise in automotive and air transportation. Much of the American workforce entered the service industry.
5. The **Satellite-Electronic-Jet Propulsion Epoch** (1970-present) has thus far shown increased levels of international interaction, specialization, and constraints on expensive energy sources, and the development of a global village.

Eras of Intraurban Structural Evolution in North America

Developments in transportation technology and industrial energy affected urban areas in North America on a local scale. **Intraurban growth**, like national urban evolution, may be organized into stages:

- During the **Walking-Horsecar Era** (prior to 1888), cities had to be compact due to the time required for long travel by pedestrians.
- The **Electric Streetcar Era** (1888-1920) saw the invention of a motor that could be attached to horsecars; this decreased travel time significantly and thus enabled urban expansion. This, in turn, enabled more specialized land use.
- The **Recreational Automobile Era** (1920-1945) was characterized by increased accessibility to the outer metropolitan ring, due to the impact of automobiles and highway expansion. The city core reached its peak during this era, which also saw an increase in suburbanization and the partitioning of residential space.
- The **Freeway Era** (1945-present) has demonstrated the full effect of individual automobile transportation on high-speed expressways; urban sprawl has resulted in distances up to 30 miles between the city's center and outskirts.

Rostow's Model of the Development Process

In the 1960s, economist **Walt Rostow** formulated a model of the process of economic development (the **Rostovian take-off model**). Rostow asserted that each of the world's countries follows a five-stage path toward development:

1. In the first stage, **traditional society**, people engage in agricultural production at subsistence levels. Nations in the first stage tend to adhere to a rigid social structure and resist technological change.
2. The second stage, **preconditions for take-off**, involves the introduction of a progressive leader (or leaders) who steers the nation toward greater diversification and flexibility. Traditional beliefs and practices are discarded, agricultural activity and birth rates decline, and infrastructure improves.
3. The third stage, **take-off**, generally involves an industrial revolution as well as urbanization and technological advancements.
4. The fourth stage, **drive to maturity**, is reached when technology disperses throughout a nation, enabling industrial specialization and increased trade.
5. A nation in the fifth stage, **high mass consumption**, exhibits high income levels and a majority of workers in the third and fourth sectors of industry.

Neolithic Revolution

The Neolithic Revolution was a period of conversion from hunting and gathering methods of subsistence to **agricultural** methods of production; this transition began approximately 10,000 years ago. This "revolution" is so named because of the long-lasting effects of social and economic changes in human society that resulted from this conversion. The causes of these changes are **climatic changes** associated with the end of the last ice age (namely, warmer, drier climates), which led hunter-gatherers to settle near stable water sources, and a food crisis perpetuated by the extinction of several species of large mammals during the late Paleolithic era. The transition to agricultural production involved the development of permanent settlements (as well as a decrease in nomadic lifestyles), the domestication of plants and animals, human modification of the natural environment, the evolution of notions of land ownership, economic specialization, and the development of trading systems. Many of the characteristics of present-day "**civilization**" (for instance, social hierarchies, advanced, specialized technologies, and cities) began with the **Neolithic Revolution**.

Industrial Revolution

The term *Industrial Revolution* generally refers to the conversion from an economy based on **manual labor** to one supported by **industry and machine manufacture**, which took place in Britain during the late 18th and early 19th centuries (though other countries experienced industrial revolutions after Britain's). The numerous causes of this revolution are complex. They include the presence of a large workforce, due to improvements in disease control; the agrarian revolution, which made agriculture a less labor-intensive endeavor and forced workers into other spheres; colonial expansion, which improved Britain's international trade market and increased its available capital; the existence of a sizeable domestic market; and the availability of abundant natural resources. Developments of the Industrial Revolution included improvements in iron smelting, based on the use of coal (converted into carbon-rich coke) as an energy source, and the invention of the steam engine, adapted for use in the textile, mining, manufacturing, and transportation industries. Innovations developed during the Industrial Revolution spread through Europe and to North America and eventually diffused across the globe.

> **Review Video: The Industrial Revolution**
> Visit mometrix.com/academy and enter code: 372796

Dust Bowl

The Dust Bowl (1930-1941) was a period of American history characterized by a high incidence of dust storms in the Oklahoma Panhandle region. The instability of the world agriculture market during World War I led to **overproduction** in the 1920s. Even lands previously considered unsuitable for agricultural use were leveled and developed. This excessive activity devastated the plains of the Oklahoma Panhandle, eliminating the natural vegetation that could have prevented the massive soil movement that occurred during the drought and strong winds of the 1930s. Thus, this ecological disaster occurred in large part due to the activities of humans in the region. In turn, the **Dust Bowl** led to a large intra-realm **migration** of humans in North America; hundreds of thousands of people migrated from Oklahoma to California. The events before, during, and after the Dust Bowl, as well as the environmental event itself, provide key examples of the complex processes of interaction between humans and their environments.

Perceptual Region

A perceptual geographic region is one that is shaped by people's shared feelings and attitudes about an area. **Perception** is the process whereby individuals use their senses to collect information about their situation or environment. A person's perception is affected by his or her past experiences and cultural background. The delineation of a **perceptual geographic region** is thus a subjective process. Perceptual geographic regions are often influenced by people's **mental maps**. The theoretical organization of parts of Earth's surface into perceptual regions may help to develop an individual's sense of the world's structure; however, since such regions are delineated based on personal viewpoints, they may reflect inappropriate (and sometimes prejudicial) stereotypes.

Geographic Realms

A geographic realm is the largest geographical unit into which Earth's surface can be divided. **Geographic realms** are sometimes referred to as "**global neighborhoods**." All places within a realm share at least one **overarching characteristic**, whether that factor is physical (such as climate type) or human (such as mode of production). Realms are also distinguished by the type of **interaction** that takes place between human society and the natural environment. In other words, the ways in which humans alter the land on which they live, including the features they erect upon it, affect the area's position in the global regionalization scheme. Finally, a geographic realm must encompass a "**great cluster**" (population concentration) of humans. China, for example, exists at the center of one such cluster. Like all regional classifications related to human activity, geographic realms change over time. Today, geographers identify twelve realms: Europe, Russia, North America, Middle America, South America, North Africa/Southwest Asia, Sub-Saharan Africa, South Asia, East Asia, Southeast Asia, Australia, and the Pacific Rim.

Earth's Three Largest Population Clusters

Earth's three largest population clusters are East Asia, India, and Europe.

1. **East Asia**, centered on China, is home to the world's largest population cluster, incorporating the eastern coastal zone from the Korean Peninsula to Vietnam. Population density is highest near the coast and ebbs as one moves inland; members of this cluster are also concentrated in the valleys of China's major rivers. The majority of people in East Asia lives in rural areas and engages in agricultural production.
2. **India** exists at the center of South Asia, the second-largest population cluster, which also includes Pakistan and Bangladesh. The highest concentration of humans in this region is located near the Ganges River. This realm is also largely agricultural. High levels of population growth in South Asia have problematized sustainable production.
3. **Europe** is the third-largest of the world's population clusters. In contrast to the other two largest clusters, the highest population density in this cluster runs along an east-west axis, corresponding to a zone of raw industrial materials. As one of the most industrialized realms, Europe is highly dependent on these resources.

Transition Zones

A transition zone is an area of spatial change between global neighborhoods. Such zones are characterized by gradual changes in the physical and human characteristics which differentiate one realm from another. Like other geographic boundaries, the divisions between geographic realms are often blurred. As these boundaries are theoretical, it not surprising that they do not practically differentiate adjacent realms. **Cultural amalgamation** and **international economic activities** often take place in transition zones. The high degree of interaction between residents of neighboring realms that takes place in these areas often leads to regional change.

Culture Hearth, Cultural Mosaic, Transculturation

A culture hearth is a principal source area and center of cultural innovation from which migrating peoples transport traditions and beliefs to their new homes. Mesoamerica, a region that spans the area between central Mexico and the northwestern boundary of Costa Rica, is an example of a **culture hearth**. Populations from this hearth expanded and worked for advancements in the spheres of, for instance, science, architecture, agriculture, and religion; these advancements spread to other regions and influenced further developments. The term *cultural mosaic* is used to describe a society in which distinct ethnic, language, and culture groups exist side by side. This concept is largely synonymous with the idea of cultural pluralism and is the opposite of a culturally assimilated society. **Transculturation** is the process whereby different cultures merge and converge. It refers specifically to the tendency of humans to work toward the resolution of conflicts, be they political, ethnic, or social.

Culture Spheres

A culture sphere is a cultural region within a larger region. The identification of general culture spheres may be useful in the description of the cultural mosaic of a pluralist society. For instance, geographers have delineated five generalized **culture spheres** within the South American realm. The tropical-plantation region is characterized by a dispersed settlement pattern, a high level of plantation agriculture, and a culture dominated by the descendants of African slave laborers who were brought over to work on those plantations. The European-commercial region is populated largely by Europeans, specifically those with affiliations to Hispanic culture. This region is economically more developed than the rest of the realm. The Amerind-subsistence region is characterized by a feudal socioeconomic structure, a holdover from former Spanish conquerors. This region contains some of the realm's poorest areas. Culture in the Mestizo-transitional region is a fusion of Amerind and European elements. It is also a zone of transition between the commercial and subsistence economic areas. The undifferentiated region consists of regions with unclassifiable cultural characteristics.

Balkanization, Shatter Belt, Ethnic Cleansing

There are several geographic terms with roots in the region of Eastern Europe that are used to describe the collapse of established order; these terms are so designated due to the complex, transitory nature of the area.

- **Balkanization**, named after the Balkan Peninsula, is defined as the breaking down of a society (such as a region) into smaller and more hostile units.
- A **shatter belt** is a region, such as Eastern Europe, located between two or more stronger, oppositional cultural-political forces. A shatter belt region is often pressured, taken over, and divvied up by outside, rival forces.
- **Ethnic cleansing** is another term coined from events in Eastern Europe. The phrase is a euphemism used to designate the forcible elimination of people of a certain ethnic group from their homeland by more aggressive groups in search of power. The term has been used historically by the Soviets (in reference to the "resettlement" of Poles) and by Serbs in Yugoslavia (in description of the policies of Albanians against Serbs).

Centripetal and Centrifugal Forces

In political geography, centripetal forces are forces within a state which act to unify and strengthen it. For instance, an outside threat (actual or perceived) on a state often binds that state's political system and may consequently make it stronger. A particularly important and enduring **centripetal force** is the belief of the state's citizens in the state's governmental system and their committed support of that system. Historically, certain charismatic leaders, such as Charles De Gaulle in France and Mao Zedong in China, have inspired this type of loyalty. **Centrifugal forces** are those that act against centripetal forces, tending to divide or degrade states. These forces are usually internal. Interracial hostilities, religious and/or ethnic conflicts, and political strife are key factors in the disunification of states. For example, clashes among ethnic groups in Yugoslavia led to much fighting and the eventual breakup of the state in 1991. The proportion of centripetal to centrifugal forces in a state affects its stability and strength.

Urban Geography

Urban geography is the subfield of geography that involves the spatial analysis of city-centered settlements with high population densities. This area of study has been organized into four main sections:

- **Urban evolution geography** (the historical evolution component of urban geography) is interested in the forces behind urban development during each period of human development since the city's founding.

- **Interurban geography** is concerned with the interactions and relationships between urban systems at a national level. Areas of interest include city types, city functions, and spheres of influence.
- **Intraurban geography** deals with the internal spatial organizations of highly urbanized settlements. This includes study of the infrastructure of a city as well as observation of the distribution and activities of different population groups in that city.
- **Urban social geography** is the component of urban geography that investigates the spatial arrangements of people in a metropolis, with a focus on their residences.

A related field, urban economic geography, examines the distribution of commercial and recreational activities in urban areas.

Principles of Spatial Interaction

A spatial interaction is a realized movement of people, freight or information between an origin and a destination. Human contact and interaction in the realm of economics and trade is organized around three principles:

1. **Complementarity** comes about when one area produces a surplus of a certain commodity that is needed in a second area. This principle thus occurs due to spatial variations in the supply and demand of particular resources, both natural and human.
2. **Transferability** is the ease of transportation of goods between two areas. Distance (including costs and travel time) and accessibility (including travel routes and the character of the relevant terrain) are factors in the transferability of a commodity. Therefore, complementarity alone does not ensure trade between regions.
3. **Intervening opportunity** states that trade between two areas, even if the conditions of complementarity and transferability are met, will occur only through the lack of a more proximate (intervening) supply source.

Areal Functional Specialization

Areal functional specialization is a phenomenon that occurs due to variations in amounts of available resources (natural and human), levels of industrialization, and amounts of available technology, which leads certain areas and peoples to specialize in the production of certain goods. Europe, for example, exhibits a high degree of **areal functional specialization**; particular ores, minerals, manufactured goods, and agricultural products tend to be produced (in surplus) in particular areas. The needs of these specialized regions of production tend to be complementary, so each area satisfies its needs through trade with other areas. Europe, therefore, is a realm of areal (economic) interdependence.

Core Areas and Peripheral Areas

Core areas of a region or nation, which may also be referred to as heartlands, are the hubs of human and economic activity in those areas. These central regions usually exhibit at least one substantive urban area, a large population cluster, and high levels of accessibility and connectivity, which grant them influence over entire regions. **Peripheral areas** (also referred to as hinterlands, a term that literally means "countries behind") are those surrounding core regions. These areas depend on goods and services produced in those core regions, which are key influences on urban development along the periphery. Heartlands and hinterlands develop due to the presence or absence of natural resources, the degree of availability of those resources, regional variations in climate, and the degree of a region's connectivity to other regions. Contrasts in development levels exist at several different scales: local, regional, national, and global.

Core-Periphery Relationships

The structure of core-periphery relationships causes already powerful and developed core areas to continue to grow and evolve, while peripheries remain undeveloped and often unstable. Uneven development is, sadly, a fact of life on Earth. Certain countries (and regions within those nations) have advantages that other countries and regions do not have, and the gap between these haves and have-nots continues to grow. These core and peripheral regions are functionally tied together. Citizens of the periphery contribute labor and taxes to the development of the core. In other words, **core regions** would not be as they are without the contributions of **peripheral regions**. Hinterlands begin to depend on heartlands for employment (though workers from the periphery generally receive lower wages than workers in the core), specialized goods and services, and even military protection. This situation negates the possibility of economic growth in the hinterlands.

Assumptions Behind Von Thünen's Isolated State Model

In 1826, economist **Johann Heinrich von Thünen** created a geographic model to explain the effects of distance and cost of transportation on the location of productive activity. Thünen's **Isolated State Model** is so titled because he wanted to develop a secluded community with no outside influences on its economic activity in order to ascertain the basic factors in the spatial organization of an agricultural region. He based his model on four assumptions:

- That soil quality and climate characteristics were homogeneous throughout the area;
- That the area was flat and contained no divisive landforms (such as river valleys or mountains);
- That the region consisted of a centrally located city surrounded by wilderness; and
- That farmers within the Isolated State would move their own products directly to the central city (meaning that transportation costs would be directly proportional to distance).

Though Thünen's theoretical model did not represent real economic areas in Europe, the distorting factors could be applied individually to the idealized representation of agricultural economy.

Thünen's Isolated State Model

Thünen's Isolated State Model seeks to identify the ideal spatial arrangement of agricultural activities in an isolated community. It consists of a central market city surrounded by **concentric rings**. The innermost ring is a zone of intensive production (including dairying), the second zone houses a forest from which firewood and timber (an important building material in Thünen's time) can be extracted, the third area produces extensive field crops, and the fourth zone is characterized by ranching and animal husbandry. In other words, the crops that yield the highest returns and perish most easily (such as vegetables) are grown closest to the city. Extensive crops such as potatoes and grains are grown further away (outside the forest zone); ranching activities take place just inside the boundary marking the distance at which transportation costs make market agricultural production uneconomical. Today, due to improvements in transportation technologies, Thünen's model can be expanded to a **macroscale**, meaning that it centers on an entire urban area rather than a single city.

United States Geography

Major Land Regions of the United States

The United States can be divided into seven distinct **major land regions**: the Pacific Ranges and Lowlands; the Western Basins and Ranges; the Rocky Mountains; the Ozark-Ouachita Highlands; the Interior Plains; the Coastal Lowlands; and the Appalachian Highlands. Of course, this division does not include Alaska or Hawaii. Some geographers eliminate the Ozark-Ouachita Highlands from the total by classifying the Ozark Plateau as part of the Interior Plains and the Ouachita Mountains as part of the Appalachian Range. Similarly, some geographers combine the Rocky Mountains with the Pacific Ranges and Lowlands into the Pacific Cordillera. In any case, the United States has a total area of about 3.8 million square miles, or about 9.8 million square kilometers.

Pacific Ranges and Lowlands Region of the United States

The Pacific Ranges and Lowlands region of the United States extends along the western border of the North American continent. On its eastern side, it is bordered by two mountain ranges, the Cascades and the Sierra Nevadas. The Cascade Range includes Lassen Peak (California) and Mount Saint Helens (Washington), both of which are active volcanoes. The Pacific Ranges and Lowlands region runs from northern Washington State to southern California. To the west of the mountain ranges, there are expansive and fertile valleys. These include California's Central Valley, Oregon's Willamette Valley, and Washington's Puget Sound Lowland. To the west of the valleys, there are coastal ranges, some of which are quite dramatic and others of which are relatively low. The Pacific Coast features a number of large bays, including San Diego Bay, San Francisco Bay, Columbia River Bay, and the Puget Sound. In California, the San Andreas Fault extends along the length of the coastal ranges.

Rocky Mountains Region of the United States

The Rocky Mountains region of the United States primarily consists of North America's largest mountain group. The Rocky Mountains run from northern New Mexico all the way to Alaska. Some of the peaks in the chain are higher than 14,000 feet. Along the lower slopes of the Rockies, there are deep forests, but above the timberline, it is impossible for trees to grow. At the highest elevations, the only plant life that can be sustained is mosses, lichens, and grasses. These jagged mountain ranges include plentiful rivers and streams, and some of North America's most dramatic scenery. Geographers trace an imaginary line, known as the Continental Divide, along the range to separate those areas in which running water flows toward the Pacific Ocean and those in which it flows into the Gulf of Mexico, Atlantic Ocean, or Arctic Ocean. The Rocky Mountains region includes the headwaters of the Rio Grande, Colorado, Missouri, and Colorado Rivers. The first widely used pass through these mountains was at the Wyoming Basin.

Outlying Areas of the United States

Two states, Hawaii and Alaska, are not part of the conterminous United States. **Alaska** is the largest state in the nation. It has proven to be an excellent source of natural resources, like gold and oil. Because of the frigid climate, though, it has a very small population. **Hawaii** is an archipelago, or collection of islands, in the Pacific Ocean. It is home to several important American military bases. The United States also has possession of several islands in the Pacific Ocean and Caribbean. Of these, Puerto Rico is the most closely aligned with the United States, though it is still largely autonomous. Puerto Rico is designated as a commonwealth. It sends a representative to Washington for committee votes, as do American Samoa, the Virgin Islands, and Guam.

Western Basins and Ranges Region of the United States

The Western Basins and Ranges region of the United States is bordered on the west by the Cascades and Sierra Nevadas and on the east by the Rockies. From north to south, it extends from central Washington to Mexico. This region is characterized by arid terrain, including several large deserts. Death Valley in California contains the lowest point in the United States, at a little less than 300 feet below sea level. To the north, the Great Basin is a large area with several salty and shallow lakes. The largest of these is the Great Salt Lake, which is adjoined by a desert composed in part of a salt bed. On the northern end of the Great Basin, the Columbia Plateau features exceptionally fertile soil, most of which derives from volcanic eruptions in the distant past. However, for the most part, the Western Basins and Ranges region is too dry for large-scale farming, though livestock may be sustained. In the southern part of the Great Basin lies the Colorado Plateau, which includes many deep river gorges, most notably the Grand Canyon.

Ozark-Ouachita Highlands Region of the United States

The Ozark-Ouachita Highlands region of the United States is not always considered an independent geographic region, though it is difficult to group it with any of the larger regions. The Ozark Plateau and Ouachita Mountains lie north of the Coastal Lowlands and south of the Interior Plains. They run through southern Missouri, eastern Oklahoma, and northwest Arkansas. The region is marked by rough, scrubby highlands interlaced with deep gorges. Perhaps the most noteworthy features of the region are the natural caves. There has also been a great deal of profitable mining in this region, primarily for coal and iron ore. Despite a network of springs, streams, and rivers, the land of the Ozark-Ouachita Highlands is not especially good for farming.

Interior Plains Region of the United States

The Interior Plains region of the United States is an enormous expanse of mostly flat land, extending from the Appalachians in the east to the Rockies in the west. This region was mainly formed by the slow passage of massive glaciers during the Ice Age. As these glaciers descended from the north, they removed topsoil in what are now Wisconsin, Minnesota, and Michigan. These glaciers were also responsible for carving out enormous depressions, among them the Great Lakes (Huron, Michigan, Erie, Superior, and Ontario), the largest system of freshwater lakes in the world. Farther south, the glaciers flattened the land and distributed the topsoil from the north, making the land in Indiana, Illinois, Iowa, and Ohio among the best in the world for farming. The region contains a network of rivers and streams, the greatest of which is the Mississippi River. The Mississippi begins in northern Minnesota and flows all the way to New Orleans. The western part of the Interior Plains region is known as the Great Plains; it is grassland used primarily for livestock grazing.

Appalachian Highlands Region of the United States

The Appalachian Highlands region of the United States extends from northern Alabama all the way to northern Maine. It includes mountain ranges like the Blue Ridge, Smokies, Whites, Greens, and Adirondacks. The Blue Ridge Mountains are widely believed to be the oldest range in the world. They extend from northern Georgia to southern Pennsylvania. Several water gaps, or flat passages useful for transportation, are cut through the Blue Ridge by the Delaware, Potomac, and other rivers. To the west of the Blue Ridge, there is a series of high and lowlands known as the Ridge and Valley Region. It includes famous valleys like the Cumberland, Shenandoah, and Rome. The third major feature of this region is the Appalachian Plateau, which runs all the way from Alabama to New York. This area was formed by glaciers and has been mined more extensively than any other area of the United States.

Climate of the United States

The United States is an extremely large nation with a varied topography, so a number of **climate groups** are represented. In the continental United States, there are humid oceanic, humid subtropical, humid continental, desert, semiarid, highland, and subtropical dry summer regions. Climate is significantly impacted by major topographical features, like the Pacific Ocean, Rocky Mountains, and Great Lakes. The highest average temperature is 78.2 degrees Fahrenheit, in Death Valley, California, while the lowest average temperature is 9 degrees Fahrenheit, in Barrow, Alaska. It was near Barrow that the lowest temperature ever in the United States was recorded: -80 degrees Fahrenheit on January 23, 1971. The highest recorded temperature is 134 degrees Fahrenheit in Death Valley on July 10, 1913.

Review Video: Climates
Visit mometrix.com/academy and enter code: 991320

Regions of the United States

Coastal Lowlands Region

The Coastal Lowlands region of the United States runs in a strip along the Atlantic coast, expanding and heading west in the southeast until it terminates in eastern Texas. This region is typically divided into three **sub-regions**: the Gulf Coastal Plain, the Atlantic Coastal Plain, and the Piedmont. The **Gulf Coastal Plain** adjoins the Gulf of Mexico and includes such major rivers as the Mississippi and Rio Grande. The land in this area is exceptionally fertile, and there are also rich deposits of petroleum. The **Atlantic Coastal Plain** runs from Maine to Florida, gradually widening as it heads south. This area is also fertile and is primarily suited for cotton, peanuts, tobacco, and citrus fruits. The Atlantic Coastal Plain includes some large natural harbors, including those at Cape Cod, Boston, and the Chesapeake. The **Piedmont** lies just inland from the Atlantic Coastal Plain. It is characterized by gentle hills and rivers. Along the eastern border of the Piedmont is the Fall Line: rivers that run west across this line feature dramatic rapids and waterfalls, which makes shipping difficult.

Grasslands and Alpine Tundra Region

The United States includes extensive **grasslands**, beginning in the Interior Plains region and stretching out into the basins and plateaus of the Rocky Mountains. These grasslands are covered with plants like side oat, buffalo grass, needle, wheatgrass, and grama. There are also numerous wild herbs growing in these areas. Grasslands used to be grazed by huge populations of buffalo and cattle, but the buffalo were mostly hunted out of existence. The continental United States only has a few instances of **alpine tundra**, mostly in the Rocky Mountains above the tree line. In these regions, vegetation consists mostly of short grasses and flowers that bloom only for a brief period. Very few animals are hardy enough to live exclusively in the tundra.

Humid Oceanic Region

A humid oceanic climate region exists in a narrow band that runs down the northern Pacific Coast of the United States, from Washington State almost to San Francisco. The eastern boundary of this climate region is the Cascade/Sierra Nevada mountain group. A **humid oceanic climate region** is characterized by a moderately warm summer and a moderately cold winter. In other words, temperature variations are slighter in this region than in others. Humid oceanic climates are typical of the western side of continents, where the prevailing winds blow east from the sea onto the land. These regions have a moderate to high level of precipitation throughout the year, mostly in the form of rain. There are very few droughts, heatwaves, or thunderstorms. In general, the relative stability of the ocean's water temperature translates into stable temperatures just inland.

Humid Subtropical Climate Region

A humid subtropical climate region covers much of the Southeastern United States and extends up the Atlantic coast as far as New York City. This climate region exists even over the higher elevations of the southern Appalachian range. It extends into western Texas and Oklahoma. In this climate region, there are very hot summers and relatively mild winters. There is a medium amount of precipitation in all seasons. No season gets significantly more precipitation than the rest. In the winter, there are often large snowstorms related to the rapid passage of westward winds over the open spaces. There are frequent summer thunderstorms, and the southeast coast occasionally encounters tropical storms and hurricanes as well.

Desert and Semiarid Climate Regions

There are desert and semiarid climate regions in the western United States, particularly in the southwest and in the northern regions on either side of the Rocky Mountains. The **deserts** are concentrated in southern New Mexico, Arizona, and California. In both semiarid and desert regions, there is very little precipitation. The variation between day and night temperatures in these regions is often severe, in part because the air is typically very clear and dry. Moisture in the air would tend to mitigate wild swings in temperature, and clouds would retain some of the heat from the day. Deserts receive less precipitation than semiarid climates, though not by much. The **semiarid** regions are generally at a slightly higher elevation.

Subtropical Dry Summer Climate Region

A subtropical dry summer climate region exists in the United States in southern California, from the Pacific Ocean west to the Sierra Nevada Mountains. The subtropical dry summer zone extends up the coast to San Francisco and slightly farther north just inland. Los Angeles is around the southern tip of this climate zone. A **subtropical dry summer climate region** is characterized by hot, dry summers and mild winters. There is a moderate amount of precipitation in the winter and very little in the summer. This is the climate typical of the Mediterranean countries in southern Europe. The subtropical dry summer climate is generally found on the western edge of a continent. In the section of the region closest to the water, the temperatures are more moderate, and there is less variation between summer and winter weather.

Humid Continental Climate Region

A humid continental climate region covers the Northeast and much of the upper Midwest. It encompasses New England and broadens as it extends west, taking in Missouri and eastern Colorado as well as Minnesota. **Humid continental regions** are characterized by mild summers and extremely cold winters. These regions experience an average amount of precipitation in all seasons. Farther inland, the variation between winter cold and summer heat is likely to be greater. Indeed, in places like northern Minnesota, the difference between summer and winter average temperatures can be as much as 65 degrees Fahrenheit. These inland locations also tend to have a bit more precipitation during the summer. The humid continental climate region in the United States is often covered by snow for most of the winter. This snow perpetuates the cold temperatures by reflecting heat back into the atmosphere.

Highland Climate Region

Some isolated highland climate regions exist in the United States along the higher points of the Rocky Mountain and Cascade ranges. To some extent, this climate region even extends south along the Sierra Nevada range. The **highland** designation actually encompasses a number of distinct climate types that are present at different elevations. The progression of climates along the ascending edge of a mountain is not unlike that encountered during travel away from the Equator; as one gains elevation, the climate becomes closer to tundra or even an icecap. Air becomes thinner, vegetation becomes more sparse and low-lying, and precipitation is more likely to be snow or ice. At the highest points of the highland region, the temperature may never rise above freezing.

Subarctic and Tundra Climate Regions

Subarctic and tundra climate regions only exist in the United States in Alaska. The lower two-thirds, approximately, of the state is considered **subarctic**, while the top third is **tundra**. In a subarctic climate region, summers are cool and brief, while winters are long and extremely cold. There is considerably more precipitation during the summer, but any during the winter is likely to be snow and to remain on the ground until spring. Indeed, subarctic regions are typically covered for most of the year. Tundra is drier and colder. The tundra is too cold to support trees, so the only vegetation there is low grasses. A common feature of tundra is permafrost, or permanently frozen ground just under the surface. It is virtually impossible to farm in tundra.

Oklahoma Geography

Mountain Ranges in Oklahoma

The four major mountain ranges that are located in Oklahoma are the Arbuckle Mountains, the Ouachita Mountains, the Ozark Mountains, and the Wichita Mountains. The **Arbuckle Mountains** are located in the southern section of Oklahoma, just south of Oklahoma City. These mountains were originally named after Fort Arbuckle, which was a military outpost established in the mountain range in the 1850s by Brigadier General Matthew Arbuckle. The **Ouachita Mountains** are located in the southeastern section of Oklahoma. These mountains were named after the Ouachita tribe, which originally inhabited the area in which the mountains are located. The **Ozark Mountains** are located in the northeast section of Oklahoma. The exact origin of the name Ozark is unknown, but the name may originate from the French "aux Arks" or the French "aux arcs." The **Wichita Mountains** are located in the southwest section of Oklahoma. These mountains were named after the Wichita tribe, which originally inhabited the area that is now Kansas and Oklahoma.

Rivers in Oklahoma

Arkansas River, Canadian River, North Canadian River, Red River

The Arkansas River flows from the center of Colorado to the southeastern section of Arkansas. The **Arkansas River** enters the northeastern side of Oklahoma from Kansas and travels southeast through the cities of Tulsa and Muskogee. The **Canadian River**, which is also known as the South Canadian River, flows from the southwestern section of Colorado to the eastern section of Oklahoma, where it meets the Arkansas River. The Arkansas River enters the northwestern side of Oklahoma from Texas and travels southeast. The North Canadian River flows from the northeastern section of New Mexico to the center of Oklahoma, where it meets the Canadian River. The **North Canadian River** enters the northwestern side of Oklahoma from Texas and travels east past Oklahoma City. The Red River flows from the northeastern section of Texas to the center of Louisiana, where it meets the Mississippi River. The **Red River** enters the southwestern section of Oklahoma from Texas and travels east along the southern border of Oklahoma.

Role of Rivers in Region's Early Trade

The rivers of Oklahoma had an important role in the region's **early trade** because most of the early traders used canoes or other small boats to travel from Canada or Louisiana to the area that is now Oklahoma. The reason for this is that most of the explorers in the area were either French or Spanish, and the Spanish explorers of the time were more interested in treasure than trade. The **French**, on the other hand, were actually interested in trading with the Native Americans, and the

French typically used the rivers to travel to Oklahoma and other nearby areas from their outposts in Canada and Louisiana. As a result, the rivers of Oklahoma were extremely important to the region's early trade because the rivers made it easier for the French traders to transport the goods that they were willing to trade for the animal furs that the Native Americans collected.

Largest Cities in Oklahoma

The three largest cities in Oklahoma, in terms of population, are Oklahoma City, Tulsa, and Norman. **Oklahoma City** has the largest population of any city in Oklahoma, with a population of over 550,000. The city is located in the center of Oklahoma on the North Canadian River and is known for its livestock, oil, and natural gas industries. **Tulsa** has the second largest population of any city in Oklahoma, with a population of over 385,000. The city is located in the northeastern section of Oklahoma on the Arkansas River, and the city is known for the large amount of oil that it has produced since its incorporation in 1898. **Norman** has the third largest population of any city in Oklahoma, with a population of over 110,000. Norman is located in the center of Oklahoma, just south of the North Canadian River, and the city is known for its colleges and universities, including the University of Oklahoma.

Fort Gibson and Fort Sill

Fort Gibson was originally a military outpost located in the northeast section of Oklahoma that was established to help the US Army protect the area from Native American attack. However, this was not the only purpose that Fort Gibson served, as the fort was also used as an outpost for both the Confederate and the Union forces during the Civil War. The outpost was originally constructed by Colonel Matthew Arbuckle (who was eventually promoted to the rank of brigadier general) on April 20, 1824, but the camp was closed in 1890.

Fort Sill is a military outpost located in the southwest section of Oklahoma, just outside the city of Lawton. The fort was originally constructed by Major General Phillip H. Sheridan on January 8, 1869, as a military outpost that the US Army could use to protect the area from Native American attack. The camp is actually still open, but it is now used as an artillery school and a US Marine base.

Chapter Quiz

Ready to see how well you retained what you just read? Scan the QR code to go directly to the chapter quiz interface for this study guide. If you're using a computer, simply visit the online resources page at **mometrix.com/resources719/osatwhistgeog** and click the Chapter Quizzes link.

OSAT Practice Test

Want to take this practice test in an online interactive format?
Check out the online resources page, which includes interactive practice questions and much more: **mometrix.com/resources719/osatwhistgeog**

World History

1. Which of the following events did not take place in the year 1066?

a. The heirless king of the Anglo-Saxons, Edward the Confessor, died.
b. Harold of Wessex was chosen as Edward's successor.
c. William the Conqueror led forces across the English Channel to battle Harold's forces at the Battle of Hastings.
d. The English army mutinied to avoid battle, granting William power without bloodshed.
e. William brought the customs of monarchial feudalism to England.

2. Which of the following rivers did NOT play an important role in the development of the earliest civilizations?

a. The Tiber River.
b. The Yangtze River.
c. The Euphrates River.
d. The Nile River.
e. The Indus River.

3. Labor unions were legalized in Germany in

a. 1866.
b. 1871.
c. 1884.
d. 1891.
e. None of these

4. Which of the following statements is not true of the Counter Reformation?

a. It was founded by Pope Paul III.
b. The pope responded to Protestant criticisms of the Catholic Church.
c. It called for a return to spirituality and ethics among the church leadership.
d. It called for a war against Protestants.
e. It called for assemblies to clarify church doctrine.

5. Which of these best explains deism?

a. God exists and maintains a hands-on involvement in day-to-day events and individual lives.
b. God exists and set things in motion, but does not perform miracles or act on everyday lives.
c. God may or may not exist; there is no evidence to prove or disprove this, so nobody knows.
d. God does not actually exist, but is simply a concept created by human beings who need to believe in a higher being.
e. God exists, but only in the minds of the individual human beings who conceive of this entity.

6. Which of the following statements about the education of wealthy Athenian males is false?

a. Children attended group schools where they studied reading, writing, poetry, and grammar.
b. Children were taken out of their homes and placed in a grueling public education program designed to build physical and psychological endurance.
c. Children studied sports such as gymnastics, javelin throwing, and boxing.
d. Adolescents studied government, ethics, mathematics, and rhetoric in the schools of the Sophists.
e. Eighteen-year olds were obligated to spend one year in military service.

7. Which of the following scientific contributions was not made by Arabic thinkers?

a. The development of the Arabic numbering system.
b. The development of algebra.
c. Significant advances in trigonometry.
d. The invention of the abacus.
e. Advances in the use of decimals.

8. A French peasant girl, Joan of Arc, had visions from the saints. What did they tell her to do?

a. Lead French troops to attack the English.
b. Lead troops to retake control of Jerusalem.
c. Become the first female priest in the Catholic Church.
d. Overthrow Charles VII of France.
e. To lead the Children's Crusade.

9. Of the following, which was *not* related to the Greek Revolution of 1821?

a. The Ottoman Empire
b. The poet Lord Byron
c. The Treaty of London
d. The French and Russians
e. These were all related to the Greek Revolution of 1821.

10. Which of these factors did not contribute to the escalation of the Peloponnesian Wars?

a. Athens had amassed great power, which threatened other Greek city-states.
b. Athens had created a monopoly on sea trade in the region.
c. Several city-states formed an alliance with Sparta to keep Athens's power in check.
d. Athens invaded Sparta.
e. The Spartans invaded Attica, near Athens, in 431 B.C.

11. Approximately how many military deaths were caused by World War I?

a. 7 million
b. 13 million
c. 37 million
d. 27 million
e. None of these

12. Who was not a member of the Julio-Claudian line of Roman Emperors?

a. Tiberius.
b. Claudius.
c. Caligula.
d. Nero.
e. Marcus Aurelius.

13. Which of the statements below is not true of the century following the death of Alexander?

a. Alexander's generals began fighting for control over the empire.
b. Alexander's brother took power only to be executed.
c. Alexander's heir took power and was executed.
d. Alexander's son brought peace to the empire and ushered in the Golden Age of Hellenistic Culture.
e. The generals divided the conquered lands into separate kingdoms and waged war with each other.

14. Which of the following provides the correct chronological order of the groups governing France (with or without a monarch) between 1789 and 1795?

a. The National Assembly, the National Convention, the Legislative Assembly, the Directory, the Committee of Public Safety, the Paris Commune
b. The Directory, the National Convention, the National Assembly, the Legislative Assembly, the Paris Commune, the Committee of Public Safety
c. The Legislative Assembly, the Committee of Public Safety, the Directory, the Paris Commune, the National Assembly, the National Convention
d. The Committee of Public Safety, the Paris Commune, the Directory, the Legislative Assembly, the National Convention, the National Assembly
e. The National Assembly, the Legislative Assembly, the Paris Commune, the National Convention, the Committee of Public Safety, the Directory

15. Of the following, which was/were *not* associated with the organizing of labor in England?

a. The group known as the Luddites
b. The Amalgamated Society of Engineers
c. Social reformer Robert Owen
d. The Grand National Consolidated Trades Union
e. These all were associated with the organizing of labor.

16. "The river was easy to navigate because of a peculiar trait: Its strong winds blew in the opposite direction of its water's flow. The winds blew down from the north, but the river flowed up from the south. This unusual feature made it easy to transport goods back and forth from the Mediterranean Sea, which lay to the north.

Which river is most likely being described in the above passage?

a. The Tiber River.
b. The Tigris River.
c. The Nile Rivers.
d. The Yangtze River.
e. The Indus River.

17. "Because of the central role religion played in Sumerian culture, priests held much of the real power, despite the existence of a king. Beneath them a class of warrior nobles, responsible for protecting the city, held the next level of power. Less powerful than the nobles but still influential were the lower priests, scholars, and merchants who took responsibility for many of the daily operations of the government."

Which characteristic of most early civilizations does this passage reflect?

a. Agricultural surplus.
b. Population centers
c. Religious practice.
d. Development of technology
e. Government.

18. Which of the following factors did not contribute to Spain's decline as a global power in the 16th Century?

a. England's defeat of the Spanish Armada in 1588.
b. A failed invasion of France.
c. A huge trade deficit.
d. Invasions by Moors who overtook much of the region.
e. The Reconquista, an attempt to drive all non-Catholics out of Spain, which effectively cost Spain all of their talents and innovations.

19. What was the largest Nazi extermination camp of the Holocaust?

a. Auschwitz
b. Treblinka
c. Dachau
d. Sobibor
e. Buchenwald

20. "This school of thought held that certainty is an illusion because no knowledge can be absolutely true. The universe constantly changes, and what is true for one time is not true for all. Thinkers who followed this school's founder, Pyrrho, questioned all scientific and religious beliefs."

The above passage reflects which of the following school of thought?

a. Skepticism.
b. Epicureanism.
c. Cynicism.
d. Stoicism.
e. Dualism.

21. Members of this wealthy family were famous for financing many great works by Italian artists in the 15th Century. They were known as patrons.

a. The Medici.
b. The Machiavelli.
c. The Ghiberti.
d. The Brunischelli.
e. The Botticelli.

22. In 1884, the Prime Minister of England gave the right to vote to __ of the adult men in the country.

a. 40%
b. 50%
c. 60%
d. 70%
e. 80%

23. Led by Spartacus, the revolt in 73-71 B.C. reflects the disgruntlement of

a. The Praetorian Guard.
b. Senators.
c. Slaves.
d. Centuria.
e. The conquered provinces.

24. Which of the following statements does NOT describe Rome's relationship with its conquered peoples?

a. All subjects were granted the full range of rights entitled to Roman citizens.
b. The Romans allowed some degree of cultural autonomy.
c. Subjects were expected to follow Roman laws.
d. Subjects were obligated to pay taxes.
e. Subjects gave up land and supplies to the government.

25. According to tradition, who founded the Israelite people?

a. Zoroaster.
b. Abraham.
c. Aeneas.
d. Daniel.
e. Jesus.

26. Which of the following rulers was female?

a. Sargon.
b. Hammurabi.
c. Hatshepsut.
d. Nebuchadnezzar.
e. Amenhotep IV.

27. Which of the following technological advancements did not lead to increased sea travel?

a. Improvements in mapmaking.
b. Improvements in the compass.
c. The invention of the astrolabe.
d. Improvements in shipbuilding.
e. Development of the steam engine.

28. Which of the following statements is NOT true of Minoan culture?

a. The name honors King Minos.
b. Its capital was in Knossos on the island of Crete.
c. Minoan culture was overtaken by the Athenians.
d. Its capital was a maze-like structure of many chambers.
e. Much of our knowledge of Minoan culture comes from reconstructed wall paintings.

29. Which of the following is not a major work by Michelangelo?

a. Frescoes on the ceiling of the Sistine Chapel.
b. Pieta.
c. David.
d. The Last Judgment.
e. Mona Lisa.

30. Who were the Angles and Saxons?

a. Viking invaders of England.
b. Groups from French Normandy.
c. Members of the emerging middle class.
d. Merchants who travelled European trade routes.
e. Two of the many Germanic groups who competed for dominance after the fall of Rome.

31. Who is the author of *Dialogue Concerning the Two Chief World Systems, Ptolemaic and Copernican* that argued the Earth was not the center of the universe?

a. Copernicus.
b. Galileo Galilei.
c. Johannes Kepler.
d. Rene Descartes.
e. Francis Bacon.

32. In what region did the Thirty Years' War take place?

a. Eastern Europe.
b. The British Isles.
c. Spain.
d. France.
e. Italy.

33. "The first English settlement in North America, this town was primarily established as an economic venture. The colonists who arrived in the region in 1607 had been sent there for financial purposes, not necessarily for the religious freedoms that motivated later settlements. Several years passed before it turned its first profit with a tobacco crop in 1614, and the years between its settlement and its first economic successes were a period of lawlessness and starvation for many of the settlers."

What is the town described in this passage?

a. Plymouth.
b. Jamestown.
c. Charleston.
d. St. Augustine.
e. Salem.

34. Which of the following countries was *not* a member of the Quadruple Alliance?

a. Russia
b. Prussia
c. Austria
d. France
e. England

35. Before the French Revolution began, who were members of the Second Estate?

a. Members of the clergy
b. Members of the nobility
c. Bourgeoisie and peasants
d. None of these
e. All of these

36. What was one difference between France's Declaration of the Rights of Man and Citizen and America's Declaration of Independence?

a. France's declaration did not declare the right to liberty.
b. France's declaration did not assert the right to property.
c. France's declaration did not declare the equality of all people.
d. France's declaration did not give power to the people.
e. None of these differed in the two declarations.

37. Which is true regarding the United States' entry into the Second World War?

a. The US wanted neutrality from the 1930s until 1941.
b. Winston Churchill's persuasion secured aid from the United States.
c. Congress' Lend-Lease Act aided the UK and Canada.
d. Japan's attack on Pearl Harbor triggered US entry.
e. All of these are true regarding US entry into WWII.

38. Of the following, which is *not* true regarding the development of the textile industry?

a. The Watt steam engine contributed to cloth production.
b. The Watt steam engine contributed to iron production.
c. The Watt steam engine, iron, and steel led to railroads.
d. The railroads both resulted from and added to industry.
e. These statements are all true.

39. Labor unions were legalized in England in

a. 1866.
b. 1871.
c. 1884.
d. 1891.
e. None of these

40. Which of these was *not* an outcome of the French occupation of Egypt under Napoleon?

a. The Rosetta Stone was discovered.
b. Slavery in Egypt was abolished.
c. Religious taxation was abolished.
d. British Lord Nelson was defeated.
e. Torturing prisoners was abolished.

41. This organization helped protect the rights of workers who practiced a craft.

a. Charters.
b. Fief.
c. Manor.
d. Guilds.
e. Banks.

42. "In the 5th Century B.C., the most popular career choice for intelligent young Greek males was politics. To prepare children for life as a politician, many parents hired travelling teachers to instruct young pupils in such skills as rhetoric, politics, grammar, and history. The name for these educators derives from the Greek word for 'wisdom.'"

Who are the teachers described in the above passage?

a. Philosophers.
b. Sophists.
c. Rhetoricians.
d. Orators.
e. Politicians.

43. Who is the Greek goddess of war?

a. Aphrodite.
b. Hera.
c. Athena.
d. Demeter.
e. Artemis.

44. Which of these is *not* true regarding the Second Industrial Revolution?

a. The number of Germany's factories more than quadrupled during that time period.
b. The United States and Germany were tied as leaders of industry during that time.
c. The oil industry was one of the most significant components of industrial growth.
d. The steel industry was one of the most important components of industrial growth.
e. While big companies had previously existed, this was when modern "mega" businesses grew.

45. Which of the following statements is not true of the Magna Carta?

a. In 1215, powerful nobles almost overthrew King John, who signed the Magna Carta in order to stay in power.
b. It took away nearly all of the powers of the monarchy.
c. The term means "Great Charter."
d. It held monarchs to the same laws as others.
e. It provided many rights to citizens.

46. "We shall fight on the beaches, we shall fight on the landing grounds, we shall fight in the fields and in the streets; we shall fight in the hills. We shall never surrender." Who said this?

a. Adolf Hitler
b. Benito Mussolini
c. Winston Churchill
d. Franklin D. Roosevelt
e. None of these said this.

47. Which of the following statements does not describe the average European diet BEFORE the expansion of trade routes?

a. Europeans ate for survival, not enjoyment.
b. They had an abundance of preservatives such as salt that could make food last longer.
c. Grain-based foods such as porridge and bread were staple meals.
d. Spices were unavailable.
e. Luxury items such as tea, sugar, and coffee had not yet been introduced.

48. Which of the following did not make a significant contribution to Roman literature?

a. Horace.
b. Livy.
c. Plutarch.
d. Homer.
e. Virgil.

Geography

1. What causes the motion of glaciers?

a. Gravity
b. Erosion
c. Wind
d. Temperature change

2. Juan has a mill, which he uses to grind wheat into flour. This is an example of

a. Primary economic activity
b. Secondary economic activity
c. Tertiary economic activity
d. Quaternary economic activity

3. On a globe, the distance between Buenos Aires and Tokyo is 35 cm. If the globe has a scale of 1 cm for every 516 km, what is the real distance?

a. 18,060 km
b. 35 km
c. 21,080 km
d. 14,740 km

4. Which of the following layers of the atmosphere is the furthest from the ground?

a. Thermosphere
b. Troposphere
c. Stratosphere
d. Mesosphere

5. How many intermediate directions are there?

a. 2
b. 4
c. 8
d. 16

6. Which of the following is *not* one of the Baltic states?

a. Moldova
b. Latvia
c. Lithuania
d. Estonia

7. For thousands of years, Africans have cultivated the grasslands south of the Sahara Desert, an area known as the

a. Qattara Depression.
b. Great Rift Valley.
c. Congo Basin.
d. Sahel.

8. Which of the following is NOT an official language of Switzerland?

a. Italian
b. Dutch
c. French
d. German

9. Last year, 4 residents of Henrytown died. The population of Henrytown is 500. What is the death rate of Henrytown?

a. 1
b. 4
c. 8
d. 12

10. Which soil horizon consists of weathered rock?

a. A horizon
b. C horizon
c. O horizon
d. R horizon

Refer to the following for question 11:

For a geography unit, students are learning about the state of Wisconsin. To help better understand the climate of the state, students are asked to record how the elevation of certain regions correlates to temperature. They are also expected to locate and label the major cities of the state, such as Madison and Milwaukee.

11. Which of the following gives the clearest relative location of Milwaukee?

a. In Wisconsin
b. On Lake Michigan
c. 44° N, 88° W
d. 100 miles north of Chicago

12. What is the name for a brief interval of coolness in between warm periods in the Pacific Ocean?

a. La Niña
b. Tropical gyre
c. El Niño
d. ENSO

13. On a political map of India, the northernmost part of the border with Pakistan is represented as a dotted line. Why is this so?

a. Pakistan does not have control of this border.
b. This area has never been comprehensively mapped.
c. Indian Sikhs are threatening to secede.
d. The borders of the Kashmir region remain in dispute.

Refer to the following for question 14:

A biome featuring scrubby plants and small evergreen trees has a hot, dry summer followed by a wetter winter. The following food chain exists in the biome:

$$tree \rightarrow caterpillar \rightarrow frog \rightarrow snake \rightarrow hawk \rightarrow vulture \rightarrow worm$$

14. Which biome is this?

a. Taiga
b. Coniferous forest
c. Chaparral
d. Savanna

15. When a foreign power has some political and economic control over a region in another country but does not directly govern, it is said to have a(n)

a. Colony
b. Sphere of Influence
c. Settlement
d. Enclave

16. Which state covers the most area?

a. New York
b. Texas
c. California
d. Alaska

17. What are the two regions of the Czech Republic?

a. Chechnya and Slovakia
b. Moravia and Slovakia
c. Bohemia and Chechnya
d. Bohemia and Moravia

18. Which of the following was a consequence of the Mexican Revolution of 1910?

a. Land redistribution
b. National sovereignty
c. Two-party rule
d. The creation of railroads

19. Which of the following most closely resembles a communist society?

a. Colony
b. Ghetto
c. Shtetl
d. Kibbutz

20. Which map describes the movement of people, trends, or materials across a physical area?

a. Political Map
b. Cartogram
c. Qualitative Map
d. Flow-line Map

21. The apparent distance between Greenland and Norway is greatest on a(n)

a. Mercator Map
b. Conic Projection Map
c. Contour Map
d. Equal-Area Projection Map

22. Which government system vests almost all control in a central government?

a. Federation
b. Democracy
c. Unitary system
d. Confederation

23. According to Alfred Wegener, the earth originally had one continent called:

a. Pangaea
b. Eurasia
c. Transcontinentia
d. Africa

24. Which form of religion includes the belief that the natural world is imbued with spirits?

a. Monotheism
b. Pantheism
c. Animism
d. Polytheism

25. On which type of map are different countries represented in different colors, with no two adjacent countries sharing a color?

a. Physical map
b. Political map
c. Climate map
d. Contour map

26. Where is the area of greatest corn production?

a. South Africa
b. Kazakhstan
c. United States
d. Mexico

27. Which of the following languages is *not* alphabetic?

a. Spanish
b. Russian
c. Chinese
d. Arabic

28. On which type of map would Nigeria be bigger than Australia?

a. Contour map of elevation
b. Flow-line map of the spice trade
c. Mercator projection
d. Cartogram of population

29. Which type of rock is formed by extreme heat and pressure?

a. Limestone
b. Metamorphic
c. Sedimentary
d. Igneous

30. Which of the following is an example of an isthmus?

a. Panama
b. The Aleutian Islands
c. Northern Greenland
d. Florida

31. During one year in Grassley County, there are 750 births, 350 deaths, 80 immigrations, and 50 emigrations. What is the natural increase rate for this year?

a. 400
b. 830
c. 430
d. More information is required.

32. Through which of the following does the prime meridian NOT pass?

a. Equator
b. Middle of the Pacific Ocean
c. Greenwich, England
d. Tropic of Cancer

Answer Key and Explanations

World History

1. D: Each of the answers describes a key event of the year 1066 except Choice D. The English army did not avoid battle. The Battle of Hastings was a bloody conflict that resulted in the devastation of the English army. William the Conqueror took control of England and brought Norman customs and government, which shaped the culture of England.

2. A: Roman civilization developed on the Tiber River, but it is not considered one of the earliest civilizations. Major civilizations developed along the other rivers listed: Chinese civilization developed in the Yangtze and Huang River valleys; Mesopotamian civilization emerged between the Tigris and Euphrates; and Egyptian culture developed in the Nile River valley.

3. D: Labor unions were legalized in Germany in 1891 (D). In 1866 (A), America's first nationalized union, the National Labor Union (NLU), was formed. In 1871 (B), England legalized labor unions. In 1884 (C), France legalized labor unions. Since (D) is correct, (E), none of these, is incorrect.

4. D: The Counter Reformation was a 16th Century movement that wanted to reform the Catholic Church without losing its traditions. It began roughly with the Council of Trent (1545-1643) and ended with the Thirty Years War (1648).

5. B: Many of the philosophers of the 18th century's Enlightenment were deists. The most correct expression of deism is choice B. Deists believe that God does exist and that God created the world and set it in motion, but thereafter is not directly involved in everyday events or the lives of individuals. This belief promotes the concept of humanity's free will and rejects the concept of predetermined fates. Choice B that God not only exists, but is active personally in daily life, is closer to an expression of theism than of deism. Choice C that God may or may not exist, and without proof nobody knows for sure, is closer to an expression of agnosticism than of deism. Choice D that God does not exist is closer to an expression of atheism than of deism. Choice E that God only exists in the minds of humans who came up with this concept is somewhat closer to an expression of existentialism than of deism.

6. B: The harsh educational techniques were practiced in Sparta, not Athens. The remaining choices are all reflections of Athenian educational practice.

7. D: Each answer describes a significant contribution Arabic thinkers made to the sciences except D, the abacus, which predates Arabic culture.

8. A: Joan of Arc was a French peasant who had visions of saints telling her to lead the French army in an attack against the English. She eventually led the French to a victorious battle against the English in 1429. Several years later she was brought before the Inquisition by political enemies, found guilty of heresy, and sentenced to death.

9. E: These all were related to the Greek Revolution of 1821 (E). The Ottoman Empire (A), which was primarily Muslim, ruled Greece before this revolution. Nationalists and liberals in Greece started the revolution to become independent of this empire. The English Romantic poet Lord Byron (B) was among many Europeans who were interested in the Greek Revolution, not only out of agreement with the Romantic ideals of nationalism and liberty, but also out of a desire for a revival of the classical Greek democracy. In 1830, the Treaty of London (C) gave Greece independence from the Ottoman Empire but specified that it have a monarchy. The French and Russians (D) as well as the English had vested interests in the Mediterranean because of the trade routes they relied on there, so these countries all provided aid to the Greek revolutionaries.

10. D: Athens did not invade Sparta. Athens' power did create resentment among other Greek city-states. Athens' monopoly on trade accounts for a significant cause of the war. Sparta did establish an alliance to counteract the power of Athens. The Spartans did invade Attica, an area near Athens.

11. B: World War I caused approximately 13 million military deaths (B), not 7 million (A). 37 million (C) is the approximate number of total casualties, including not only deaths but also those wounded and those missing in action, not 27 million (D). Since (B) is correct, (E), none of these, is incorrect.

12. E: Marcus Aurelius, is the only emperor among those listed who was not a member of the Julio-Claudian line. The first emperor from this family lineage was Augustus. He was followed by Tiberius, Caligula and Claudius. The lineage ended in 68 A.D. with the suicide of Nero.

13. D: Alexander's son did not bring peace to the region; he was executed after taking power over the empire. Each of the remaining choices is true statements about the period after Alexander's death.

14. E: The answer providing the correct chronological order for the French governing bodies is choice E: The National Assembly, the Legislative Assembly, the Paris Commune, the National Convention, the Committee of Public Safety, and the Directory. In 1789, the Third Estate renamed itself the National Assembly and invited the First and Second Estates to join it. King Louis XVI, by then lacking the power to oppose this, ordered the First and Second Estates to join the National Assembly, but revolution broke out soon after this. The National Assembly passed laws eradicating the *ancient regime.* The Legislative Assembly had been formed by 1791, in which year the French constitution dictated that the King shared power with the National Assembly, and could veto acts passed by the Legislative Assembly but his veto could be overridden by the Legislative Assembly. This is like the United States' system with respect to the President and Congress. The Legislative Assembly in France came to replace the National Assembly. In 1792, the Legislative Assembly was mobbed by revolutionaries known as "sans-culottes" (meaning "without fine clothes"). For a time, the revolution was then run by the Paris Commune instead of the Legislative Assembly. The Paris Commune was led by revolutionary George Danton. Within a month of the invasion of the Legislative Assembly, following many executions by the Paris Commune, the National Convention took the Legislative Assembly's place and eliminated the monarchy. Within four more months, Louis XVI was guillotined. The National Convention, however, suffered from internal divisiveness. When Austria, Britain, the Dutch Republic, Portugal, Prussia, and Spain all fought against the French Revolution in an effort to bring back the French monarchy, first Danton and then Robespierre were in charge of the Committee of Public Safety, which succeeded the National Convention. This 12-man Committee performed many more executions, by guillotine as with Marie Antoinette, and by mass drownings using retired ships, during the notorious Reign of Terror. In 1794, public sentiment turned against the Paris Commune's and Committee of Public Safety's radical members as the populace tired of the revolution. Three months after ordering Danton's execution, Robespierre was executed himself. In 1795, the National Convention, which still existed even while the Committee of Public Safety had taken over its leadership, drafted a new constitution for the country. Included in this new constitution was a legislature under the oversight of a five-man Directory. This Directory continued until it was eliminated by Napoleon in 1799.

15. A: The group *not* associated with organizing labor in England was the Luddites (A), who opposed machines as threats to their jobs. The Amalgamated Society of Engineers (B) was one of the early labor unions formed in England. This union charged its members a small amount of dues weekly to provide them with unemployment insurance. Robert Owen (C) was a proponent of social reform and an organizer in England who founded the Grand National Consolidated Trades Union (D). His focus in starting this union was to campaign for an 8-hour workday. Because the Luddites (A) were not a group associated with organizing labor unions (E), these all were associated with organizing labor, is incorrect.

16. C: This passage contains two clues to the answer: one the river flows north and two the river lies to the south of the Mediterranean Sea. The Nile is the only river listed that flows south-to-north and lies to the south of the Mediterranean, making Choice C the best choice. These geographical clues can be used to exclude the other choices: the Tiber is incorrect because it lies to the north of the Mediterranean Sea. The other choices are incorrect because these rivers lie east or southeast of the sea.

17. E: This passage details the political hierarchy of the Sumerian government. Little mention is made of agricultural surplus, population centers, or technology. Choice C is incorrect because the passage primarily focuses on the structure of Sumerian government.

18. D: The Moors invaded Spain in the 700s. Although Spain's decline in power began to accelerate after the defeat of the Spanish Armada, many causes led up to the decline.

19. A: Auschwitz (A) in Poland was the largest Nazi extermination camp of the Holocaust. More than a million people were killed at Auschwitz. Treblinka (B) and Sobibor (D) were also sites where the Nazis built death camps. Dachau (C) and Buchenwald (E) were concentration camps. While many people also died there, these were differentiated from death camps in that their primary purpose was to extract forced labor from their prisoners, while the primary purpose of death camps was to kill their prisoners. While Hitler's main target was the Jews due to his rampant anti-Semitism and his belief that the "final solution" to the "Jewish question" was to kill all the Jews, who were murdered in the largest numbers, many other people were killed in these camps as well.

20. A: The most significant clue is the name Pyrrho, who founded the school of skepticism. Epicureanism held that people should seek pleasure and minimize pain to get the most out of life. The cynics promoted a life without concern for social status, physical pleasure, or wealth. The stoics placed the pursuit of wisdom above all other goals. Dualism is a generic term for a philosophy that divides the world into two parts: mind / body, spiritual / material, etc.

21. A: The Medici were a powerful, wealthy family, famous for their financial contributions to artists in Florence.

22. C: In 1884, William Gladstone, the liberal Prime Minister of England, passed the Third Reform Act, also known as the Representation of the People Act, giving the right to vote to 60% of the adult men in the country (C). This was done by extending voting rights from boroughs (or towns or cities) to the countryside, thus increasing the electorate. All men who paid a minimum yearly rent for land or who owned land valued at the same minimum amount (£10) were allowed to vote. Though this act did not provide universal suffrage, as women and the other 40% of men still could not vote, it was still an improvement. As 60% of adult men now could vote due to this act, the figures of 40% (A), 50% (B), 70% (D), and 80% (E) of adult men are all incorrect.

23. C: Spartacus was the leader of a slave rebellion.

24. A: Most of the conquered peoples were not granted Roman citizenship. Each conquered state was allowed some degree of cultural autonomy. Subjects were expected to follow the laws of Rome, pay taxes, and hand over land and supplies to the Roman government.

25. B: Abraham is considered the founder of the Israelite tradition. Zoroaster is not directly associated with the Israelite tradition. Aeneas is a character from Greek legends, sometimes associated with the founding of Rome. Though Daniel and Jesus shaped the history of the Israelite people and religion, neither is considered the founder.

26. C: Hatshepsut was an Egyptian Pharaoh whose name means "foremost of noble ladies." Sargon, Hammurabi, Nebuchadnezzar, and Amenhotep IV were men.

27. E: The steam engine was not invented until the 19th Century. The other choices describe a technological innovation that helped improve navigation and shipbuilding technology during the Early Modern period.

28. C: is the best choice because Athenian culture developed more than a thousand years later than Minoan. The remaining choices all reflect true statements, so none is the best choice for the question. The legendary King Minos is the namesake for the island. Knossos was the center of Minoan culture and its capital was on the island of Crete. The capital was a mazelike structure from which we derive the term "labyrinth." Many frescoes, or wall paintings, have been uncovered and reconstructed provide scholars a great source of information about Minoan culture.

29. E: The *Mona Lisa,* is the only painting not created by Michelangelo. The artist was Leonardo Da Vinci.

30. E: The Angles and Saxons were two of the Germanic groups who competed for power after the fall of Rome. It is from them that the term Anglo-Saxons originated.

31. B: The *Dialogue Concerning the Two Chief World Systems* was written in 1632 by Galileo Galilei. Two characters debate the merits and flaws of the Ptolemaic model, the Earth was the center of the heavens, and the Copernican model, the Earth was not the center of the universe. The Inquisition forced Galileo to publicly retract his support for the Copernican model.

32. A: The Thirty Years' War began when the Holy Roman Emperor began to drive Protestants from Bohemia and Austria in 1618. Protestants responded by rebelling, and though they were quickly suppressed, many other rebellions began. They sparked a land-grab in the region, which was finally settled in 1648 with the Treaty of Westphalia, creating several new nations in Eastern Europe.

33. B: The town described is B, Jamestown. Plymouth was founded by Puritan settlers in pursuit of religious freedom. Charleston was also known for its religious tolerance. St. Augustine was founded in 1565 by Spanish settlers and is the oldest continuously inhabited city in the US. Salem was an important seaport.

34. D: The country that was not a member of the Quadruple Alliance was France (D). The purpose of this alliance's formation in 1813 was to combat Napoleon and France. The alliance consisted of Russia (A), where Napoleon had recently been badly defeated; Prussia (B), where Napoleon had forced reforms during his invasion which ultimately backfired on him by making Prussia more nationalistic and a stronger force; Austria (C), which had had territory in the Netherlands and Northern Italy taken from it as well as privileges taken from the Catholic Church in Switzerland by the French revolutionary army before Napoleon's rise to power; and England (E), a longtime enemy of France which Napoleon wanted to destroy by stopping other European nations from trading with it.

35. B: Members of the Second Estate were nobles (B). In France, those in this class were divided into "nobles of the sword," who were descended from long lines of aristocrats; and "nobles of the robe," who were not noble by ancestry but had bought their social status. Neither division was necessarily rich. However, the nobility did not pay many taxes and possessed significant influence. They were also landlords who collected dues, such as rent, from peasants living on their land. Some of the nobles supported the revolution and some were against it. Members of the clergy (A) were the First Estate. Bourgeoisie and peasants (C) were the Third Estate. Since (B) is correct, (D) none of these, and (E) all of these, are incorrect.

36. D: One difference between France's and America's declarations was that France's did not give power to the people (D). In America's declaration, individuals united by a common cause were named as having power, but France's declaration stated that "all authority rests essentially in the nation." Thus, according to some historians, nationalism in the modern sense began with the French Revolution and its Declaration. France's declaration did declare the right to liberty (A) just as America's did. Both countries' declarations also asserted the right to property (B). Both declarations also stated that all citizens were politically equal (C). Because (D) is a difference between the two, (E), none of these was a difference, is incorrect.

37. E: All of these are true regarding US entry into WWII. The United States decisively preferred to maintain a neutral position from the mid-1930s until 1941 (A) when Japan attacked Pearl Harbor, Hawaii. Even though the American public attitude was supportive toward Great Britain in 1940, the US still did not want to be involved in the European war. However, the UK's Prime Minister, Winston Churchill, was very persuasive (B), and he convinced the American government to trade its old warships to Great Britain for military bases in Newfoundland and the West Indies, as well as convincing the US to provide war supplies to Britain, which would pay America for them after the war. The US Congress passed the Lend-Lease Act (C) enabling this transaction to take place. While America's formal position on the war was still one of neutrality, it also aided England and Canada at the same time. The end of US neutrality was when Japan, an ally with Germany, attacked America's Pacific Fleet in Pearl Harbor, Hawaii on December 7, 1941 (D); the next day America declared war on Japan. Shortly thereafter, Hitler declared war against the US by Germany.

38. E: All of the statements are true regarding the development of the textile industry. James Watt's invention of the steam engine in England provided a source of power for new cotton mills (A). Soon the steam engine was also applied to the process of making iron (B). The production of iron and steel together with the steam engine enabled England to build its first railroad (C). By the middle of the 19th century, many cities in England were connected by railroads, and in another 70 years there were railroads in America, Canada, Europe, Asia, Africa, and Siberia. The railroads resulted from industry and feeders of industry (D) as their existence created additional demand for metal, oil, and machine power.

39. B: Labor unions were legalized in England in 1871 (B) to improve conditions for employees, including pay, work hours, workplace conditions, and benefits such as paid vacations, mandatory breaks, and workers' compensation. England was the first European country to legalize unions due to its history of liberalism and industrialization. In 1866 (A), America's first nationalized union, the National Labor Union (NLU), was formed. In 1884 (C), France legalized labor unions. In 1891 (D), Germany legalized labor unions. Since (B) is correct, (E), none of these, is incorrect.

40. D: Lord Nelson being defeated was not an outcome of France's occupation of Egypt under Napoleon. This leader of the British navy defeated the French navy in Aboukir Bay, which ended the French occupation of Egypt. Before it ended, though, the period of occupation brought certain reforms to Egypt. These included the abolition of slavery (B), of religious taxation (C), and of the practice of torturing prisoners (E). Napoleon also introduced many scientists to Egypt, which resulted in the discovery of the Rosetta Stone (A). This stone, by its inclusion of the same texts in both Egyptian hieroglyphics and the ancient Greek language, enabled hieroglyphs to be translated for the first time since ancient history.

41. D: Charters refer to land grants that allowed citizens of towns certain rights. Fief refers to a land granted by a lord to a vassal, a lower noble, in exchange for loyalty and protection. Manor refers to a lord's landholdings. Banks refers to moneychangers.

42. B: The word derives from the Greek word for wisdom, which is also the root of "philosophy" and "sophisticated." Philosophers is not as accurate as sophists. Rhetoricians and orators refer to public speakers, not private tutors. Although the sophists vetted their students for a life in politics, politicians were primarily educators.

43. C: Athena was the goddess of war, wisdom, and the arts. Aphrodite was the goddess of love. Hera was the goddess of marriage. Demeter was an Earth goddess, whose name comes from a combination of the words "Earth" and "mother." Artemis was often depicted as the goddess of the hunt.

44. B: It is not true that the US and Germany were equal in leading industry (B). Although Germany's factories did more than quadruple in number (A) during the Second Industrial Revolution, evidencing enormous growth, the United States was still the world leader of industry. The oil and steel industries (C and D) were two of the most important contributors to additional industrial development. Though large corporations (such as the British East India Company) had previously existed, the Second Industrial Revolution beginning in the late 19th century was the time when "mega" corporations, as we are now familiar with them, came into being (E) all over the Western Hemisphere, but particularly in the United States, due in large part to the immigration of millions of Europeans (see question #71).

45. B: Each of the answers is true except Choice B. The Magna Carta did not take the powers of the monarchy away. It did, however, hold the monarchy to the same rule of law as commoners.

46. C: Winston Churchill (C), the British Prime Minister during World War II, said this. Despite their desire for and appropriation of absolute power, neither Hitler (A) nor Mussolini (B) made this statement of resolution never to give up fighting. American President F.D. Roosevelt (D) did not speak of refusing to surrender, but rather of finding a lasting peace. Since (C) is correct, (E), none of these said this, is incorrect.

47. B: Salt and other preservatives were known in Europe long before major trade expansions, but they were costly and not abundant for most people; therefore, the claim of an 'abundance of preservatives' is inaccurate.

48. D: Homer is the ancient Greek author of the *Iliad* and the *Odyssey*. Horace was a Roman poet, the source of many popular Latin phrases, such as *carpe diem*, "seize the day." His works include *Odes, Satires*, and *Ars Poetica.* Livy was a famous Roman historian whose only surviving work is the *History of Rome*. Plutarch wrote many works. One of his best known works is a collection of biographies, referred to as *Lives*, which recount the lives of great Greek figures and compare them to great Romans. Each contains a philosophical reflection on the lessons to be learned from each figure's accomplishments and character. Virgil is best known for his epic, the *Aeneid*, which recounts the mythical history of Rome and connects the country's origins to the great Greeks who fought in the Trojan War.

Geography

1. A: Glaciers move because they are incredibly heavy, and the force of gravity slowly pulls them lower. Erosion is a result rather than a cause of glacier movement. Although large glaciers may only move a few inches a year or may not move at all, some valley glaciers in Europe move as much as 600 feet annually. The result is a rounded valley and a trail of rock and soil debris known as a moraine. The Great Lakes in the United States were formed by the passage of glaciers long ago.

2. B: Grinding wheat into flour is an example of secondary economic activity. A secondary economic activity is one in which raw materials are converted into a more valuable product. Another secondary economic activity would be weaving cotton into yarn. A primary economic activity is a direct use of natural resources. Hunting is one example of a primary economic activity. Service jobs are considered to be tertiary economic activities. These jobs do not necessarily entail the acquisition and use of raw materials. Lawyers and bus drivers are just two examples of tertiary economic actors. Quaternary economic activities entail the acquisition, synthesis, and production of information. Teachers and writers are among those who make up the quaternary level of economic activity.

3. A: The distance between Buenos Aires and Tokyo is approximately 18,060 km. The process of converting a scaled distance to a real distance is fairly simple. In this case, multiply the number of centimeters by the number of kilometers represented by each of these centimeters. The calculation can be expressed as (35 cm) (516 km/1 cm). Because centimeters are in the numerator of the first term and the denominator of the second term, they cancel out, leaving kilometers as the unit.

4. A: Of the options listed, the thermosphere is the furthest from the ground. There is very little air in the thermosphere. The stratosphere lies just above the troposphere and includes the ozone layer. The mesosphere is in between the stratosphere and the thermosphere, 30 to 50 miles above the surface of the earth.

5. B: There are four intermediate directions. They are northwest, northeast, southwest, and southeast. The intermediate directions are midway between each set of adjacent cardinal directions. The cardinal directions are north, south, east, and west. On a compass rose, the cardinal directions are typically indicated by large points, while the intermediate directions are represented by smaller points.

6. A: Moldova is not one of the Baltic states. Latvia, Lithuania, and Estonia all border the Baltic Sea, which has enabled them to become major traders. Unfortunately, the smallness and advantageous locations of these nations has made them attractive to invaders. The Soviet Union took over these lands in 1939, and it was not until 1991 that they regained independence. All three of these nations are now struggling to establish themselves as viable economic actors.

7. D: The Sahel, a belt of grasslands just south of the Sahara Desert, has long been a focus of agricultural efforts in Africa. This semiarid region has provided sustenance to people and animals for thousands of years. In the last thousand years, stores of salt and gold were found there, giving rise to empires in Ghana and Mali. Changes in climate have expanded the Sahara, however, and pushed the Sahel farther south. The Qattara Depression is a low-lying desert in Egypt. The Great Rift Valley is a region of faults and rocky hills that extends along the southeastern coast of Africa.

The Congo Basin is a repository of sediment from the Ubangi and Congo rivers. It is in the northern half of what is now called the Democratic Republic of the Congo.

8. B: Dutch is not one of the four official languages in Switzerland, a nation unique in Europe for having several distinct cultures within its borders. The official name of the country is the Swiss Confederation. The majority of Swiss speak German, and cities like Zurich and Bern are predominately German in architecture and culture. Geneva, on the other hand, is a largely French-speaking city. There is a local Swiss dialect, known as Romansch, which is spoken by many people. Some areas, such as Ticino, have considerable Italian-speaking populations.

9. C: The death rate of Henrytown is 8. Death rate is calculated as the number of deaths every year for every thousand people. Of course, the population of Henrytown is only 500, so it requires a quick calculation to obtain the death rate. This can be accomplished with the following equation:

$$\frac{4}{x} = \frac{500}{1000}$$

This equation basically means "4 is to 500 as x is to 1000." The equation is solved by first cross multiplying, which yields $4{,}000 = 500x$. Then, both sides are divided by 500 to isolate the variable. This indicates that x is equal to 8.

10. B: The C horizon of soil consists of weathered rock. A soil that has been in the same place for a long time will begin to develop unique layers known as horizons. The bottom layer is called the R horizon; it consists of unweathered bedrock. Just above is the C horizon, which is composed of weathered rock fragments. Next up is the B horizon, made up of minerals and drier soil. Above that is the A horizon, or topsoil, which has a great deal of organic matter in it. The top layer is known as the O horizon. It is a thin layer of humus.

11. D: A relative location for Milwaukee is 100 miles north of Chicago. Relative location is a description of placement in terms of some other location. The latitude and longitude of Milwaukee are its absolute location because they describe its placement relative to an arbitrary but inalterable system of positioning. To say that Milwaukee is in Wisconsin or on Lake Michigan does not provide as much detail as answer choice D because Wisconsin is a big state and because Lake Michigan is a large body of water.

12. A: La Niña is a brief interval of coolness in between warm periods (El Niño) in the water of the Pacific Ocean. For a long time, La Niña was considered only in terms of its relation to El Niño. Increasingly, however, it is being studied as a climate event in its own right. A tropical gyre is a circle of winds made up of equatorial currents in one direction and countercurrents in the other direction. There are tropical gyres in both the Northern and Southern hemispheres. El Niño is an annual event, though some years it is considerably more pronounced. It is an increase in the temperature of coastal Pacific water, sometimes by as much as 2° Celsius. El Niño has a great impact on fishing and weather in the areas that border the Pacific Ocean. The El Niño–Southern Oscillation (ENSO) occurs during a particularly intense El Niño; the flow of equatorial wind and water during an ENSO actually reverses course.

13. D: The northernmost border between India and Pakistan is represented on political maps as a broken line because the borders of the Kashmir region remain in dispute. Both nations lay claim to this mountainous region, which has great water resources. This has been just one of the issues to complicate relations between these neighbors in South Asia. Although India controls most of Kashmir at present, the boundaries have not yet been fully resolved, and, on a political map, such undefined borders are usually represented with dotted lines.

14. C: The chaparral biome features scrubby plants and small evergreen trees and also has a hot, dry summer followed by a wetter winter. This biome is mainly found around the Mediterranean Sea, though there are also chaparrals in Australia, South Africa, and the American Southwest. The taiga is a colder biome found primarily in northern Europe and Asia. The vegetation of the taiga is mainly scattered stands of coniferous trees. A coniferous forest, meanwhile, is a warmer forest composed of trees that have needles and cones rather than leaves. These trees are better suited for a cold climate than are deciduous trees. A savanna is a tropical grassland with only a few trees. Savannas are clustered around the equator.

15. B: A sphere of influence is a region in which a foreign power has some political and economic control but does not directly govern. One classic example is the sphere of influence held by European nations in China in the nineteenth and early twentieth centuries. These regions were ostensibly still part of China but had their politics and trade manipulated by the governments of foreign nations. Spheres of influence are less formal than colonies or settlements, which are directly under the control of the foreign government. An enclave, meanwhile, is a country that is entirely surrounded by some other country.

16. D: Alaska is the largest state in terms of area. It is about 660,000 square miles, while the second-largest state, Texas, is about 270,000 square miles. Despite its immensity, however, Alaska is sparsely populated, with fewer than 630,000 permanent residents. Much of the state is covered in ice year round, and there are several months during the winter in which the sun barely rises at all. Nevertheless, Alaska is an incredible source of natural resources for the continental United States. In particular, Alaska supplies large amounts of oil, timber, and fish to the rest of the nation. There is a continuous conflict between environmentalists and those who want to harvest the state's natural resources more aggressively.

17. D: The two regions of the Czech Republic are Bohemia and Moravia. Bohemia is the western half of the country, including Prague. Moravia is the eastern half of the Czech Republic. Czechoslovakia became two separate nations, the Czech Republic and Slovakia, in 1993. This separation was spurred by Slovak resentment of the domination of the government by the Czech majority.

18. A: Land redistribution was one consequence of the Mexican Revolution of 1910. Up to that point, all the arable land in the country was controlled by a select group of aristocrats. There were approximately 8,000 haciendas, which could only be farmed by certain people. After the Mexican Revolution ended in 1920, the newly formed government moved to purchase these haciendas and provide access to peasant farmers. Much of this land is distributed in what are called *ejidos*, or collective farms owned and operated by several people. Nevertheless, to date, the Mexican government has only succeeded in redistributing about half of the original haciendas. As for the other answer choices, Mexico had already become a sovereign nation in 1821 after a long struggle with Spain. The Mexican Revolution did not usher in a period of multi-party rule; in fact, it was not until the election of Vicente Fox in 2000 that the country had a president who was not a member of the Institutional Revolutionary Party. Finally, the massive construction of railroads in Mexico had already taken place during the late 19th century, mainly to provide foreign economic interests with access to Mexico's natural resources.

19. D: A kibbutz is a collective farm in Israel in which the economy closely resembles that of a communist society. Those who live on a kibbutz do not own private property; rather, they share living space with one another. Children are raised by the entire community. Although the kibbutz has become slightly less popular in recent years, there are still many of these arrangements in Israel. A colony is any settlement controlled by the government in another country. A colony could be administered like a communist society, but it need not be so. A ghetto is an impoverished urban district primarily populated by people of a certain race, religion, or ethnicity. A shtetl is a Jewish community, especially one in eastern Europe, that existed over the past few centuries.

20. D: A flow-line map describes the movement of people, trends, or materials across a physical area. The movements depicted on a flow-line map are typically represented by arrows. In more advanced flow-line maps, the width of the arrow corresponds to the quantity of the motion. Flow-line maps usually declare the span of time that is being represented. A political map depicts the man-made aspects of geography, such as borders and cities. A cartogram adjusts the size of the areas represented according to some variable. For instance, a cartogram of wheat production would depict Iowa as being much larger than Alaska. A qualitative map uses lines, dots, and other symbols to illustrate a particular point. For example, a qualitative map might be used to demonstrate the greatest expansion of the Persian Empire.

21. A: The apparent distance between Greenland and Norway will be greatest on a Mercator map. The Mercator map is a type of cylindrical projection map in which lines of latitude and longitude are transferred onto a cylindrical shape, which is then cut vertically and laid flat. For this reason, distances around the poles will appear increasingly great. The Mercator map is excellent for navigation because a straight line drawn on it represents a single compass reading. In a conic projection map, on the other hand, a hemisphere of the globe is transposed onto a cone, which is then cut vertically (that is, from rim to tip) and laid flat. The apparent distances on a conic projection will be smallest at the 45th parallel. A contour map uses lines to illustrate the features of a geographic area. For example, the lines on an elevation contour map connect areas that have the same altitude. An equal-area projection map represents landmasses in their actual sizes. To make this possible, the shapes of the landmasses are manipulated slightly, and the map is interrupted (divided into more than one part).

22. C: In a unitary system of government, almost all control is held by the central government. The central government makes the laws, and the local governments are not allowed to overrule them. Although the unitary system is often associated with repressive regimes like that of North Korea, it also exists in countries like Japan and Great Britain. A unitary system tends to work better in countries with homogenous populations and relatively little cultural difference between regions. A federation, meanwhile, is a system in which the central government has some powers but grants others to local governments. The United States is a federation. A democracy is a system in which the people elect government officials. A democracy could be a unitary system, but it does not have to be. In a confederation, the central government has much less power than the regional and local governments. In such a system, the central government is usually only responsible for defense and trade with other nations.

23. A: Alfred Wegener was a German scientist credited with developing the idea of Pangaea, the original supercontinent from which today's large landmasses were formed. Wegener created this name from the Greek words for *all* and *earth*. The continental drift theory asserts that Pangaea began to break up approximately 180 million years ago. Wegener was inspired in part by his observation that many of the continents seemed to fit together. He also discovered a number of prehistoric fossils that suggested similarities between animals and plants from different continents.

24. C: Animistic religions include the belief that the natural world is imbued with spirits. Animists believe, for example, that trees, rocks, and animals are divine in some way. This sort of belief system is typical of Native Americans and the indigenous peoples of West Africa (for instance, the Asante). Many sociologists have noted that animist cultures often demonstrate greater reverence for the natural world. Monotheism is a belief that there is only one God. Christianity, Judaism, and Islam are all monotheistic religions. Pantheism is the belief that everything is a manifestation of the

Divine Spirit. Polytheism is a belief in multiple gods. Hinduism is the most popular polytheistic religion.

25. B: On a political map, countries are represented in different colors, and countries that share a border are not given the same color. This is so that the borders between countries will be distinct. Political maps are used to illustrate those aspects of a country that have been determined by people: the capital, the provincial and national borders, and the large cities. Political maps sometimes include major physical features like rivers and mountains, but they are not intended to display all such information. On a physical, climate, or contour map, however, the borders between nations are more incidental. Colors are used on these maps to represent physical features, areas with similar climate, etc. It is possible that colors will overrun the borders and be shared by adjacent countries.

26. C: The greatest area of corn production is in the United States, specifically in the so-called Corn Belt that runs from northern Florida and eastern Texas all the way up to Iowa and Pennsylvania. Corn has traditionally been the specialty grain of the Americas, although it is now grown as a subsistence crop all over the world. Indeed, all the incorrect answer choices are areas that produce significant amounts of corn, though not as much as the Corn Belt. Corn is useful because it can grow in various climates and can be converted into a number of different products.

27. C: Chinese is not an alphabetic language, which means that it is not written as a series of different sequences of letters. In English, for instance, all the words are made up of combinations of 26 letters. There are upper-case and lower-case forms of these letters, but these forms are constant. The same is true of all alphabetic languages, including Spanish, Russian, and Arabic. Chinese is a logographic language that uses characters that typically represent syllables or morphemes rather than individual letters. Learning to read a logographic language requires the mastery of thousands of ideograms. Functional literacy in Chinese typically requires knowledge of a few thousand characters, although large dictionaries list over 20,000 characters.

28. D: On a cartogram of population, Nigeria would be bigger than Australia. Even though the area of Australia is several times greater than that of Nigeria, Nigeria has a much larger population. A cartogram is a map on which countries or regions are sized according to a certain variable. So, in a cartogram of population, the country with the most people will be the biggest. The countries would be depicted at their usual size in a contour map of elevation or in a flow-line map. On a Mercator projection, Nigeria would actually be smaller relative to Australia because it is closer to the equator.

29. B: Metamorphic rock is formed by extreme heat and pressure. This type of rock is created when other rocks are somehow buried within the Earth, where they are subject to a dramatic rise in pressure and temperature. Slate and marble are both metamorphic rocks. Metamorphic rocks are created by the other two main types of rock: sedimentary and igneous. Sedimentary rock is formed when dirt and other sediment are washed into a bed, covered over by subsequent sediment, and compacted into rock. Depending on how they are formed, sedimentary rocks are classified as organic, clastic, or chemical. Igneous rocks are composed of cooled magma, the molten rock that emerges from volcanoes. Basalt and granite are two common varieties of igneous rock.

30. A: An isthmus is a narrow strip of land connecting two larger landmasses. The strip of land should be bordered by water on either side. The nation of Panama is the most classic example of an isthmus in Central America because it is so narrow. This is why it was chosen as the site for a great canal connecting the Atlantic and Pacific Oceans. The Aleutian Islands are an example of an archipelago, or cluster of islands in an ocean. Northern Greenland is an example of a tundra, the coldest of the biomes. There are no trees in the tundra. Florida is an example of a peninsula, a strip of land extending out into a large body of water, in this case the Atlantic Ocean.

31. D: More information is required to calculate the natural increase rate for Grassley County during this year. Natural increase rate is the growth in population measured as the surplus of live births over deaths for every thousand people. The calculation of natural increase rate does not take account of immigration or emigration. The natural increase rate for Grassley County cannot be calculated because the original population of the county is not given. As an example, if the beginning population of the county had been 10,000, the natural increase rate would be 40; $400 \times 1{,}000/10{,}000 = 40$.

32. B: The prime meridian does not pass through the middle of the Pacific Ocean. It is 0°, the line from which longitude is measured. There is no special reason why it passes through Greenwich, other than that the observatory there was one of the first to devise a system for measuring longitude and therefore put itself at the base of the system. The international date line is 180° longitude; it passes through the middle of the Pacific Ocean. Both the equator and the Tropic of Cancer are lines of latitude and therefore intersect the prime meridian. The equator circles the earth at its broadest circumference, equidistant from the North and South poles. The equator has a latitude of 0°. The Tropic of Cancer, 23°26′22″ North latitude, represents the northernmost point at which the sun is directly above the earth. In other words, at no point during the year will the sun be directly above any point north of the Tropic of Cancer. This line is mirrored in the Southern Hemisphere by the Tropic of Capricorn.

Online Resources

Due to our efforts to try to keep this book to a manageable length, we've created a link that will give you access to all of your online resources:

mometrix.com/resources719/osatwhistgeog

It's Your Moment, Let's Celebrate It!

Share your story @mometrixtestpreparation